HENRIK IBSEN

Ibsen in 1863, aged 35. Signature from a letter, 1845.

Michael Meyer

HENRIK IBSEN

The Making of a Dramatist 1828-1864

Rupert Hart-Davis *London 1967*

© Michael Meyer 1967
First published 1967

Rupert Hart-Davis Limited
3 Upper James Street
Golden Square
London W1

Printed in Great Britain by
C. Tinling & Co. Ltd
Liverpool, London and Prescot

Note
All translations of passages from languages
other than English are original, unless
otherwise indicated.

For Casper and Dilys Wrede

Contents

List of Illustrations

'I consider that my Almighty Author has given me some glimmerings of superior understanding and mental gifts; and I should reckon it the very worst treason against Him to neglect improving and using to the very utmost of my power these His bountiful mercies. At some future day it shall go hard but I will stand above these mean men whom I have never yet stood *with*.'

Thomas Carlyle to his mother
Edinburgh, 2 June 1822

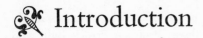 Introduction

NEARLY FORTY YEARS have elapsed since the publication in 1928 of Halvdan Koht's monumental two-volume biography of Ibsen (though a revised and partly rewritten edition appeared in 1954). Koht knew Ibsen and was one of his executors; he was acquainted with Ibsen's work as few other men have been, and was able to call not merely on his own memories of the dramatist but on those of Ibsen's family and acquaintances. He was, too, an historian of distinction, and his book must be the foundation stone for any new study of Ibsen.

But for all its many and admirable qualities, Koht's work has long been regarded as not wholly satisfactory. It omits a good deal of factual information, and is written from a narrowly nationalistic standpoint; Koht himself grew up as a young man during the period of Norway's struggle for political independence, and this theme frequently occupies the centre of his biography, with Ibsen reduced to the status of a foreground, sometimes even of a background figure. Ibsen's attitude towards his country's political problems was that of an independent observer rather than a committed patriot, and Koht could not always forgive him for not, on certain occasions, having behaved and written like Bjørnson. Koht, again, was not a man of the theatre, and Ibsen interested him more as a writer for the printed page than as a dramatist who was exploring and revolutionising the business of stagecraft. Finally, Koht was born in 1873, only thirteen years after Chekhov, and his judgments are those of his generation. They are not necessarily the less correct for that, but a writer of Ibsen's stature means something different to every generation, and requires re-examination in every age.

The present biography attempts, firstly, to present all the factual information available about Ibsen's life; secondly, to reconsider his development as a man and as a writer; thirdly, to revalue his works, both individually and as a whole; fourthly, to portray the changing theatrical world of his time; and fifthly, to show the impact of his life and work on his contemporaries and the generations which have succeeded them.

13

Of the many people who have helped me in my work, I must especially thank the poet's grandson, Mr Tancred Ibsen; Professor Francis Bull, who knows more about Ibsen than anyone, and should have written this book himself; Mr Øyvind Anker, the Librarian of Oslo University, and his staff; the staffs of Oslo Bymuseum, the University Library of Bergen, the University Library of Stockholm, the Royal Library of Stockholm, the library of University College, London, the British Drama League, and the British Museum; Dr Elias Bredsdorff, Mr Nils Lie, Mr Gordon Hølmebakk and Dr Einar Østvedt.

I also pay respectful homage to Ibsen's earlier biographers: Paul Botten Hansen (1863), Henrik Jæger (1888), J. B. Halvorsen (1892), Edmund Gosse (1907), Gerhard Gran (1916–17), Halvdan Koht (1928) and A. E. Zucker (1929). The first six all knew Ibsen personally, and he provided Botten Hansen, Jæger and Halvorsen with much of their material; he checked the proofs of Halvorsen's long survey of his life and work in *Norsk Forfatter-Lexicon*, and later vouched for its correctness. Gosse and Gran were both distinguished historians and men of letters, and their biographies admirably express the attitude of, respectively, the Edwardian and the early Georgian ages towards Ibsen. Of Koht's great work I have already spoken. Zucker disclaimed any pretensions to literary criticism, but gathered some valuable reminiscences of Ibsen from those who knew him. My debts to other writers are acknowledged in the bibliography which appears at the end of this book. I owe, and gratefully acknowledge, a debt of a different kind to Mr Casper Wrede and Mr Michael Elliott, who between them taught me whatever theatrical insight into Ibsen's work I may have acquired. From them I learned to consider Ibsen as a man writing for the theatre rather than for the printed page, and it is, primarily, from that viewpoint that I have written this book.

London, 1967   MICHAEL MEYER

HENRIK IBSEN

ONE

Ancestry and Childhood

(1828–1843)

HENRIK JOHAN IBSEN was born on 20 March 1828 in the small trading town of Skien on the east coast of Norway, a hundred miles south of the capital Christiania (now Oslo). He was the second child of a merchant, Knud Ibsen, and his wife Marichen, *née* Altenburg.

Ibsen is a Danish name (Ib is an old Danish form for Jacob), and in later years when he felt more than usually ill-disposed towards his native country, Henrik Ibsen was wont to assert that he had not a drop of Norwegian blood in his veins. In fact, thirteen of his sixteen great-great-grandparents were Norwegian, and as far as can be calculated he was approximately two-thirds Norwegian, one-sixth Danish and a little less than one-sixth German, with a slight admixture of Scottish. Apart from his father, his paternal ancestors had for over two hundred years been sea-captains; and towards the end of his life Henrik Ibsen is said to have looked, and walked, more and more like a sea-captain himself.

The earliest of his ancestors to have been traced was one Simen Ibsen-Holst, who was born in Bergen in the 1570's and obtained his captain's certificate there in 1604. He often travelled to Stege on the Danish island of Møen, and there, in due course, he married a wife and settled. His son Rasmus dropped the Holst from the family name; he, too, was a skipper, combining this activity with those of merchant and farmer. In about 1720 three of Rasmus Ibsen's sons went to live in their grandfather's birthplace of Bergen, where they married the three daughters of an emigré merchant named Heinrich Holtermann. In 1726 the youngest of the three sons, Peter, and his wife Birgitta had a son whom they named, after his German grandfather, Henrich. It was thus that the name which the dramatist was to inherit entered the Ibsen family.

This Henrich Ibsen, the dramatist's great-grandfather, married (we do not know when) a girl named Wenche Dishington, whose ancestors had long ago, at least four generations previously, come to Norway from Scotland. He was also of course a skipper and died in 1765 aged thirty-nine. Soon after his death Wenche bore a son whom, in memory of his father, she christened Henrich

Petersen. A little later she remarried with a clergyman, Jacob von der Lippe. In 1771 he was appointed to a living at Solum, near Skien; thus the family moved from western to eastern Norway.

Henrich Petersen Ibsen, the dramatist's grandfather, was remembered as 'a witty, clear-minded man, with many lively and eager interests; of a sanguine temperament, always full of jests and pranks'.[1] Like his father, he died young. On 22 November 1797, when he was thirty-two, the vessel of which he was both owner and captain went down with all hands off Hesnæs, near Grimstad, a tiny port a hundred miles south of Skien where, half a century later, his grandson was to write his first play. Only a few fragments of the wreck, including one bearing the name of the ship, drifted to land to tell the tale. Two years earlier he had married the daughter of a local merchant, Johanne Cathrine Plesner (1770–1847). Both her grandfathers were Danish and, like her husband, she also had German blood; she is said to have been 'a cultivated woman, by the standards of the day; she took an eager interest in contemporary movements, her character was strict and earnest, and she is reported to have been deeply religious, which was not general in circles such as hers...She was withdrawn and taciturn, in a way that made her not easily accessible'.[2] She gave her husband two sons before he died. Their firstborn, Jacob von der Lippe Ibsen, named after his step-grandfather, died in 1805 as a child of nine; their second, born in 1797, they called Knud Plesner Ibsen after his maternal grandfather.

The year after her husband's death in 1798, Johanne Ibsen married again, with a shipmaster named Ole Paus. She bore him eight children, four boys and four girls. Two of her sisters had married into rich merchant circles, so that she considerably raised the social standing of the Ibsens, and young Knud grew up with his eight half-brothers and half-sisters at a house in the parish of Gjerpen, just outside Skien, in an atmosphere of greater pretension than any earlier Ibsen had known.

On 1 December 1825, Knud Plesner Ibsen married Marichen Cornelia Martine Altenburg; he was twenty-eight, she twenty-six. She was also of Danish and German as well as Norwegian blood, and was an excellent match. Her father, Johan Andreas Altenburg (1763–1824), who had died the previous year, had been a wealthy shipmaster, and also, later, a merchant; in 1804–1805 he is known to have been worth twenty to thirty thousand riksdaler, or over five thousand pounds, a considerable fortune in the Norway of those days. Portraits of Johan Altenburg and his wife Hedevig Christine, the dramatist's maternal grandparents, have survived; he appears oval-faced in a high collar,

---

[1] Henrik Jæger, *Henrik Ibsen, et livsbillede* (Christiania, 1888), p. 5.
[2] *ibid.*, p. 4.

she square-faced and severe in a white frilled cap. Little is recorded of Johan Altenburg's character; there is a tradition in Skien that the dramatist had him in mind when he wrote of Rasmus Gynt, that thrifty grandfather of Peer Gynt whose son Jon so wastefully squandered his inheritance. A girl who was brought up in the house remembered Hedevig Christine Altenburg many years later as 'an authoritative woman, strict with children; clever and thrifty, keeping her house in exemplary order'.[1] She was the sister of Knud Ibsen's stepfather Ole Paus, and Knud had frequently visited the Altenburg house as a child, so that he and Marichen had virtually grown up together.

Knud and Marichen Ibsen had their first child, a boy, Johan Altenburg Ibsen, on 3 October 1826, but he died at the age of eighteen months on 14 April 1828. Three and a half weeks before this unhappy event, on 20 March, a second son was born. They named him Henrik Johan, after his two grand-fathers. He was baptised at home on 28 March, which suggests that he may have been weakly, and again in church on 10 June. Three citizens of substance stood as godfathers: Ulrich Cudrio, merchant and shipmaster, Jacob Bakke, sea-captain, and J. Stenersen, sea-captain; also a humbler figure, Jacob Boyssen, storekeeper at a works, probably a member of the church committee. Marichen Ibsen herself and Knud's half-sister Mariane Paus were registered as the child's godmothers. Knud and Marichen Ibsen had four more children during the next seven years, all of whom survived into adulthood: Johan Andreas Altenburg (1830– ?), Hedvig Cathrine (1831–1920), Nicolai Alexander (1834–1888) and Ole Paus (1835–1917). Henrik Ibsen thus grew up as the eldest of five.

The house in which he was born stood in the main square of Skien and was named Stockmannsgaarden. It no longer stands, having been destroyed, like most of the other houses in the centre of the town, by the great fire of 1886. A contemporary water-colour portrays it as a pleasing wooden edifice of two storeys with tall windows divided into tiny panes. When Henrik was two, his father bought his widowed mother-in-law's house, Altenburggaarden, a larger and more opulent building with its own paddock, just around the corner in Prindsensgade (now Henrik Ibsens gate), and they moved there in the following year, 1831.

Ibsen's first biographer, Henrik Jaeger, writing in 1888, described the Skien of Ibsen's childhood as being 'a homely little town of wooden houses, con-taining scarcely three thousand inhabitants. But, small as it was, it was the scene of much busy life and a not unimportant centre of trade'.[2] The town had made considerable economic progress since the turn of the century; many ship-

---

[1] Oskar Mosfjeld, *Henrik Ibsen og Skien* (Oslo, 1949), p. 17.
[2] Jæger, *op. cit.*, p. 6.

masters and captains had earned useful fortunes during the Napoleonic wars
and the export of timber to England had also proved rewarding. Edmund
Gosse compared it to 'a kind of Poole or Dartmouth...existing solely for
purposes of marine merchandise, and depending for prosperity, and life itself,
on the sea'.[1] It possessed a flourishing timber trade and in the eighteen-twenties
boasted four spectacular weirs and some forty sawmills. Many years later, in
1895, Ibsen described it as 'the town of the storming, soughing, seething
waters. Over the whole town there is, as it were, a song in the air from all the
weirs. So at least I remember it...It is not for nothing', he added, 'that I was
born in the town of rushing waters'.[2]

The natives of Telemark, the province in which Skien lies, are, temperamen-
tally, a race apart from their fellow-countrymen. Foreigners who know Norway
only through Oslo, the west coast and the northern and central ski resorts have
written of Ibsen as an untypical Norwegian. He was by no means an untypical native of Telemark. 'They appear sanguine but are often melancholic',
a Norwegian historian has written. 'They analyse and pass judgment on themselves.'[3] Another, speaking of the people of Skien in particular, observes:
'They are proud and stiff, combative when anyone threatens their interest,
dislike being told. They are reserved and cautious towards strangers, do not
easily accept their friendship, and are not very forthcoming even towards their
own kin. Strangers who go to live there often feel isolated. The people of Skien
are afraid openly to surrender to a mood, or let themselves be carried away;
this apparent lack of spontaneity is what Ibsen calls "the shyness of the soul".
They have an alert critical sense, but their criticism is not mercilessly direct
and honest such as, for example, one finds in the people of Bergen. The citizens
of Skien prefer to express theirs in quiet, ironical observations, in subtle satire,
in mimicry. An unlucky and thoughtless utterance can easily be remembered
so long that it becomes a proverb.'[4]

Apart from a few weeks in 1814, and we must remember this when considering Ibsen's early artistic and spiritual problems, Norway had not known true
independence for nearly 450 years. This proudest of people had come under
Danish rule in 1387, when the crown had passed to a member of the Danish
royal house, and had remained thus, an Ireland to Denmark's England until in
1814 the Treaty of Kiel at last freed her from this unwilling union. She at once
tried to assert her independence by setting up a constitution, which still stands;

---

[1] Edmund Gosse, *Ibsen* (London, 1907), p. 2.
[2] Letter to Hildur Andersen, 29 July 1895.
[3] Vetle Vislie in *Norge, 1814–1914*, ed. N. Rolfsen and E. Werenskiold: Vol. II (Christiania, 1914), p. 164.
[4] Mosfjeld, *op. cit.*, p. 57.

but the Great Powers, led by England and Russia, promptly handed her over to Sweden as a reward for the latter country's support of their cause against Napoleon. The Norwegians took up arms in defence of their liberty, but the new King-elect[1] of Sweden, Napoleon's long-nosed former marshal Bernadotte, shortly to become Carl XIV Johan, defeated them in a brief campaign and forced them into yet another unwilling union; although he permitted them to keep their constitution and retained only a suspensive, not an absolute veto on the decisions of the Storthing, the Norwegian Parliament. Norway had thus merely exchanged the Danish yoke for a Swedish one. Politically, she was a province of Sweden; culturally, she remained a province of Denmark. Her citizens read Danish novels, or Danish translations from the English and French; even the written Norwegian language, *riksmaal*, was virtually indistinguishable from written Danish, though a movement was afoot to utilise the natural rhythms and idiomatic richness of the country dialects—a situation very similar, linguistically as politically, to that which was to exist in Ireland half a century later.[2]

Unlike Ireland, however, Norway had virtually no literature to boast of: only one writer of international standing, the eighteenth century dramatist Ludvig Holberg (1684–1754)—and he, though born in Norway, had done all his writing in Denmark for Danish readers[3]—and in the nineteenth century two distinctive and interesting poets, Henrik Wergeland and J. S. Welhaven. Otherwise, there were only the old ballads and folk takes, which were now being reclaimed as, in the previous century, scholars such as Bishop Percy had reclaimed the Old English and Scottish ballads and, more recently, the brothers Grimm the folk-tales of Germany. The Icelandic Sagas, written six centuries earlier by Norwegian emigrants to Iceland, were no more intelligible to nineteenth-century Norwegians than the Anglo-Saxon Chronicles are to modern Englishmen.

At the time of Ibsen's birth, Norway was still a very primitive country. Many of the houses in the remoter rural areas were windowless, as they had been in the Middle Ages, with only a hole in the roof to let out the smoke. Farming methods were extraordinarily antiquated; 'the cattle', we learn, 'wintered in stalls built without light or standing-room, so as to give the maximum of warmth, from which they were lifted out as living skeletons when spring came; the accumulated muck was then shovelled out on to the fields'.[4]

---

[1] The old king, Carl XIII, was childless, and the Swedish Parliament had chosen Bernadotte to succeed him.

[2] See Appendix B.

[3] See Appendix A.

[4] T. K. Derry, *A Short History of Norway* (London, 1957), p. 142.

Fishermen still used the line instead of the costlier but far more effective net; and, as late as the middle of the nineteenth century, leprosy was still to be found along the west coast, in some areas affecting as high a proportion as 1 per cent of the population. The towns were tiny. Even the capital, Christiania (which had been Oslo until 1624, but was not to regain its old name until 1925) boasted less than 30,000 inhabitants. The country possessed no coal. Little of her mountainous soil was cultivable (even today the figure is less than 3 per cent), and a quarter was covered by forests. Her people depended largely upon the sea for their livelihood and for their communications; Ibsen was a grown man before the first railway was seen in Norway.

In 1881 Ibsen jotted down some childhood memories, the only extended fragment of autobiography to which he ever committed himself:

'When a few years ago the streets in my birthplace of Skien came to be named, or perhaps I should say re-named, I had the honour to have one street called after me. Or so at any rate the newspapers have reported, and I have also heard it from reliable travellers.[1] They tell me that this street stretches from the main square down towards the harbour, or *muddringen*.[2]

'But if this news is correct, I cannot think on what grounds the street came to bear my name; for I was not born in it, and have never lived in it. 'I was born in a house in the main square, Stockmannsgaarden, as it was then called. This house stood directly opposite the front of the church, with its steep steps and lofty tower. To the right of the church stood the town pillory, and to the left the town hall, with its cell for delinquents and "lunatic-box". The fourth side of the square was occupied by the Grammar School and Lower School. The church stands isolated in the centre.

'This prospect was accordingly the first sight of the world that greeted my eyes. Only buildings; nothing green; no rural, open landscape. But above this square of stone and timber the air was filled all day long with the softly booming whisper of Langefoss and Klosterfoss and the many other weirs; and through their watery roar there penetrated, from morning to dusk, something resembling the sharp cries of women, now shrieking, now moaning. It was the hundreds of sawblades working out on the weirs. When later I read of the guillotine, I always thought of those saw-blades.

'The church was of course the town's most imposing building. When one Christmas Eve towards the end of the last century, thanks to the care-

---

[1] Ibsen had, at the time of writing, been resident in Italy and Germany for seventeen years.
[2] Derived from *mudre*, to dredge.

lessness of a servant-girl, Skien was burned down, the old church was burned too. The servant-girl was, not surprisingly, executed. But the town, which was rebuilt with broad and regular streets covering its hills and hollows, gained thereby a new church, of which the citizens used to claim with a certain pride that it was of yellow Dutch clinker, had been raised by a Copenhagen master builder, and exactly resembled the church at Konigsberg. These merits I understood at that time insufficiently to appreciate them; but what inscribed itself powerfully in my memory was a large, white, heavy-limbed angel which on weekdays hovered high up under the vaulting with a bowl in its hands, but on Sundays, when a child was to be baptised, descended softly among us.

'Almost more than the white angel, however, another resident of the church excited my imagination; the black poodle, which dwelt at the top of the tower where the watchman called the hours at night. It had glowing eyes, but was not often seen; indeed, as far as I know it only showed itself once. It was a New Year's Eve, just as the watchman shouted "One!" through the window in the front of the tower. Then the black poodle came up out of the staircase behind him, stood still, just looked at him with its glowing eyes, that was all; but the watchman fell through the window on to his head in the square, where they saw him lying dead, all the good people who walked that New Year's morning early to mattins. Since that night, the watchman never shouts "One" through *that* window in the church at Skien.

'This business with the watchman and the poodle happened long before my time, and I have since heard tell that similar events occurred in olden times in several other Norwegian churches. But that same tower window held for me, when I was a child, an especial significance, in that it was there that I received the first conscious impression that has remained with me. My nursemaid carried me one day up into the tower and let me sit alone in the open window, safely held from behind, of course, by her faithful arms. I remember clearly how impressed I was at being able to see the crowns of people's hats; I looked down into our own rooms, saw the window frames, saw the curtains, saw my mother standing down there in one of the windows; yes, I could see over the rooftop and down into the courtyard, where our brown horse stood tied to the stable door swishing its tail. On the stable wall I remember there hung a pail. But then there was a hubbub, and a crowd of people, and a waving upwards from down there in the doorway, and the maid pulled me hurriedly away and ran down with me. I don't remember the rest; but afterwards they often told me how my mother had caught sight of me in the window of the tower, had shrieked, had fainted, as people did then, and later, having got me back, had wept and kissed and petted me. As a boy I never afterwards crossed the square without looking up at the window in the tower. I felt that that window belonged to me and the church poodle.

'I have kept only one other memory from those earliest years. As a christening gift I had been given, amongst other things, a large silver coin with a man's head on it. The man had a high forehead, a big hooked nose and a protruding underlip; he was, moreover, bare-necked, which I found strange. The nursemaid taught me that the man on the coin was "King Fredrik Rex", and once I tried to bowl it along the floor, with the unfortunate result that the coin rolled down into a crack. I think my parents interpreted this as an unlucky omen, it being a christening gift. The floor was taken up and they searched and dug around assiduously, but King Fredrik Rex never saw the light of day again. For a long time afterwards I could not help regarding myself as a wicked felon, and when I saw the town constable, Peter the German, emerge from the town hall and make his way towards our door, I ran as fast as I could into the nursery and hid myself beneath the bed.

'As things turned out we did not live long in the house on the square. My father bought a bigger house, into which we moved when I must have been about four [sic] years old. This new home of mine was a corner house, sited a little higher up in the town, just at the foot of Hundevad Hill, so called after an old German-speaking doctor whose majestic wife drove around in something we called "the glass coach", which in winter was used as a sleigh. This house had many large rooms, both downstairs and upstairs, and much entertaining went on. But we boys did not spend much time indoors. The main square, where the two biggest schools stood, was the natural meeting-place and battlefield for the youth of the town. The Grammar School was at that time ruled by the eminent and exceedingly lovable old Dr Ørn; while in the Lower School the principal authority was, I believe, the janitor Iver Flasrud, an equally impressive old man who also acted as the town barber. Between the boys of these two schools many a violent battle was waged around the church; but I, being a pupil of neither, was for the most part merely an attendant spectator. In any event I was as a child not, as a rule, combatively inclined.[1] For me there resided

---

[1] 'He was one of those children who seem old.
Lacking the will to join his wild companions
In their free play, he but looks quietly on,
Sufficient to himself.'
(Epic version of *Brand*, 1865).

a far more potent attraction in the aforementioned pillory, and in the town hall with all its presumably sinister secrets. The pillory was a reddish-brown post of about the height of a man; above, it had a big round knob which had originally been painted black. By now this knob looked like a friendly and inviting human face, cocked slightly askew. On the front of the post hung an iron chain and from this an open hoop, which seemed to me like two small arms waiting gleefully to fasten themselves around my throat. This had not been used for many years; but I remember well that it stood there all the time I was in Skien. Whether it still stands I do not know.

'Then there was the town hall. Like the church, it had a steep flight of steps. Beneath were the cells, with barred windows looking onto the square. Behind those bars I have seen many pale and sinister faces. One room deep down in the cellars was known as the "lunatic box" and must in fact, improbable as it now seems to me, have been used in its time to confine lunatics. This room had barred windows like the others; but behind the bars the whole of the small window space was filled with a massive iron screen, bored with innumerable tiny holes so that it resemb-led a cullender. This place was also said to have served as residence for a famous criminal of the time known as Brandeis, because he had been bran-ded; and I believe it was, too, once occupied by an escaped slave who had been recaptured and was flogged up in Li Square. Of this last fellow eye-witnesses told how he had danced as they led him to his place of punishment, but that when the time came for him to return to prison he had to be carried in a cart.

'Skien was, in the years of my childhood, an unusually gay and sociable town, very much the opposite of what it was later to become. Many highly cultivated, esteemed and prosperous families lived there then, either in the town itself or on the great estates outside. Most of these families were either closely or distantly related, and balls, dinner parties and musical gatherings followed each other in rapid succession, winter and summer. Many travellers also visited the town and, since there were then no proper hotels, they stayed with friends or relations. We almost always had people staying in our large and roomy house, which at Christmas and Fair-time would be full, an open table being kept from morning to night. Skien Fair was held in February, and was an especially happy occasion for all us boys; a full six months ahead we would begin to save our pennies so as to be able to watch the jugglers and the rope-dancers and the "equine artists", and buy gingerbread in the market stalls. Whether this Fair greatly contributed to the commercial prosperity

of the town I do not know; I remember it principally as a great popular
feast which lasted for something like a whole week on end.[1]

'The 17th of May[2] was not in those days an occasion of particular
festivity in Skien. A few young people fired off popguns out on Bleaching
Hill, or let off fireworks, but that was about all.[3] I think this reserve in
our otherwise ebullient town arose mainly from respect to a certain
worthy gentleman whose ancestral home lay in the neighbourhood and
whom for various reasons people were reluctant to offend.

'But we made up for this on Midsummer Eve. This was not communally
celebrated, but the boys and young men of the town would divide up into
five or six groups, each devoted to gathering material for its own bonfire. As early as Whitsuntide we would start going around in packs to the
shipyards and shops to "beg" empty tar-barrels. One curious custom had
survived from time immemorial. What was not freely given us we stole,
without either the owner or the police ever considering laying a com-
plaint against such outrageous behaviour. A group would thus gradually

---

[1] These February fairs were revived in 1835 after having been dropped for about fifty
years. They were held down by the wharfs, and seem to have been mainly for the sale of
hides; many people came from all over Telemark, and even foreigners. The local newspapers, *Bratsberg Amtstidende* and *Ugebladet*, tell us some of the entertainers who appeared,
and whom Ibsen may have seen. In 1841 and 1842, for example, there was Balabrega,
whose *kunstcabinet* contained "mechanical artifices, a collection of illuminations, and all
the Swedish Kings and ruling Queens from Gustav I to the Present Monarch"; Guidotti
with his Cabinet of Extraordinary Waxworks; Alexander and his Equestrian Artists.
G. Francke announced that he would send up two hydrogen-filled "Acrostatic Figures",
namely, "An Observation Balloon with the Norwegian Tricolour" and "A Turk, Life-
Size, with a Globe in his Hand"; P. Dahl and Company advertised a great display of
"Gymnastics, Equilibrianism, Rope-Dancing, Indian and Malabara Conjuring, and Feats
of Strength"; and the Norwegian sprinter and clown Hermann offered to race "The
Town's Horsemen" for a wager. In March 1844 a big circus came to Skien, Gautier's
Equestrian Company, boasting no less than fifty-two performers and forty horses; they
marched into the town from the quay with instruments playing, like the circus performers
in *The Pillars of Society*. (Mosfjeld, *op. cit.*, p. 47).

[2] The anniversary of the promulgation of the Norwegian Constitution in 1814.

[3] The 17th of May does not always seem to have been as dull as Ibsen suggests. In 1842
Bratsberg Amtstidende describes the scene at Skien as follows: 'At around six o'clock signs
of life began to appear in the streets, and a crowd such as our town seldom offers to the eye
gathered in the vicinity of the square. To the accompaniment of music and with the beautiful tricolour flag at their head hundreds of people set forth across the bridges to the Abbey
Wood, whither many had already repaired, to celebrate the Day of Liberation in God's
blessed nature. Here all the people now mingled, and a general dance began, in which rank
and social distinctions were for some hours laid aside. As well as the modern dances, our
nimble mountain lads aroused lively interest by their smartness and agility in the Halling
and the Leap. The Song of Liberation was frequently heard from the enthusiastic multitude.
The whole ended with a grand firework display and the sending aloft of an Air Balloon,
a rare occurrence in this parish.' (Mosfjeld, *op. cit.*, p. 55).

assemble a whole pile of empty tar-barrels. We enjoyed the same time-honoured right over old boats. Should we happen to come upon any of these drawn up on land, and succeed in dragging one or another of them away undetected and keeping our prize safely hidden, then our right of ownership was thereby conceded, or was anyway never challenged by anyone. Then, the day before Midsummer Eve, the boat would be carried in triumph through the streets to the place of our bonfire. Up in the boat would sit a fiddler. I have on several occasions witnessed a procession of this nature, and once myself took part in one.'

Here Ibsen tantalisingly concludes his reminiscences. When he was seven, for reasons which will shortly be described, his childhood suddenly became clouded by misfortune and disgrace, and even in old age he evidently had no desire to commit those later memories to print.

Knud Ibsen had, as already stated, chosen not to follow the seafaring tradition of his forefathers. He ran a *bondehandel*, a general store which sold practically everything: groceries, dairy produce, glass, hardware, ice cream, wine and schnapps. This last commodity he distilled himself; indeed, his was the second largest distillery in town. He also acted as a general importer, and the customs records indicate the extent of his trade. From Bordeaux he imported wine, grape brandy and groceries; from Flensburg, dolls, pewter, ivory combs, glassware, hardware and catgut; from London, woollen and cotton goods; from Altona, aniseed, coriander and fennel seed, presumably for schnapps-making; from Hamburg, woollen goods; and from Newcastle, malt mustard, stone goods and whetstones.[1] He did well; in the year 1833–4, only sixteen private individuals in the district had a higher income, and around the middle of 1833, anxious no doubt to keep pace with his relatives and friends, the Pauses, Altenburgs, Cudrios, Boysens, Bloms and Cappelens, he indulged in the luxury of buying a small country house with forty acres of land at Venstøp in the parish of Gjerpen, a couple of miles outside Skien, for 1,650 specie-dollars (about £410).

No photograph or portrait of Knud Ibsen exists. He is remembered as having been 'under medium height, slight-limbed, oval-faced, with a rather long and slightly crooked nose and a small mouth; narrow between the eyes, with a somewhat sly expression; fair and rather long hair',[2] and as 'a wag, a satirist, and very foxy.'[3] Another witness who met him as an old man found

---

[1] Skiens customs records, quoted by Mosfjeld *op. cit.*, p. 62.
[2] J. A. Schneider, *Fra det gamle Skien*, Vol. (Skien, 1924), p. 249.
[3] Mosfjeld, *op. cit.*, p. 23.

him 'a trivial little fellow of the most ordinary kind with no distinguishing
characteristics, who, however much he talked, never said anything of the
faintest interest';[1] but that was when he was nearly eighty and the years of
failure, poverty and drink had taken their toll. In his youth he seems to have
been a good raconteur with a large stock of funny stories and a quickly in-
ventive tongue. He loved trotting and was a great hunter (there were many
wolves in the district then). In his last years he 'came every morning at
eleven o'clock to a baker whose shop stood next to the old school. In the
back room of the bakery was a little café, where Knud Ibsen would take a
schnapps and a glass of beer. As he sat there enjoying himself, the boys from
the school would often come and bang on the window and shout abuse to
annoy him. Then he would become raging mad and rail at them furiously, but
at the same time so wittily that the words fairly crackled. It was like a firework display.'[2] His son was to paint three different but equally recognisable
portraits of him in his plays: as Jon Gynt in Peer Gynt, Daniel Hejre in The
League of Youth, and Old Ekdal in The Wild Duck.

Knud Ibsen's wife, Marichen (pronounced Marken) is said to have been very
beautiful. A silhouette of her as a young girl (the only likeness we have) shows
a pleasing profile with a retroussé nose. As a young girl she was keen on drawing
and painting (some water colours by her which have survived show a not
negligible talent); and she was, then, merry and gay, and worried her family
by her passionate interest in the theatre. Evening after evening she would slip
away to the performances that travelling Danish players gave in the town. Her
parents were also disturbed by her fondness, even when she was a grown girl,
for playing with dolls; an expression, it has been suggested, of her frustrated
theatrical passion. She played the piano and sang, was lively and spontaneous,
small and dark-haired, with deep and sensitive eyes.

Such were Henrik Ibsen's parents for the first seven years of his life: a gay
and prosperous couple, keeping open house. But this state of affairs was not
to last. In 1834, when Henrik was six, his father's troubles began. On 10 June
of that year the authorities closed his schnapps distillery, and he was distrained
for thirteen dalers for tax arrears. This was less than a year after he had had the
seventeenth largest private income in the town and had bought himself a
country house. During the latter half of 1834, most of 1835 and part of 1836
he was forced to mortgage or sell most of his possessions, one after the
other. The newspaper Ugebladet contains repeated advertisements of forthcoming auctions to this end. In January 1835 his domestic animals, six cows,

---

[1] ibid., pp. 23–24.
[2] ibid., p. 23.

four horses and four pigs, were put up for sale; on 2 May the proud Altenburg mansion, to meet the bills of the Hamburg house of Kragelius; on 9 June the furnishings thereof, including 'bedclothes, two rare carpets and two large mirrors'; and in August, two boat-houses. His creditors did not, as has been supposed, bankrupt him, for his name remained on the list of citizens entitled to vote, from which bankrupts were excluded. They left him his small country house at Venstøp, and to this, probably early in June 1835, Knud and Marichen retired with their four children, and a fifth on the way.

Financial ruin has been known to alter a man's character for the better. It was not so with Knud Ibsen. He became combative, sarcastic and bitter towards those who were not his friends, and also very litigious. The legal archives of Skien are full of petty suits which he brought against this person and that, including even his servants. Oskar Mosfjeld, who interviewed several people who had known Knud Ibsen, or whose parents had known him, comments: 'He wanted to dominate everyone...and if people did not bow to his wishes he became coarse and uncontrolled, especially when he had a little drink inside him. One can imagine what bitterness the sense of social deg-radation must have unleashed in a man of his temperament, how difficult it must have been for him to accept the fact that no one any longer looked up to him. He found people unjust and ungrateful, and struck at them with the only weapon he had left; his sharp tongue. When misery got the better of him, he sought refuge in the bottle and dreamed of the day when he should regain the social position which befitted him. He lacked balance and did not understand how to accept his downfall with dignity. Had he done so, things might in some measure have righted themselves, for his half-brothers were well-to-do and amiably disposed towards him, and he had every opportunity to have worked his way up again had he set his mind to it. But such now were his state of mind and his conduct that many felt embarrassed at being called friends of Knud Ibsen; and when his acquaintances one after another turned away from him, the reason was not, as he supposed, that they despised him for being poor, but because his less fortunate characteristics had come to the surface and made him disagreeable company. At home he felt no inhibitions to his passion for dominance, which at times bordered on brutality. Here he took his revenge for all the frustration which he encountered elsewhere, and made his wife and children pay for it. He could still be polite in company and sociable at home when he chose. But he was moody and incalculable and, when the inclination took him, he gave his touchiness full rein.'[1]

Marichen Ibsen, too, became a different person. The gay young woman with

---

[1] *ibid.*, pp. 20–21.

a passion for the theatre developed into a withdrawn and melancholy recluse. We are told that she hardly dared to speak to people after her husband's degradation, but hid herself away so as to attract as little notice as possible. 'Knud Ibsen scared the wits out of her,' an old lady told Mosfjeld, 'so that in the end she became like a changeling';[1] and other witnesses confirmed that throughout the years at Venstøp she was silent and withdrawn. But she remained loyal to Knud Ibsen. Her daughter Hedvig, many years later, described her as 'a quiet, lovable woman, the soul of the house, everything for her husband and children. She always sacrificed herself; bitterness and fault-finding were unknown to her'.[2]

To the disgrace of his father's financial ruin and social degradation was added another source of embarrassment which must profoundly have affected Henrik Ibsen's childhood. It was openly rumoured that Henrik was not Knud Ibsen's son, but that of an old admirer of his mother named Tormod Knudsen. Marichen had met Knudsen in 1825, shortly before her marriage, when he had come to work as a clerk in the local sheriff's office, and although she was then already engaged, there is a strong tradition in Telemark that she and Knudsen were lovers. This tradition furthermore asserted that the affair continued after her marriage, and that Tormod not only was Henrik's father, but even claimed to be. Knudsen's legitimate son, Knut Knudsen, knew of this rumour years later, and believed it.[3] An old lady who lived on in Skien until the nineteen-thirties told Mosfjeld that she knew something 'terrible' about Marichen Ibsen, but had sworn never to reveal it; and Mosfjeld adds that this informant 'was by no means of the sensation-mongering type, but on the contrary exceedingly reliable, sober and truthful'.[4] Henrik Ibsen himself knew of these rumours. His friend Christopher Due recorded that once at Grimstad, when Ibsen was in his late 'teens and drunk, he blurted out his suspicions to Due and to their friend Ole Schulerud. 'As he spoke', writes Due, 'he gradually became very excited, said in plain words that there were irregulatities connected with his birth, and bluntly named Tormod Knudsen.' Due adds that he never liked to press Ibsen on the subject, and that Ibsen never mentioned it again.[5]

Whether this rumour was true we shall never know. But one important piece of evidence is against it. Henrik Ibsen never remotely resembled Knudsen,

---

[1] ibid., p. 27.
[2] Letter to Henrik Jæger, op. cit., p. 5.
[3] Mosfjeld, op. cit., p. 32.
[4] ibid., p. 33.
[5] Albert Bœck, Små randgloser til Ibsens biografer, in Nordisk tidskrift för vetenskap, konst och industri, häft 4, (Stockholm, 1940).

whom photographs show as having a long face with a pointed jaw and a protruding underlip; but he very closely resembled Knud Ibsen. Professor Francis Bull tells that people in Skien used to say of Henrik Ibsen in his later years that 'it was like seeing old Ibsen [i.e., Knud] resurrected'.[1] J. A. Schneider quotes persons who knew both Knud and Henrik Ibsen as saying that they had something in common in 'appearance, character and habits';[2] and J. Borchsenius writes that Knud Ibsen in old age wore that same peculiarly tight expression around the mouth that we see in Henrik Ibsen's photographs.[3] Against all this we have only rumour. Knudsen's own claim to have been the father means little. Men who covet another man's wife and are known or thought to have been intimate with her before marriage often claim to be the father of one of her children, especially if they are as vain as Tormod Knudsen is reputed to have been. But 'an unlucky and thoughtless utterance can be remembered so long that it becomes a proverb', and the rumour reached Henrik Ibsen's ears when he was a child, probably from other children who had heard it from their parents. He believed it, as would most children who heard rumours of their illegitimacy if, like Ibsen, they had no respect for their father, and it was something from which he was never to escape. Bankruptcy and illegitimacy recur spectre-like throughout his work. Hardly a play he wrote, from *The Pretenders* to *Rosmersholm*, but has its illegitimate or supposedly illegitimate child: Haakon and Peter in *The Pretenders*, Gerd in *Brand*, the Ugly Brat in *Peer Gynt*, Dina Dorf in *The Pillars of Society*, Hedvig in *The Wild Duck*, Rebecca West in *Rosmersholm*.

Such was the background against which Henrik Ibsen spent the next eight years of his childhood, from seven to fifteen. We know little about his early education. He began to read the Bible at the age of six or seven, and it was to remain his favourite book, though he was never a practising Christian. He may possibly have gone to a primary school in Skien before the move to Venstøp; after that, he may, as would seem logical, have been a pupil at a school near the Ibsen house which existed primarily for the benefit of employees at a local factory, but which other children were also permitted to attend. If so, he was fortunate. The headmaster was a young man of thirty-seven named Hans Isaksen who had travelled abroad, knew several languages and was celebrated for the beauty of his handwriting. Alternatively, he may have been educated by one Sexton Lund, who was a good friend of Knud Ibsen and had an excellent private school not far away, much patronised by children from

---

[1] Ibsen, Samlede verker, hundreårsutgave, xx (Oslo, 1930), p. 8.
[2] Schneider, *op. cit.*, III, p. 243.
[3] J. Borchsenius, *Skien for branden 1886* (Oslo, 1934), p. 85.

Skien. Lund is known to have said of Ibsen as a child that he would become 'a great man', possibly from having known him in the classroom.[1]

The house at Venstøp had been somewhat ramshackle when Knud Ibsen bought it, having stood unoccupied for two years; the previous owner, a seaman's widow, had died in 1831. Her husband, a certain Niels Jørgen Hirscholm, had lived a romantic and dangerous life. Among other adventures, he had been a convict in England and a slave in the Barbary States, and had acquired the nickname of 'The Flying Dutchman'. He had died in 1828, the year of Henrik Ibsen's birth. Many of his books remained in the large loft at Venstøp and, although a lot were in English and therefore unintelligible to him, the young Ibsen gained much of his early knowledge from reading them. They included an old illustrated edition of *Harrison's History of London*, that book which was so to excite Hedvig Ekdal's imagination in *The Wild Duck*. 'There's a great big book called *Harryson's* [sic] *History of London*—I should think it must be a hundred years old—and it's got heaps and heaps of pictures in it. On the front there's a picture of Death with an hour-glass, and a girl. That's horrid, I think. But then there are lots of other pictures of churches and castles and streets and great ships sailing on the sea...There was an old sea captain who used to live here once and he brought them home. They called him The Flying Dutchman. It's funny, because he wasn't a Dutchman...In the end he got lost at sea and left all these things behind'.

Ibsen as a boy resembled his father, with the same short build and strong nose, though he had his mother's dark colouring. Apart from painting and reading, his chief passion seems to have been clothes. Old Mr Lund, the father of the aforementioned sexton, was something of a Beau Brummell, and had a special uniform which he used to don on festive occasions comprising velvet breeches, a waistcoat of brown and yellow striped silk, a brown broad cloth coat, a starched cravat and buckled shoes. Ibsen loved to be allowed to come while the old man put all this on. He liked also to paint people in fine clothes and glue them on to bits of wood. He amassed a collection of these, and would arrange them in groups as though in conversation, as in a puppet theatre. No one else was allowed to touch them. Sometimes, as he looked at them, he would 'sit laughing silently to himself, so that he shook'. He would also arrange living tableaux, a pastime in vogue then, and enjoyed joining in

---

[1] Sexton Lund's daughter, who was at school with Ibsen (either at her father's establishment or at Fossum) recalled three-quarters of a century later that Ibsen as a small boy sometimes used to go to school in a red woollen cap, and that when there was snow on the ground the top of his cap could be seen over the wall of a bridge he had to cross well before he himself, being small, came into sight. (J. Brunsvig, *Ibsen-huset på Snipetorp, Ibsen-årbok* 1953, Skien, 1954).

when they went *på julebuk*, going from house to house at Christmas to collect
money like carol singers. Then he would 'dress up grandly, and cut the
finest figure of them all'.[1]

By the entrance to the kitchen at Venstøp (the house still stands, a spacious
and agreeable wooden building of two storeys, with a fine view across the
valley), one may still see the little porch with the closet where Henrik Ibsen
as a child used to lock himself in with his books, dolls and drawings. Soon he
started his own puppet theatre. An old lady, Benedikte Paulsen, who saw
these puppet shows as a small girl in 1841 or 1842, has described them:

'In the early eighteen-forties Henrik Ibsen ran a puppet theatre at
Venstøp. The house had an extension to the north which incorporated the
wash-house, the servants' quarters, a storehouse and various other rooms.
The storehouse served as a theatre. At one end a raised platform had been
built, consisting of several broad table-tops, behind which was a gallery
hidden by a curtain. From this gallery the movement of the puppets was
controlled with the assistance of strings. Henrik himself was responsible for
this, abetted by a trusty assistant, usually Theodor Eckstorm from Grini. It
cost a halfpenny to attend the performance. But some people got in free.
People came a long way to see these performances. Some of the boys came
to make fun of the proceedings.

'Of the female puppets the star attraction was Isabella of Spain. How
splendid she was! Coal-black ringlets, a crinoline of rose-red silk. She
moved elegantly across the boards, to the delight of the little girls. Then
Fernando came riding on to the stage. Feathered hat, scarlet costume laced
with gold. He moved slowly and aristocratically towards Isabella. Then,
alack, there suddenly appears, swift as lightning, a blackamoor, who seizes
her and makes to carry her off. But Don Fernando buffets him so heartily
that he falls to the ground and stays there, whereupon Fernando and
Isabella bow to the audience. Such was the play. But one spring day, when
a gala performance had been advertised at Venstøp and the stage decorated
with blue anemones, there was an unexpected *denouement*. Ole Paulsen from
Gulset and Peder Lund Pedersen from Limi cut the strings. Then Henrik
became really angry. He went for Ole, though the latter was much bigger.
Peder had to go to his friend Ole's help for, though Henrik was small, he
was tough. The young audience yelled and screamed, and the din was fearful. Then a voice was heard which drowned them all: "What's all this?"

---

[1] Interview in *Nationen*, 4 August 1920. This interview actually took place in 1910, but
the two old ladies who were questioned asked that it should not be published until after
the death of Ibsen's sister, Hedvig.

It was Knud Ibsen, Henrik's father. When he saw the combatants, he grasped the situation at once, for he said: "Can't you leave Henrik and his dolls in peace?"

'Henrik did not lose heart, but got new strings for his puppets. His mother said she could well understand why she ran so short of clothes lines. Midsummer Night that year the performance was repeated. Then they lit bonfires on Venstøp Hill, and a large crowd attended, adults as well as children. Henrik exploited the occasion to make a lot of money for his theatre.'[1]

Ibsen also learned some skill as a conjuror; how to make a watch disappear from someone's pocket and replace it there unseen, or pound a watch in a mortar and restore it whole; and other tricks, including ventriloquism, with the aid of his young brother Nicolai concealed in a box. 'Often on a Sunday evening,' his sister Hedvig wrote to Henrik Jæger, 'he obtained leave to give a performance in one of the sitting-rooms, and the neighbours were invited to come and watch. I can see him now in his round jacket, standing behind a large chest, which was brought in and dusted for the occasion; and he would perform miracles which to the astonished onlookers seemed truly magical. None of them, of course, knew that Henrik's younger brother was sitting in the chest, having been well paid to do so; for otherwise he threatened to make a scandal and, since that was the worst Henrik could imagine, he always promised whatever the boy asked'. He also made a little money by constructing small painted cardboard houses and so forth, which an old woman named Maren Mela sold at her fruit stall in the market square. He had inherited something of his father's satirical turn of mind; once, when he had been asked to paint a nice face on a doll for his sister, she found him working on it and laughing unpleasantly to himself. She ran to her mother, crying: 'Oh, now he's laughing again!' But when asked why, he replied that he was merely thinking of the face he *could* have painted. He loved to draw caricatures, and would occasionally harangue his brothers and sisters, standing on a barrel.

At the age of thirteen, Ibsen was enrolled at a small private school started that year (1841) by two young men with theological degrees, Johan Hansen and W. F. Stockfleth. This lay in Skien itself, on Telemarksgaten, not far from Ibsen's birthplace. It had only twenty pupils, but appears to have been well thought of, as at least one distinguished local worthy sent his son there. Ibsen attended this school for two years. His favourite subjects were history, especially that of classical antiquity, and religion, when he would sit for hours

[1] Mosfjeld, *op. cit.*, pp. 106–7.

looking up the passages in the Bible to which references were given.[1] He also learned German, and had private lessons in Latin from Hansen, whom he later praised highly as a teacher, adding that he had 'a mild, amiable temper, like that of a child'.[2] When Hansen died in 1865, Ibsen mourned him; he was practically the only person connected with his childhood, apart from his sister, for whom he retained any affectionate sentiment. The local sexton (not Lund), who helped with the lessons, recalled the young Ibsen as 'a quiet boy with a remarkable pair of eyes, but with no particular cleverness apart from an unusual gift for drawing',[3] One of his fellow-pupils remembered him as 'a little hasty of temper, sharp-tongued, and of a satirical bent, but at the same time friendly and sociable',[4] adding 'I remember too, how one day the whole class sat dead silent while Ibsen read us a composition of his own, in which he related the following dream:

"While wandering across the mountains we were surprised, confused and weary, by the darkness of night. Like Jacob of old we lay down to rest with stones beneath our heads. My companions soon slumbered; I could not sleep. At length weariness overcame me; then in a dream I saw an angel standing over me saying: 'Arise, and follow me'. 'Whither wilt thou lead me in this darkness?', I asked. 'Come', he replied. 'I will show thee a spectacle, human life in its reality and truth.' So I followed, afraid, and we descended as though down huge steps till the mountains bowed over us in mighty vaults and there before us lay a great city of the dead with every dreadful mark of death and corruption; a whole world turned to corpses, all fallen under the stroke of death, its glory faded, withered, quenched. Over the whole hung a weak twilight, sad as that which church walls and whitened crosses cast over a churchyard, yet brighter than anything it could impart to the bleached rows of bones which filled the dark void in endless rows. The sight cast an icy horror over me as I stood there by the angel's side: 'Here seest thou, all is vanity'. Then there came a murmur like the first weak mutterings of an approaching storm, as though of a thousand melancholy sighs, rising to a shrieking blast so that the dead moved and stretched out their arms towards me...and with a scream I awoke, wet with the cold dew of night'.

'On being questioned', continues the reminiscence, 'Ibsen wrote that he well remembers having written this composition, which resulted in a coolness

---

[1] Jæger, op. cit., p. 20.
[2] J. B. Halvorsen, Norsk Forfatterlexicon, III (Christiania, 1892), p. 3 footnote.
[3] ibid., p. 3.
[4] Provst B. Ording, quoted by Halvorsen, op. cit., p. 3.

between him and the master who taught us our mother-tongue, of whom, however, he speaks as an otherwise admirable and cultivated man. The master had, in fact, taken it into his head that the boy had copied his theme out of some book, and when he put forward this hypothesis in class, " I rejected it", says Ibsen, "with more energy than he approved of." [1]

Ibsen took art lessons from a painter named Mikkel Mandt and painted local scenes and romantic subjects, including some based on illustrations in the Flying Dutchman's books. If his father had continued on his earlier, prosperous career, Henrik Ibsen might well have chosen to become a painter. But fortunately for posterity, in those days any Norwegian painter with serious intentions had to go abroad for the necessary technical training, usually either to Dresden, where the great Norwegian landscape artist J. C. Dahl lived (and where he was to act as cicerone to Ibsen when the latter visited the city in 1852 to study theatre) or to Dusseldorf. So that career was closed to him.

He was not interested in any kind of sport, except fishing, swimming and, perhaps surprisingly, dancing, though he was physically tough and resilient. 'Withdrawn' is the word used again and again to describe him at this time, as throughout his life. His sister records that when she and their four brothers were romping together out of doors, he would retire into a little room by the kitchen entrance and bolt himself in. 'He was never a sociable companion', she told Henrik Jæger,[2] 'and we always tried our best to disturb him by throwing stones or snowballs at the wall or door. We wanted him to play with us, and when he couldn't stand our taunts any longer, he would rush out and drive us away—but since he had no talent for any kind of athletic exercise, and violence was foreign to his character, nothing further ever came of it. When he had chased us far enough, he would go back into his room.'

His more boisterous companions found him self-important, a judgment which, again, is confirmed by almost everyone who knew him at this period. He seems to have reacted to the family's plunge into poverty, as so often happens in such cases, by standing on his dignity; he was unwilling to accept the country lads who were his neighbours as his social equals, and is even said to have given them money so that they would not accompany him to school. When he finally left for Grimstad, the local children shouted after him: 'Good riddance, ugly mug!' ('Reis med dig styggen!')[3] Several of these early traits— withdrawnness, social formality, obsessive interest in dress—he was to retain until his death.

---

[1] Halvorsen, op. cit., p. 5 footnote.
[2] Jæger, op. cit. pp. 19–20.
[3] Brunsvig, op. cit.

With the other sex, in general, he got on better. The two old ladies interviewed in 1910 remembered him as 'nice, quiet, reticent, neat, not shy exactly,
but unassuming and withdrawn. But you couldn't call him constrained; he
was never at a loss for an answer. His fellows didn't care for him; they thought
him pompous.' 'Yes, and they gave him a good hiding for it at least once,'
said Fru B. 'And,' she added, 'I think he was a bit uppish.' 'But,' said Fru A.,
'we girls liked him. He was nice looking and well set up. When he came and
asked us to dance, we regarded it as a great honour.' 'Yes,' said Fru B., 'we
were highly flattered. And he was a great ball-goer. He loved dancing, and
was good fun at parties. And once he had started dancing with a girl he would
dance the rest of the evening with her, every single dance...Occasionally he
joined in the other boys' games, as when they went round the houses dressed
up at Christmas, and then he cut the best figure of them all. He liked to dress
up grand.' 'Whom was he closest too?' 'His sister Hedvig. She was very quiet
too, and resembled him in many ways. His brothers were more boisterous,
though they were nice children. His mother was taciturn and became more and
more withdrawn and melancholic. Henrik loved her very much. But I think
there was less understanding between him and his father. His economic position
was one cause of Henrik's bitterness. But his father was a clever, sharp man.
Henrik inherited his talents from him. And his father was very fond of Henrik
and always gave him the best possible clothes...Knud Ibsen was strict in his
own house, but generally speaking he was a merry, lively man, and a great
one for parties. He could be fun too. When he lived at Venstøp I remember he
came to my home one day and we small girls got him to do a solo dance for us.
That was the kind of man he was.'[1]

Knud Ibsen never succeeded in reinstating himself financially, and seems
to have lived the last years of his life largely on the charity of his relatives. He
applied repeatedly for a post in the customs—in 1836, 1837, 1838, 1842 and
1843. His application in 1838 reads sadly: 'To return to my former business
has proved impossible; my possessions, having been mortgaged for debts
which I was unable to pay, were sold; my home likewise was sold at the behest
of a trading company in Hamburg, my distillery at the behest of the Bank,
and my three warehouses to pay the residue of my excise duty and other taxes;
and my other taxes are unhappily so great that I see no possibility of satisfying
my creditors, nor does the financial position of my relatives hold out any hope
of a solution, that of my old parents being especially precarious. For they are
dependent upon their children, I myself having contributed to their support
while my business prospered; so that through no fault of my own I am come

---

[1] Interview in *Nationen*, 4 August 1920.

into most unfortunate straits.'² Repeatedly in his applications he stresses that
his financial troubles have occurred through no fault of his. Local worthies
wrote in his support, praising his conscientiousness and meticulous attention
to detail, characteristics which his dramatist son was to inherit to a marked
degree. In his old age Knud Ibsen ran a chicken farm, and the pedantic detail
with which he recorded his daily output of eggs is very similar to that with
which Henrik Ibsen was to keep the account books of the Bergen Theatre and,
later, his own.

Knud Ibsen failed to obtain any of the customs posts for which he applied. He
took on a variety of minor odd jobs, still, apparently, keeping himself largely
by borrowing. In 1849, when the America fever was at its height, he acted
as agent for ships carrying passengers across the Atlantic. In 1850, we find him
named as enlistment officer and inspector of pilots, and also as agent for Danes
selling grain and dairy produce and Dutchmen selling glazed tiles, onions and
tobacco. But during the four years from 1848 to 1852, he had to appear no less
then seventeen times before the commissioners to answer for unpaid debts.
For a brief while he held a minor post at the Savings Bank; but before long
he was categorised in the tax records of Skien as a 'pauper', from whom no
tax was required, and for the last twenty years of his long life (he lived to be
nearly eighty) he appears to have had no regular work, doing the odd job,
making a little from his chickens, borrowing (mainly from his half-brothers,
the Pauses) and sustaining himself with schnapps and daydreams. As Oskar
Mosfjeld has observed: 'He had long since ceased to play the role of Jon Gynt,
and was henceforth to alternate between the roles of Daniel Hejre, Old
Ekdal and John Gabriel Borkman.'

How much theatre Ibsen saw during his childhood at Skien we do not know;
but he had ample opportunities. The town was visited during the eighteen-
thirties and -forties by a variety of touring companies, mostly Danish, and the
advertisement columns of the local newspaper, *Bratsberg Amtstidende*, give us
some idea of the fare offered. In 1838, Messrs Olsen and Miller announced
eleven performances, comprising a total of eighteen items, mostly contemporary French comedy and romantic melodrama: *Le Jeune Mari*, a comedy
in three acts by Mazère; *Le Mort de Napoleon*, a historical drama in three acts
by Dupeuty and Regnier; *Valeur et Compagnie*, a comedy in one act after
Bayard and Devorne; Scribe's *La Lune de Miel* and *Les Premières Amours*, etc.
In 1839, their repertoire included two more plays by Scribe, *Le Budget d'un
Jeune Ménage* and *Etre aimé ou Mourir*, and Kotzebue's comedy *Blackmail*. In

---

² Mosfjeld, *op. cit.*, p. 83.

1840, G. W. Selmer's company performed Goldsmith's *She Stoops to Conquer*, Oehlenschläger's five-act tragedy *Axel and Valborg* and no less than six Scribes, *Les Premières Amours* (again), *La Pensionnaire Mariée*, *La Somnambule*, *Yelva*, *Le Quaker et la Danseuse* and *Une Fante*. In 1843, the fare offered by Carl Petersen's company included Scribe's *Clermont*, *Une Verre d'Eau* and a repeat of *Le Quaker et la Danseuse*, and fictitious introductions to the greatest English actor and actress of recent times, the elder Dumas's five-act play *Kean*, *l'Acteur Anglais*, and a drama of unnamed authorship entitled *Mistress Siddons, the English Actress*. The list is interesting, for it coincides to a remarkable degree with the repertoire that Ibsen was to find himself compelled to stage as a theatre director in Bergen and Christiania ten and even twenty years later. The titles give a frightening picture of the theatrical taste of the time; and it must not be supposed that this list had been tailored to suit provincial palates, for most of the plays were taken from the repertoire of the Royal Theatre at Copenhagen, Det Kongelige, one of the most accomplished and enlightened theatres then to be found in Europe.

Ibsen left school in the spring of 1843, shortly after his fifteenth birthday, and on 1 October of that year he was confirmed with several other boys in the church at Gjerpen. The order of the candidates was arranged strictly according to their social standing, and Ibsen was placed third, behind Theodor Eckstorm and Peder Lund Pedersen, the boy who had cut the puppets' strings. Knud Ibsen regarded this as a considerable social humiliation and groused about it for years; the only reason he could find was that the parents of the other two boys had given the pastor a fine joint of veal, while he had not been able to afford any such gift. The humiliations of life have a different effect on different people. They drove Knud Ibsen to drink and illusions, and turned his son into a dramatist.

That October, Knud and Marichen Ibsen moved from Venstøp to a house at Snipetorp, in the outskirts of Skien on the road to Bratsberg. Set on a slight hill away from the heart of the town, this building, two-storeyed like Stockmannsgaarden and likewise of wood, escaped the conflagration of 1886 and stands today. It was to be the family home for over twenty years, until 1865, but Henrik Ibsen was to live there for only a few weeks, during which time he decorated some of the door panels with large painted caricatures of his brothers and sister as animals; Johan as a monkey, Hedvig as a bear, Ole as a fox and Nicolai as something that has never been satisfactorily identified.[1]

Now that Ibsen was nearly sixteen, it was time for him to seek a living; and he cannot have been sorry to go. There was constant strife between his

---

[1] These paintings have survived, and may be seen in the Folk Museum at Skien.

parents, his mother was withdrawing more and more into herself, and food was so short that the main meal of the day often consisted only of potatoes. Moreover, the America fever was at this time at its height. During 1842 and 1843 especially, many people emigrated across the Atlantic from the Telemark district, and the local newspapers of those years contain frequent letters from Norwegians who had made their homes in America, mostly in Wisconsin, Minnesota and Dakota, praising the conditions of freedom and opportunity which they had found in the New World. The windows of Snipetorp faced towards the harbour, and from his room the young Ibsen could watch the emigrants embark. In that unhappy house, he must surely have felt the longing to set out, like those hungry families, 'towards the new, towards the unknown, towards the strange shore and the saga that is to come'.[1] A friend of his father's, a travelling salesman, undertook to look out for a post for him, and found him one as assistant to an apothecary at Grimstad, a tiny huddle of houses around a harbour a hundred miles to the south.[2] Two days after Christmas, on 27 December 1843, he departed from Skien in a tiny sailing-ship appropriately named *Lykkens Prøve*, the *Lucky Chance*.

Those eight years between the ages of seven and fifteen left a scar that was never wholly to be healed. In his last years, according to his niece Anna, he often spoke of returning to his birthplace, but could never bring himself to do so. He would, she records, shake his head slowly, and say: 'It is not easy to go to Skien.'[3]

---

[1] *The Pretenders*, Act 4.

[2] Fru Mülertz, whose husband had bought half the Venstøp estate in 1837, owned an apothecary's shop in Skien called the Swan, and it has been suggested that Ibsen may have helped there after leaving school and so gained some knowledge of the work.

[3] Mosfjeld, *op. cit.*, p. 59.

TWO

The Apothecary's Apprentice

(1844-1850)

IBSEN ARRIVED AT GRIMSTAD in the *Lucky Chance* on 3 January 1844, two months short of his sixteenth birthday. He was to remain there for six and a quarter years.

Grimstad is a town that has been much maligned by Ibsen's biographers. Edmund Gosse dismissed it as 'a small, isolated, melancholy place, connected with nothing at all, visitable only by steamer. Featureless hills surround it, and it looks out into the east wind, over a dark bay dotted with naked rocks. No industry, no objects of interest in the vicinity, a perfect uniformity of little red houses where nobody seems to be doing anything.'[1] Simple it certainly was, and is; but, visiting it on a sunny winter's day in 1965, I found it a pleasing cluster of wooden houses, many of them dating from Ibsen's time, attractively situated on its inlet and generally resembling the more agreeable kind of Cornish fishing village. The surrounding landscape, less rugged than that around Skien, is of a gentle and unpretentious charm.

Similarly, Gosse, like Halvdan Koht after him, assumed that Ibsen's years there, spent in extreme poverty, formed a particularly unhappy period of his life. But the evidence of those who knew him at this time suggests precisely the contrary, as does a letter which Ibsen wrote four months after his arrival to a friend at Skien named Poul Lieungh:[2]

Dear Poul,

You must please forgive me for not answering your letter before, but I have had so much to do that I haven't been able to do so earlier, and even now I can't for lack of time write a long letter. Hedevall will already have left by now, and I am sure he will find things to his liking, I at any rate am very happy here and have never regretted coming, as Reimann is very good to me and does everything possible to make me keen on this chemistry work, which I wasn't very at first. With his wife, on the other hand,

---

[1] Gosse, *op. cit.*, pp. 11-12.
[2] Lieungh was a year senior to Ibsen, and the two families were old friends; Knud Ibsen was Paul Lieungh's godfather.

I don't get on nearly so well, and we often quarrel, since it's impossible to do anything right in her eyes. Reimann is also the postmaster, so you can tell my brother Johan to enclose your letters in his, by which means you will be saving postage. I must tell you that Grimstad, and the surrounding countryside especially, is extremely beautiful, and the ladies, though not as galante as those of Skien, are also very acceptable, and you can be sure I do everything to win their favour, which is quite easy to obtain. Since the steamer calls at Grimstad twice weekly I hope to make a trip with it to Skien, if no obstacle arises, which I don't think will. I have several questions to ask you, which you must answer by the next post. First and foremost you must tell me how J.J. took the news of her sweetheart's death, and who is the lucky man who has taken his place; for I know her too well to suppose she is still mourning for him. Then you must tell me whether Carl Aamodt is still writing poetry, and if so please don't forget to ask him to send a short specimen so that I can see if he has made any progress. Though I have more to tell you I must stop now for lack of time, but you may rest assured that my next letter will be longer. Will you please send the copy of William Tell *which Hedevall borrowed back to our house, as it isn't mine? Good luck, and best wishes to all my good friends, from your affectionate*

Henrik J. Ibsen

Please don't let anyone see this, as I have scribbled it in great haste.

With its eight hundred inhabitants, Grimstad was no smaller than many a Norwegian coastal town then; Molde, for example, was no bigger. At first sight, it appeared something of a backwater. Christopher Due, who came there eighteen months after Ibsen, and who well into the present century in extreme old age set down some of the most valuable reminiscences of the early Ibsen that we possess, recorded: 'When I arrived one dark autumn evening in 1845, I at once received the impression of a primitive and impecunious place. There was no street lighting whatever. The feeble light from such windows (by no means few in number) as had no curtains, so that even in the so-called main street one could see families seated around tables illuminated by only a single tallow candle, merely served to make the street darker, and it was not undangerous to walk there because of the gutters down the middle.'[1] Grimstad had no church of its own until December 1849, a few months before Ibsen's departure, and, more regrettably for posterity, no newspaper of its own until 1856 when *Grimstads Adressetidende* was founded. Nor does it seem to have had any good school, for the better families sent their children away to be educated.

But it was not a sleepy town. On the contrary, with its fine natural harbour and amply accessible timber it was, despite its smallness, a bustling and prosperous centre of shipbuilding. 'In every inlet,' noted Due, 'and there are many

---

[1] Christopher Due, *Erindringer fra Henrik Ibsens ungdomsaar* (Copenhagen, 1909), p.13.

inlets in or near the town, one saw a hull on the stocks and, as soon as this had been launched, the frame was erected for its successor...Everyone who had any savings, or could manage to borrow some, bought shares in a ship. The priest, the doctor, the justice, not to speak of the seamen and tradespeople, the artisans and even the servant-maids, were all, in greater or less degree, ship-owners...To own a share in a ship was reckoned as safe as, and much more profitable than, investing one's money in the Savings Bank. It not seldom happened that, freight rates being what they were then, a ship repaid the cost of its construction in two or three voyages. The greater part of the male population went to sea immediately after confirmation, and thereafter spent only the winter months at home...The people were frugal, undemanding and, above all, peaceably inclined, living out their quiet and modest lives within their narrow circle.'[1]

Hans Eitrem, who in about 1909 spoke to several survivors from Ibsen's time there, concluded that Grimstad was, for its period, a tolerant and friendly little town.[2] The pietism that was to dominate it, like so many other Nor-wegian towns, later in the eighteen-fifties had not yet taken root; the local pastor, who bore the unchristian-sounding name of Pharo, was a worldly and eccentric figure. There was a billiards hall, where you could sit with a toddy; dances were held, sometimes masked, and 'excursions with dance' were a popular diversion. In the early forties at least there were amateur theatricals, and the plays performed included Beaumarchais' *The Marriage of Figaro* and works by Ludvig Holberg,[3] Kotzebue and J. L. Heiberg;[4] in 1909 Eitrem reported that whole chests were still to be found full of scripts. Troupes of wandering players also visited the town, as they did Skien, living from hand to mouth; and when the summer came and the citizens no longer wished to spend their evenings indoors, (and the tallow candles which formed the only source of stage illumination could no longer fight the sunlight), they eked out their precarious existence as dancing and fencing masters until the autumn dusk began to close in. Ibsen was to recall these amateur groups and strolling players when, thirty years later, he wrote *The Pillars of Society*, a play that is full of Grimstad memories.

In a town that lived on its shipping, Ibsen must, through his work, have mixed a lot with sailors. There still lived in Grimstad several men who had been in prison in England during the Napoleonic Wars (in which Norway and

[1] Due, *op. cit.*, pp. 14–15.
[2] H. Eitrem, *Ibsen og Grimstad*, written in or around 1911 but not published until 1940 (Oslo), pp. 41–46.
[3] See Appendix A.
[4] See page 110.

Denmark sided with France), and others who had been prisoners in Gothen-
burg during the brief war against Sweden in 1814. Many foreign ships took
refuge from storms in the harbour; the references to American sailors in *The
Pillars of Society* make it clear that the inhabitants were well used to having such
aliens in their midst. In Christmas 1847 an Italian ship destined for St. Petersburg took refuge in Grimstad because of ice in the Baltic, got frozen in and had
to stay until the following May; the sailors' band marched through the streets
of the little town with banners flying, singing O *bella Napoli*.[1]

Reimann, the apothecary to whom Ibsen was apprenticed, was an amiable
but unpractical man of thirty-nine whose business was on the slide. His shop
lay in a poor quarter of the town, occupying part of 'a small and exceedingly
humbly furnished house, with small-paned windows in both of its two low
storeys'.[2] The remainder of the house (i.e., that part not taken up by the shop)
served as accommodation for the Reimanns, their numerous children, their
two maids and their new apprentice. Everyone slept upstairs in three rooms.
The inmost was occupied by the Reimanns and the smallest children, the second
and central room by Ibsen and the three elder sons, and the third by the two
maids. Only the last of these had direct access to the staircase, so that when, as
happened frequently, anyone came with urgent requirements in the night,
Ibsen had to go through the maids' room with his candle to answer the door.[3]

The ground floor comprised the shop, a tiny waiting room and the kitchen.
When Ibsen had to prepare anything that required heating, he had to do it
over the open fire in the kitchen, often with one of the maids cooking a meal
beside him. 'When he came to the kitchen fire with his pots and pans, and
wanted all the room, we had words,' one of these maids, Marie Thomsen, told
Eitrem sixty-five years later.[4] Christopher Due, as a very old man, vividly
recalled the background against which he saw Ibsen for the first time:

'As I passed [the shop] one day with a friend, the latter asked me if I had
seen the apothecary's apprentice, remarking that there was something odd
about him. I should explain that long after his arrival there were many
people who had not set eyes on him unless they had had any business with
the apothecary, since Ibsen was never to be seen outside, at any rate in
daytime. Curious to inspect him I soon went into the shop. This comprised a tiny room, so low that I could almost touch the ceiling with my
hand, and extremely shabby—undusted, dark and displeasing. As an

---

[1] Eitrem, *op. cit.*, pp. 52–53.
[2] Due, *op. cit.*, p. 18.
[3] Marie Thomsen to Eitrem, *op. cit.*, p. 19.
[4] *ibid.*, p. 20.

apothecary's it was primitively equipped in every respect...There was no one to be seen, nor any sound to suggest that anyone was present, so I had ample time to make these observations; but on banging upon the counter, I perceived some movement behind the so-called prescription cabinet, and soon afterwards there emerged somewhat abruptly a small young man with an attractively vital face. I should here mention that Ibsen in his youth wore a handsome full brown beard, unusually well developed for one so young, which gave his face an energetic and at the same time harmonious expression...The total impression was that of a handsome young man with a good, shapely figure.'[1]

Since Reimann, according to Marie Thomsen, 'spent most of the time walking outside and did little work,'[2] Ibsen had to see to practically everything. He was perpetually boiling and compounding, breaking off only to serve a customer or to deal with the town's post, for which, as Ibsen explained in his letter to Lieungh, Reimann was officially responsible. He had desperately little free time ('You never saw him in the streets of a weekday,' another informant told Eitrem[3]), earned the most miserable of salaries, and did not have enough to eat.[4] Nevertheless, by stinting himself of sleep, he managed to pack far more into each twenty-four hours than most youths of his age. He painted a great deal, drew caricatures of the local citizens, wrote lampoons about them, and serious poetry as well. He also read much; he had brought a whole box of books with him from Skien, and among the authors he devoured were Dickens, Scott, Holberg, Voltaire (whom he especially admired), the contemporary Swedish novelist Fredrika Bremer and the Danish novelist Fru Gyllembourg. Reimann was a member of a reading circle, and allowed Ibsen to borrow books through him.[5]

Not content with such general reading, he studied at night for his matriculation, in the hope that he might eventually qualify to go to the University; and this, as we shall see, was to provide him with the inspiration for his first play.

---

[1] Due, *op. cit.*, pp. 18–20.

[2] Eitrem, *op. cit.*, p. 22.

[3] *ibid.*, p. 22.

[4] Fru Staff told Eitrem (*op. cit.*, p. 135) that even Reimann's own children hardly had any butter on their bread.

[5] A *læseselskab*, or book club, had been formed in 1835 with twenty-seven members; Reimann and his successor, Nielsen, both belonged, and Ibsen, who could not afford the eight crowns subscription, borrowed books through them. It possessed in Ibsen's time over six hundred volumes, including (in translation) such foreign authors as, in addition to those mentioned above, Dumas, Victor Hugo, Bulwer, Fenimore Cooper and Captain Marryat, also that *World History* of Becker which Peer Gynt intended to consult. (Eitrem, *op. cit.*, p. 44).

On the infrequent occasions on which he found himself free in the daytime, he took long solitary Wordsworthian walks, often armed with a paintbox, and would occasionally go for a row.

Jørgen Peder Eriksen, who had known Ibsen from the time of the latter's arrival in Grimstad at the age of fifteen, was still alive, a vigorous old man of eighty-four, when Eitrem visited the town in 1909. 'Yes, of course I remember the lad,' he told Eitrem. 'He was always wanting to do handgrips and wrestle... and we used to lift weights to see who was the strongest. He looked strong, too; he was well built, but small.' Eriksen well recalled Ibsen's arrival at the apothecary's: 'He came in a "candle-snuffer" [i.e. a coat fitting tightly at the waist, a novelty in Grimstad then, though it was the fashion in the capital]. He wasn't at all sullen; very talkative, and mixed a lot with the other local youths. But he looked so old; he had a coarse face, full of pimples.' Eriksen's sister, Marthe, recalled that 'he used to lie on the hill and toboggan with the young girls. With every one of them. There wasn't such a difference between boys and girls then. They were mostly the daughters of sailors and woodcutters.'[1] Jørgen Eriksen also remembered that Ibsen was often to be seen reading or painting on Vestre Varden, a high crag above the town.[2]

Another portrait of Ibsen during his first two years at Grimstad comes from a schoolmaster, H. Terland, who in 1900 delivered a lecture to the Christiania Philological Society which was printed in the newspaper *Eidsvold*.[3] 'Quiet and withdrawn as he was, he made no effort to gain an acquaintance with the families of the town. Nor, certainly, could he be regarded as an acquisition to the social circles of Grimstad, being a mere boy and of a very unprepossessing exterior. Small and thin, but squarely built, of swarthy complexion, with a dark lock of hair hanging down over his forehead, and a shy glance which he continually averted—thus do old inhabitants of Grimstad depict the young Ibsen's appearance...He was certainly no beauty, and when one recalls that he also had a curious introspective, old-mannish face, and an enclosed personality, it is not in the least surprising that people regarded the sixteen or seventeen year old boy as a queer fish...He was taciturn and withdrawn, didn't say much, but wrote short poems with extraordinary facility, always in rhyme...One must remember that Ibsen was still in the hobbledehoy stage, and the need that boys have then to poke fun at the world and play-act found expression in him through this medium.'

---

[1] Another old lady who as a girl had known Ibsen in Grimstad recalled how he liked to pull their plaits. (*Selskab for Grimstad bys vels medlemsskrift* nr. 22, 1956).
[2] Eitrem, *op. cit.*, p. 18.
[3] *Eidsvold*, 8 October 1900.

The apparent contradiction between Terland's account and that of the Eriksens and others need not trouble us. It is evident that Ibsen was one person when in the company of simple people, with whom he had no sense of social inferiority, and another when with ladies and gentlemen of 'good family'.

Ibsen does not appear to have made any close friends at Grimstad during his first couple of years there (he probably did not meet Due until some time in 1846). Then, two and a half years after his arrival, the thing that he could least afford happened.

One of the maids at the Reimanns was named Else Sofie Jensdatter. She was ten years older than Ibsen, having been born on 11 January 1818 in Børkedalen in Vestre Moland. Else was not, as many commentators have taken for granted, a kitchen slut; her ancestors had been gentlemen farmers, and the family had become impoverished in an honourable cause. Her grandfather, Christian Lofthuus, had led a rebellion of the Norwegian peasants against their Danish overlords in the previous century, as punishment for which his farm had been burned, his property declared forfeit, and he himself chained to a block in the fortress of Akershus, where, ten years later, he died.

Else was one of the two servant girls who slept in that outer room through which Ibsen had to pass on his way to answer the night bell. She was, moreover, his *husmor*, which means that it fell to her to see to his personal needs, such as mending. She attended to other needs too. On 9 October 1846, when she was twenty-eight and Ibsen was eighteen and a half, she bore him a son. The birth did not take place in Grimstad; she returned for the occasion to her parents in Børkedalen, so that the affair did not receive the full local publicity which would otherwise have been accorded it. But Ibsen had, out of his almost non-existent salary, to pay paternity costs towards the child's upbringing until he reached the age of fourteen.

Else named her son Hans Jacob Henriksen; and we may turn aside briefly from the story of Ibsen's own life to summarise the unhappy history of his illegitimate son and the latter's descendants. Hans Jacob lived with his mother at Børkedalen, east of Lillesand, until he was twenty-nine, eking out a hard living as a blacksmith. They were very poor; his mother seems to have been unable to do any kind of work, and there is an unconfirmed tradition that she went blind. When, finally, her parents' house was taken from them, Hans Jacob scrawled on a rock the grim word *Sultefjell*—Starvation Hill. Else moved to a 'small, grey hut' on a hillside at Tyttebærmœn, west of Lillesand, and died there, a pauper, on 5 June 1892, aged seventy-four. Hans Jacob became, according to one who remembered him late in his life, 'a very interesting man, who read a great deal, taking especial pleasure in history, geography and travel books. He was also a bit of a fiddler and fiddle-maker, in general a well appointed man; but unhappily he was a victim of drink.'...In fact, he became an alcoholic and ne'er-do-well. He married three times and had seven children, but their fate, too, makes sad reading. Six died young; the fate of the seventh is unknown. We have no record of what happened to the eldest, Jens, born out of wedlock in 1876. Hans Jacob married the mother, Mathilde Andreasdotter, but she died five years later of tuberculosis. The following year, 1882, he married one Trine Marie Gunvaldsen; she bore him a daughter, Marie, two months afterwards, but the child lived only a fortnight and the mother died nine days later. In 1883 Hans Jacob made his third and final marriage, with Ida Gurine Olsdatter, who bore him five children. Ole (born 9 April 1884) died as a baby. Isak (born 9 March 1885) died on 7 April 1888, aged three. Inge (born 10 August 1888) was drowned off Rockall in the *Norge* on 28 June 1904, on her way to America, aged fifteen. Gunda (born 24 April 1892) died on 17 September 1896, aged four. The fifth and last child, Jenny, (born 8 March 1895) seemed likely to break this tragic sequence; she lived to the age of twenty-seven, working as a seamstress, but died on 22 September 1922 of tuberculosis shortly before she was due to be married. Hans Jacob himself lived on until 20 October 1916; he had no contact with his famous father until he saw him for the first time, briefly and dramatically, towards the end of the latter's life.[1]

Shortly before the birth of Ibsen's illegitimate son, the unfortunate Reimann's debts at last caught up with him, and in August 1846, at the demand of a fellow apothecary in Christiania to whom he owed nearly thirteen thousand crowns (about £650), his business was put up for auction and bought by one O. A. Haanshus. Early the next year Haanshus resold it to a former apprentice of Reimann named Lars Nielsen, the twenty-three-year-old bachelor son of a well-to-do local shipmaster. Nielsen transferred the shop from Storgaden 75 to a better locale at Østergade 13, a house owned by a stone-deaf and eccentric widow named Geelmuyden, who spent her whole day in a chair, occupied solely with her snuff-box.[2] Here, Nielsen leased two decent-sized rooms on the ground floor. The outer room, into which the front door opened, was the shop; the inner room, to the rear, served as waiting room, laboratory, parlour, dining-room and bedroom for the young apothecary and his 'qualified assis-

---

[1] For the information contained in this paragraph I am indebted to Fru Ingeborg Björklund-Bexell, who included it in her unpublished thesis, *Ibsens Vildanden, en studie*, written in 1962. Her informant who remembered Hans Jacob Henriksen at Lillesand was J. Ager-Hansen.

[2] Fru Geelmuyden's maid, Sofie Høglund, who came to her in 1847 at the age of seventeen and stayed two years, told Eitrem that Ibsen as a lodger was 'nice, a really nice person, never complained'.

tant' (*examinerade medhjelper*), for Nielsen raised Ibsen to this status from his previous one of apprentice and increased his salary. Reimann had given him an excellent reference, saying that he was unusually skilful at his work, conscientious and industrious. The building at Østergade 13 still stands, a pleasant wooden house of two storeys a stone's throw from the sea, and the two rooms are preserved much as they must have been in Ibsen's time, except that then the walls of the parlour were hung with Ibsen's own paintings, few of which have survived. In the shop itself perched a large stuffed owl, which had been shot in the tree outside Ibsen's window and which figures in one of his early poems.

A portrait of Ibsen at work as an apothecary comes to us from the other of the Reimanns' two maids, Marie Thomsen. She remembered him as 'very quiet; badly dressed; his clothes were as shiny as that stove; you could tell from them that he was hard at it all day.' There was an old man called Svend Fjeldmand (Svend the Hillman), who used to wash up and do odd jobs in the shop; he and Ibsen became friends and often took a walk together on Sundays to Fjære churchyard half an hour away. Svend died shortly before Ibsen left Grimstad and Marie recalled that Ibsen painted a picture and put it on Svend's grave at Fjære 'with something he'd written'. He did a lot of paintings; Marie and the Eriksens were agreed on this. At work he was perpetually boiling and mixing, breaking off only to attend a customer. He was neat at his packaging. Sometimes, in the kitchen, he would get bad-tempered and stump off into the shop. But 'a moment later he'd come out again, and the mood would have left him. "Feel better now?" I'd ask him. I could put him in the right humour, I could..."If you grow up and get married you'll plague the life out of your wife," I told him. "I bet he was a terror in his own house?" she asked suddenly.' But when Eitrem replied that he was very nice, she didn't find it surprising. 'No, he didn't say much; but he wasn't surly or miserable. He was fun really. He liked playing jokes...That Henrik was a terrible one for reading. He had a whole box bursting with books—but no clothes. He spent nearly the whole night writing and reading. Never in bed before two. Light? Yes, he had a tallow candle—I never heard them refuse him one. Sometimes I'd open the door and say: 'You go to bed now, lad. You'll get fuddle-headed with all this reading'... More than once he said: 'I'll never live to see the day when I get on the right shelf'. He never said what kind of a shelf that might be. We never knew what was going on in his mind, and didn't ask...Most of his spare time he spent drawing and painting. The whole house was full of his pictures. Oh yes, they let him hang them up. No frames on them, though. He painted quick as lightning. Sometimes he'd paint in the shop, sometimes in the storehouse. I don't know whether he painted the shop sign outside [of a swan]. It was certainly

D

done while he was there. He used pencils too. Drew us all—in our working clothes—as we stood washing ourselves and looking dreadful. Old Pharo, the father of the priest at Fjære, he did a drawing of him. He was the one who always went past the window with a finger through a hole in his coat. And he drew people who came to the shop. When he'd drawn anyone he'd come out to us in the kitchen and show it to us'.[1]

She confirmed that he liked climbing the hills around Grimstad, and rowing, and denied that he was miserable; the apothecary (Reimann), she said, made much of him. 'If he'd been father to the boy he couldn't have been kinder to him'. A fine man, the apothecary. Not at all bossy, nor was his wife really, only she was always so poorly. One Christmas they hadn't a bite to eat. My mother went down to Crawfurd's shop and got food from the English lady. The apothecary became angry when he heard this and wouldn't take it. "Well, if you want your family to starve, that's your business," I said. But in the end he let us keep it. Quite untrue that Ibsen starved—that's a lie. But he [Reimann] drank too much. Ibsen was quick in his movements, silent and quick as an owl."[2]

With the children, he was not always so popular. J. Schulerud, whose brother Ole was to become one of Ibsen's few really close friends, recalled: 'We small boys didn't like him, he was always so sour. When we went to the apothecary's to buy liquorice, he gave us miserably little for our halfpennies. Old Reimann gave us much more.' Schulerud added that he only once heard Ibsen laugh 'good and heartily, like other human beings'.[3]

Nielsen, Ibsen's new employer, was a quiet and *soigné* young man, very different from Reimann. He ate all his meals at his parents' house a few minutes away, and at his suggestion Ibsen took lunch with them and had his breakfast and supper brought up to the shop. When they had visitors in the evening, they often invited Ibsen, leaving the maid Sofie to look after the shop and run down to fetch Ibsen if anyone should call. Old Nielsen, the apothecary's father, was a jovial man with a good stock of travellers' yarns; his drawing room contained two large mirrors and twelve lamp brackets. Among his ships was one named *The Palm Tree*, which was to figure, like so many other Grimstad memories, in *The Pillars of Society*. Fru Nielsen was a different type, pious and narrow-minded, and she disapproved of the radical opinions to which Ibsen sometimes gave expression.   One of her friends, Fru Damsgaard, once said to her: 'I don't know why you talk to that horrid Ibsen, he's so coarse and ill-mannered

---

[1] Eitrem, *op. cit.*, pp. 18 ff.
[2] *ibid.*, p. 18.
[3] Interview in *Verdens Gang*, 23 and 24 June 1910.

he isn't worth answering.' But Fru Nielsen, to her credit, replied that she believed that he didn't speak thus to offend but because he had a doubting and enquiring mind, and liked to hear other people's opinions.[1]

No real friendship sprang up between Ibsen and his young employer. Ibsen used to refer disrespectfully to him in his absence as 'the animal', and when he borrowed Nielsen's galoshes called them 'the animal's hind footwear'; he was also heard to utter remarks about 'empty heads and full pockets'.[2] Ibsen himself later wrote of Nielsen that he was 'good and clever, but entirely preoccupied with his work'[3] (which included being cashier at the local Savings Bank, a task which took up more of his time than the shop). Like Reimann, he left the preparation of medicines and the reception of customers almost entirely to Ibsen. A thrifty man, he died in 1865 aged forty, leaving a sizeable fortune.

Among the people Ibsen met at the Nielsens was an old Scottish lady named Miss Crawfurd. Her brother Thomas Crawfurd, an engineer from Carron in Stirlingshire, had settled in Grimstad in 1822, and she had joined him. She was known in the town as *Tanten*, the old maid, but was a much respected figure, and one of the few people in the town to have a good private library. She took a liking to the abrupt and awkward young newcomer, with his radical views, and her nephew, Jens, told Eitrem sixty years later how, as a boy of fourteen, 'I often took books from my old aunt to Ibsen.'[4] He remembered that she owned Kierkegaard's *Either-Or*, published only a few years earlier in 1843, and she may well have provided Ibsen with his first introduction to Kierkegaard's work.[5]

It may also have been through Miss Crawfurd that Ibsen first discovered the plays of Adam Oehlenschläger, the great Danish poet then approaching the end of his career. Oehlenschläger, as a dramatist, lay somewhere between Corneille and Schiller, the latter being his idol; his plays, like theirs, are written in distinguished, dignified and sometimes eloquent verse, but to a modern reader seem static and declamatory, the kind of theatre that has been unkindly described as grand opera without the music. But we must remember that Ibsen, at this time, could read neither English nor French, and German only with difficulty, and he can have gained little from the poor Scandinavian translations then available of Shakespeare and other foreign dramatists; nor, until he went to Copenhagen in 1852, did he have the chance to see any great tragedy

---

[1] Family tradition quoted by Eitrem (*op. cit.*, p. 38).
[2] Due, *op. cit.*, p. 39.
[3] Preface to the second edition of *Catiline* (Copenhagen, 1875).
[4] Eitrem, *Maal og Minne* (Oslo, 1910), p. 47.
[5] On the possible influence of Kierkegaard on Ibsen, see page 198.

on the stage. Oehlenschläger's poetic dramas, mostly set in Scandinavia during
the heroic age, (*Earl Haakon the Mighty*, *The Vikings in Byzantium* and so forth),
were Ibsen's first glimpse of theatrical tragedy; and Oehlenschläger was to be
his first model, though he was quickly to discard him, as he was to discard his
other influences.

Jens Crawfurd also remembered that his aunt possessed the poetical works
of Henrik Wergeland, the Norwegian poet of freedom (1808–1845) of whom
it has well been said that 'few theological students of any university have
figured so frequently in the police court' and that 'it is a little bit as though
Shelley had also been Cobbett'.[1] Wergeland was a great admirer of Shakespeare, and revered England as the home of the liberty that he was perpetually
preaching. Christopher Due told Eitrem that he read Wergeland's enormous
720 page poem, *Creation, Man and Messiah*, with Ibsen in Grimstad.[2] The
earliest poems that we possess by Ibsen, dating from 1847 and 1848, are very
much in the Wergeland manner; carrying titles such as *Resignation*, *By the Sea*,
and *Doubt and Hope*, they are, in content, the usual adolescent mixture of eager-
ness and suicidal melancholy, and are interesting only for an unusual technical
maturity, especially in the rhyming. Ibsen's extraordinary facility for writing
verse, especially rhymed verse, in practically any metre was to dominate his
early play-writing to its disadvantage. In his first ten plays, he is almost always
at his best when subjecting himself to the tougher discipline of prose.

Ibsen gave some of his poems to old Miss Crawfurd as he wrote them, and
on returning to her home after a Sunday at the Nielsens she would read them.
She died in 1865 at the age of eighty-seven, late enough to learn of his success
the previous year with *The Pretenders* and, we may hope, to hear in the year
of her death of his greater triumph with *Brand*, and perhaps to read it.

By the end of 1847, Ibsen was reading hard for his matriculation. The
subjects in which he had to prepare himself included Latin and Greek; these,
and other subjects, he read with two theological students who visited the shop,
S. C. Monrad and Emil Bie. He also wrote Norwegian compostions for a
tutor in Christiania, some of which have survived. One, dated 3 February
1848, dealt with a theme which was to preoccupy him throughout his life:
On the Importance of Self-Knowledge. It is written in a remarkably lucid and
mature style for one whose schooling had been so brief.

'Of all the branches of thought', it begins, 'the investigation of our own
nature is among those in which the sharpest observation and impartiality
are necessary if one is to arrive at that which is the goal of every enquiry,
namely, the truth. Self-knowledge demands the most careful study of

---

[1] Derry, *op. cit.*, p. 149.
[2] Eitrem, *Maal og Minne*, p. 47.

ourselves, our inclinations and actions, and only by the results of such an analysis is it possible for a human being to reach a clear and truthful understanding of what he really is.' He concludes: 'Even if a man, by acquiring this self-knowledge, gets to know his worst characteristics and thereby finds himself required to humble himself in his own eyes, such humiliation can in no way impair his self-respect, since it provides evidence of a strong will and an honest quest for what should be man's goal in life—the development of his spiritual gifts and a care for his temporal well-being.'

By now, much to his delight and profit, Ibsen was seeing more of Christopher Due, and a close bond sprang up between the two. Due writes:

'I felt more and more strongly drawn to him. His intelligence and bubbling humour fascinated me all the more because these characteristics were lacking in my other acquaintances. Gradually I became a daily visitor to the shop, mostly in the evenings, when Ibsen would be sitting peacefully in his room. I used to look forward all day to these meetings. It was a new and entrancing experience to listen to his witty utterances, those independent and, to me, largely new views of life, somewhat audacious, to be sure, as they seemed to me, and full of paradoxes, but always interesting. And he found in me a grateful listener, enthusiastically following him in his occasionally somewhat wild flight from the prosaic material situation in which he lived and which, by this means, he, as it were, cast off, to our mutual advantage. As is usual among young persons, we discussed everything between heaven and earth, not least marriage. Among Ibsen's extravagant caprices I remember that he contended with a curious ardour that he and his wife, if he ever acquired one, would have to live on separate floors, see each other at meal-times, and not address each other as "Du". This was at that time his ideal of marriage...Gradually people began to notice this intelligent and witty young man, and the waiting room of the apothecary's shop soon became, especially on Sundays and of an evening, a favourite meeting-place, to which new friends were continually introduced. It was always fun, with Ibsen as the centre-point of the grateful circle, for he bubbled with humour, and, admittedly, with sarcasm too, and despite the poverty of his circumstances he was always in an excellent temper. One never got any feeling that he was depressed. He possessed to a high degree the elasticity of youth.'[1]

Due goes on to confirm that Ibsen often indulged his wit in the form of sharply satirical poems and caricatures. 'He had an astonishing talent for writing fluent

---

[1] Due, *op. cit.*, pp. 21–22.

verses, and was a very talented artist. His pencil swiftly and surely made its point.' Due quotes a kind of strip cartoon which Ibsen composed about a man and his horse, the horse eventually proving far more cunning than the man. He also wrote 'an excellent poem in rhyme' about a local youth, fitted to the melody of a popular Danish vaudeville of the time from which the youth in question was always singing extracts. Ibsen then got the subject of the poem to sing it to a gathering of friends, all of whom, except the singer, knew that it referred unflatteringly to the latter.

'To see Ibsen's pleasure at the merriment which reigned among us when we persuaded the object of our Harcellas to sing the verses of which he was himself the comic hero, was indescribable. Ibsen's eyes glittered like fire... In addition to such amusements, we occasionally held a card party of an evening in Ibsen's room. Only the more trustworthy among us were selected for these occasions, men who could keep silence about such enormities as that we drank punch from ointment pots which, should we be surprised by some suspicious intruder, were swiftly emptied and stuffed into our pockets. As midnight approached, one of the more thoughtful among us might suggest that Ibsen needed some peace, since we all knew that he used part of the night in studying for his examination, but he always assured us that there was still plenty of time left for both study and sleep.

'Ibsen's capacity for work and physical resilience, [continues Due], were phenomenal. Apart from a very few hours he literally worked throughout the day and night. Most of his day was of course taken up with the business of the shop. Since there was then only this one apothecary's business between Kristiansand and Arendal, a matter of some seventy kilometres, there was obviously a deal to do, and since the apothecary himself was much occupied with his duties as cashier and book-keeper at the local savings bank and was moreover in uncertain health, the result was that Ibsen did most of the work at the shop. This was, like the older shop [i.e., Reimann's], even by the humble standards of those days, very inadequately equipped. For example, there was no special room set aside as a laboratory. When any complicated potions had to be prepared, resort was made to the kitchen belonging to the lady who owned the house. She lived in one half of the ground floor of the little house while the apothecary's shop and waiting room occupied the other half. I have actually seen Ibsen in the kitchen over an open fireplace, without even a stove, busy preparing medicines next to Madame Geelmuyden's cooking pots. For smaller preparations a small spirit lamp in the shop served. In those days there was no such thing as a petroleum apparatus. With such primitive equipment the work of the shop was naturally extremely arduous and took a disproportionately long time, to Ibsen's chagrin, since it meant that he could spend less time on what most interested him...

'It was quite incredible how much Ibsen got through in each twenty-four hours. Apart from his work in the shop, which as stated took up most of the daytime, he had his matriculation studies, which he had to pursue largely without assistance...These caused him considerable worry and trouble. Then, from a natural inner compulsion, he felt urged to spend part of the day or night writing, which more and more obsessed his thoughts. And yet he also found time to employ his talent as an artist in many directions. Not only was his pencil continually active, he also painted landscapes...When one remembers that visits from his friends occupied part of each day too, it will be appreciated that there was little time left for sleep or rest. But I never heard Ibsen complain of being tired. His health was always exemplary. He must have been uncommonly tough physically. For example, his financial situation compelled him to exercise the strictest imaginable economy, to the point of having to manage without underpants and even, later. without socks. Since there was among the many female charmers of Grimstad a young lady towards whom he was inclined, I jestingly told him that he was acting *Love without Stockings*.[1] We had a good laugh over this. Ibsen was always ready to take a humorous view of his painful circumstances. These sartorial experiments of his succeeded even in winter, when he had, moreover, no overcoat, for I never knew him to catch cold, or suffer from any physical ailment.'[2]

One day Grimstad was surprised by the arrival of a young 'student' (i.e., someone who had passed the matriculation examination). 'A *student* was a rare sight in those parts,' comments Due. 'Among the natives of the town, for many years there had only been two. One looked up to an *akademiker* with a kind of involuntary respect.' This newcomer was Ole Carelius Schulerud, born 1827. Due, who knew Schulerud's father, quickly introduced him to Ibsen, and the three soon became firm friends. 'Apart from our mutual sympathy and literary interests—in those days one eagerly studied Søren Kierkegaard's books, *Either-Or*, *The Works of Love*, etc., and not least Oehlen-schläger's tragedies, and *Clara Raphael's Letters*[3]—we were, all three, in contrast to our other comrades, "as poor as church mice". One of us had, for

---

[1] A parody of neo-classical French tragedy by J. H. Wessel (1742–1785), set to music by Paolo Scalabrini.

[2] Due, *op cit.*, pp. 29–35.

[3] One of the first calls for female emancipation.

economic reasons, to do without lunch, the second could manage both
board and lodging but seldom found the pocket money for a cigar, and the
third, Ibsen, had from his pitiful salary to buy clothes and books, pay his matriculation tutor, and even, as 'apothecary's journeyman' (for thus, to his
rage, he was described in the tax register), contribute to the town rates. Most
of our fellows had, in varying degrees, shares in ships, and were therefore
comfortably off. They could afford many things that we three had to deny
ourselves. Their situation provided a marked contrast to that of the 'Trium-
virate', with our humble get-togethers, and created, not least in Ibsen, a
bitter resentment against 'empty brains with full wallets'...There were a few
families where a more intelligent life was carried on, but Ibsen never moved
in their circles.'[1]

In so small and conservative a community as Grimstad, respectable citizens
had begun to notice and shake their heads at the young radical, with his
atheistic and republican views. For Ibsen was already a heretic in such matters
as marriage, love, morality and religion. He had broken away from his early
religious teaching, and was unwilling to believe in a God, except in generalised
and agnostic terms. He had, as we know, studied Voltaire, and Due tells
how 'he championed the latter's Deism and Pantheism...He denied the
existence of a personal God. In this he met strong opposition from one or two
of us, and we tried our best to move him from his position of complete
religious disbelief, but in vain.'[2]

To so restless and questioning a soul, it was natural that the idea of republicanism should appeal, especially in a Norway which, for over thirty years,
after the briefest period of independence from her old Danish yoke, had
languished discontentedly under the suzerainty of a Swedish King and his
appointed Norwegian cabinet. When therefore, in February 1848, the people
of Paris rose against their King and, on the second day of the street fighting,
24 February, Louis Philippe abdicated and bolted to a villa in Surrey, and
France proclaimed herself a republic, the effect on the young Ibsen, a fortnight short of his twentieth birthday, was explosive. According to Edmund
Gosse, who once met and talked to Ibsen, this proclamation was 'the first
political event that really interested him'. There was much more of the same
kind to interest him in that tumultuous year. During the spring, revolution
spread through Italy, touching Rome, Turin, Leghorn, Pisa, Florence and
Milan. Even the mighty Austrian Empire was affected. On 13 March, a
single day's rioting overthrew Metternich, a figure seemingly as impregnable

[1] Due, op. cit., pp. 38–39.
[2] ibid., p. 40.

as the Pope, if not more so, and gave Vienna to the people. At this news, even Venice bestirred herself and declared a republic. Later the same month there was rioting and bloodshed in Berlin as a result of Frederick William IV's delay in granting reform, and he was forced to permit the formation of a Parliament. In May the Lombards rose and expelled their Austrian garrison. Nearer home, in response to the revolutionary feeling in Germany, the twin duchies of Schleswig and Holstein were up in arms.[1] To the young Ibsen, as to the young Wordsworth in 1789, it must have seemed that a new and glorious dawn was breaking for mankind.

Under the influence of these events, relates Due, Ibsen 'gradually became a full-blooded Republican. With him as inspiration social gatherings were arranged at which there was much jollification and speeches were made, with the ideals of republicanism as the leading theme. After the French pattern, we arranged a so-called "Reform Banquet", at which Ibsen made a fiery oration against all Emperors and Kings, the vermin of society, and in defence of Republicanism, the "only possible" form of government'.[2]

It was in this exalted mood that Ibsen, during the summer of 1848, paid a short visit to his family in Skien—possibly his first since he had left them four and a half years before.[3] We need not read any particular significance into his not visiting them during this period; he may well have had no holidays, and in any case probably could not afford the journey. We know nothing of what he found or felt on seeing his family again, nor how long he stayed. While he was there, however, the hopes that had been raised in him, as in so many others, by the revolutions of the spring began to be dashed one by one. In June there was civil war in the Paris streets, and Prince Windischgrätz turned his guns on Prague to crush the Bohemian rebellion. On 30 October, after Ibsen's return to Grimstad, the reactionary Jellačić defeated a Hungarian army marching to relieve Vienna against Windischgrätz on the plain of

---

[1] Holstein was within, Schleswig without the confines of the German Confederation, but both had been governed by the King of Denmark continuously since 1490. The Danes were, in 1848, planning to incorporate Schleswig in their monarchy and sever its connection, long deemed insoluble, with Holstein. German opinion was united in holding that the two Duchies must be subject to a single ruler. Confused and indeterminate fighting was ended by the intervention of the Powers only in 1852. King Frederick VII of Denmark had no male issue and by the Treaty of London that year it was decided that on his death Christian of Glucksburg should succeed him and rule in both Denmark and the Duchies. This settled the matter until Frederick died in 1863, when the whole trouble flared up afresh.

[2] Due, op. cit., p. 42.

[3] One of Reimann's sons, with whom Ibsen shared a bedroom at the old shop on Storgaden, told Eitrem that Ibsen had once brought him back toys from a visit to Skien; but this could have been in 1848, when he may still have been in touch with the children.

Schwechat. There was to be no more democracy in Vienna for nearly three-quarters of a century. In November, Frederick William IV dispersed the Berlin Parliament; in April of the following year he ruthlessly stamped out revolt in Saxony, Baden and Hanover; in June the French crushed Mazzini's Roman republic, despite a courageous defence by Garibaldi, recently returned from a nomadic existence in South America; and on 24 October, the Venetian republic also fell. Before long Louis Bonaparte was to stage a *coup d'état*, dissolve the Paris Chamber and make himself master of France.

Twenty-seven years later, Ibsen described his reaction to this volcanic upheaval in Europe. 'It was a momentous era. The February revolution, the risings in Hungary and elsewhere, the Schleswig war—all this had a powerful and maturing effect on my development, long though it took for that process to unfold. I wrote resounding poems to the Magyars exhorting them in the name of freedom and humanity to continue steadfastly in the struggle against "the tyrants". I wrote a long sequence of sonnets to King Oscar [of Sweden and Norway], mainly, as far as I can recall, entreating him to put aside all petty scruples and straightway, at the head of his army, to rally our brothers to defend the furthermost frontiers of Schleswig. Since I now, unlike then, doubt whether my winged appeals would markedly have assisted the cause either of the Magyars or of Scandinavia, it is probably fortunate that they remained in the semi-privacy of manuscript. But, my motives being so lofty, I could not refrain from expressing myself in a passionate manner, as befitted the mood of my poems, which, however, brought me but doubtful reward both from my friends and from those less amiably disposed towards me, being hailed by the former as demonstrating a bent for the unconsciously ridiculous, while the latter deemed it remarkable that a young person in my humble position should take it on himself to debate matters on which even they themselves did not presume to hold an opinion. I must in truth add that my conduct in more than one respect held out no great hope that society might count on any accession in me of civil virtues, the less so since I had, by reason of certain epigrams and caricatures, fallen out with individuals who deserved better of me and whose friendship I in fact valued. To sum up, while a great age thundered outside I found myself in a state of war with the little community within which, by the circumstances of my work, I sat imprisoned. Such was the situation when, preparing for my examination, I read Sallust's *Catiline*, and Cicero's speeches against the latter.'[1]

The sonnets to King Oscar have, perhaps fortunately, disappeared, but two

---

[1] Preface to the second edition of *Catiline* (Copenhagen, 1875).

of Ibsen's exhortatory poems have survived, *To Hungary*, in which he com-
forts the Magyars with the assurance that, in years to come, their name will
serve as a battle-cry for the new generation that will 'topple the pillars of
tyranny', and *Awake, Scandinavians!* a similarly unremarkable though lively
piece, like inferior Kipling. Where, however, these contemporary rebels
failed to inspire Ibsen to any uncommon literary achievement, the rebel who
had died two millenia previously, and had been condemned by historians as
an arrogant and misguided felon, succeeded. François Mauriac has written that
a sinner is closer to a saint than are the vast majority of harmless, middle-of-the-
way mortals, because the requisite zeal and passion, and often even the self-
lessness, are there; it is simply that, perhaps through no fault of the individual,
they are misdirected. The figure of the misguided reformer was one that was
to fascinate Ibsen throughout his life, and the line of mighty, twisted figures
that includes Brand, Julian the Apostate in *Emperor and Galilean*, Gregers Werle
and John Gabriel Borkman began, in the ante-room of the apothecary's shop
at Grimstad, with *Catiline*.

In his preface to the second edition published in 1875 Ibsen explained:

> 'My play was written at night. From my employer, a good and able man
> who, however, had no interests outside his work, I had virtually to steal
> free time in which to study, and from these purloined hours I thieved
> further moments in which to write. So I had little time left to me but the
> hours of night. I think this must be the unconscious reason why almost the
> whole action of the play takes place at night...As may be seen, I did not share
> the two old Roman authors' opinion of Catiline's character and conduct,
> and I still incline to the view that there must have been something great, or
> at any rate noteworthy, about a man with whom so indefatigable and
> esteemed an advocate as Cicero did not dare to cross swords until events
> had taken such a turn that he could do so without fear of the consequences.
> It should also be remembered that there are few historical personages whose
> posthumous reputations have been more entirely dictated by their enemies
> than Catiline.'

He wrote the play in the first three months of 1849, in blank verse, with occasional excursions into the rather unusual metre of rhymed trochees.
Catiline, as portrayed by Ibsen, has a guilty secret; he once seduced a woman,
who, in despair, drowned herself. Disillusioned with the corrupt rulers of
Rome, he dreams of 'greatness, power and eternal fame'. His gentle wife,
Aurelia, tries to dissuade him from mixing in politics, so that he can retire
with her to a peaceful life in the country; but her influence is defeated by
that of Furia, the first of those domineering and destructive women whom

Ibsen was to portray at intervals throughout his work: Margit in *The Feast at Solhaug*, Hjørdis in *The Vikings at Helgeland*, Rebecca West, Hedda Gabler, Hilde Wangel, Rita Allmers. She urges him to rebellion:

> I am your genius.
> I must lead you whithersoever you go.
> I am an image out of your own soul.

Furia then betrays his conspiracy, revealing herself to be the sister of the drowned woman. Finally, Catiline kills himself.

When in his later years Ibsen was asked what books he had read in his youth and which authors had influenced him, he tended to shy away from the question almost pathologically. Two of the few influences to whom he admitted were Ludvig Holberg and Oehlenschläger, and in 1880 he told Henrik Jæger that, as far as he could recall, they were the only two dramatists he had read when he wrote *Catiline*. Structurally, it is difficult to see what the play owes to either: it has nothing in common with the swift-moving, short-scene, colloquial comedies of Holberg, or with the static and ponderous tragedies of Oehlenschläger, though the latter may have served as a model poetically. The dramatist to whom the play seems to owe an obvious debt is one with whose work Ibsen can hardly have been totally unfamiliar even at that early stage in his career: Shakespeare. The character of Catiline himself has much in common with that of Brutus in *Julius Caesar*, and the scenes between Catiline and his fellow conspirators, and that of his final suicide after his defeat in battle, seem plainly indebted to the same play, He could of course have learned Shakespeare's technique at second-hand, through the works of Schiller or, for that matter, through Oehlenschläger. But Miss Crawfurd, who guided Ibsen's reading so helpfully at this time, can surely not have omitted to draw Ibsen's attention to at least this fellow-countryman of hers; and although Ibsen's English, if it existed at all at this time, would certainly not have been good enough to read Shakespeare in the original, he would have had no difficulty in obtaining him in Danish translation.[1]

---

[1] Edmund Gosse thought that Sallust's account of the Catiline conspiracy which, Ibsen had been studying for his matriculation examination, had a considerable effect on both the style and viewpoint of Ibsen's play. 'If we seek for the master-mind that started Ibsen,' wrote Gosse in his 1907 biography, 'it is not to be found among the writers of his age or of his language. The real master of Ibsen was Sallust. There can be no doubt that the cold and bitter strength of Sallust; his unflinching method of building up his edifice of invective, stone by stone; his close, unidealistic, dry penetration into character; his clinical attitude, unmoved at the death-bed of a reputation; that all these qualities were directly operative on the mind and intellectual character of Ibsen, and went a long way to mould it while moulding was still possible.' Gosse, steeped in the British nineteenth-century passion for

Nevertheless, *Catiline* is far from being a mere pastiche. Apart from the considerable skill of the verse, a signpost to the flexible and muscular dramatic poetry that was to come in *Love's Comedy, Brand* and *Peer Gynt,* the sharpness of the characterisation, the continuous movement of the plot, and, rarest of talents in a playwright, the ability to construct and develop not merely a character but a human relationship, are all evidence of uncommon maturity in a largely self-educated youth approaching his twenty-first birthday. Ibsen has rather touchingly described the emotions with which he re-read the play after a lapse of a quarter of a century. 'I had almost forgotten the content, or anyway the details; but on reading it afresh, I found that it contained a good deal that I was still able to acknowledge, especially when one considers that it was my maiden play. Much that my later work has dealt with—the conflict between aspiration and capacity, between will and ability, the overlapping of tragedy and comedy, whether on a general or an individual scale—is already mistily indicated here.'[1]

If, as has been argued, everything we write mirrors our internal conflict at the time we wrote it, it is possible to draw certain parallels between the content of *Catiline* and Ibsen's position at Grimstad during that winter of 1849. Like his hero, Ibsen must have been nagged by a sense of being insufficiently appreciated and an ambition for higher things; also, no doubt, by the consciousness of having shrugged off his responsibility towards a woman with whom he had had an affair. Perhaps, as some critics have suggested, the two women who contended for the possession of Catiline represented the conflict that takes place in every artist between settling for a peaceful life and the danger and uncertainty of an artist's career.

In this same preface to the second edition of *Catiline,* Ibsen recalled the enthusiasm with which Due and Schulerud received the news that he had written a play, and the efforts they made to launch it:

'An occupation as incomprehensible to my associates as playwriting had of course to be kept dark; but a twenty-year-old poet cannot easily continue without confidants, and I therefore entrusted my guilty secret to two friends of my own age. We three built great hopes on *Catiline* once it was completed. First and most important, it had to be fair-copied so that, over a

---

the ancient classical writers, probably overstates his case; but it is a theory not to be dismissed.

Gosse also remarks that in October 1848, only a few weeks before Ibsen began his play, a new drama about Catiline by Alexandre Dumas *père* had been staged in Paris, and that although Ibsen could not have read it he may well have seen a mention of it in a newspaper, perhaps in connection with the political events then taking place in France.

[1] Preface to the second edition of *Catiline.*

pseudonym, it might be submitted to the theatre in Christiania; after which it was to be offered to the public in print. One of my loyal disciples [Due] took it upon himself to produce a handsome and legible copy of my rough and uncorrected draft, a task which he performed so conscientiously that he did not omit a single one of the innumerable dashes which, in the heat of composition, I had employed whenever the appropriate expression had not immediately occurred to me. The other friend, whom I take leave to name since he is no longer among the living—Ole Schulerud, then a student, later a lawyer—went with this copy to Christiania. I still remember one of his letters, in which he tells me that *Catiline* has now been delivered to the theatre; that it will soon be performed, of that there can be no possible doubt, since the directorate of the theatre is composed of highly perceptive gentlemen; equally, it is beyond question that all the booksellers of the capital will compete for the honour of paying a good round honorarium for the first edition; the only problem, in his view, being to ascertain which will make the worthiest offer.

'After a long and hopeful period of waiting, however, certain difficulties began to reveal themselves. The theatre returned the play to my friend with an exceedingly courteous but none the less conclusive letter of rejection. He then took the manuscript from bookshop to bookshop; but they, with one voice, all expressed the same opinion as the directors of the theatre. The best he could get was an offer to print the play for such and such a sum without any question of any money being paid to the author.

'All this, however, far from dispelled my friend's confidence in ultimate victory. On the contrary, he wrote to me that what had happened was for the best; I would myself step forward into the limelight as publisher of my own drama; he would advance me the necessary money; the proceeds we would share, in anticipation of which he would take charge of all the business side—apart from the proof-reading, which he thought would be unnecessary, since the printer would have so beautiful and clear a manuscript to work from. In a later letter he declared that with such promising prospects in view he was thinking of giving up his studies entirely in order to devote himself wholly to the publication of my works; he thought I should have no difficulty in composing two or three plays a year, and by a sober reckoning the profit must in a short while enable us to make the journey we had so often agreed, or at any rate discussed, across Europe to the Orient.'

This was in October 1849. The previous month, an important and encouraging event had occurred for Ibsen; for the first time, a work of his appeared in print.

It was a poem entitled *In Autumn*, and its publication was entirely thanks to Due who, on hearing Ibsen read the poem aloud, sent it to the *Christiania Post*, for which he acted as local correspondent. It was published as being by 'Brynjolf Bjarme', a pseudonym which Ibsen was to use for some time (*Catiline* was also to appear under it'. We do not know what made him coin this name. When Due received the issue of 28 September containing the poem, he relates: 'I was very impatient for evening to come, when the shop would be quiet and I could show Ibsen the newspaper. Enthusiastically, and with a certain triumph at my friend's success, I displayed to him his first "poem in print". At first Ibsen turned quite pale with emotion, but soon a flush of joy streamed over his face.'[1] In 1858 he was to recall the occasion in his poem *Building Plans*.[2]

Three letters which Ibsen wrote from Grimstad to Schulerud while the latter was trying to sell *Catiline* in Christiania have survived. The first, dated 15 October 1849, was evidently written as an apology for an impatient and suspicious earlier letter of the kind which Ibsen was often to pen in his maturer years, and which Schulerud, in obedience to Ibsen's expressed wish, must be presumed to have destroyed:

My dear friend!

Your last letter made me doubly happy, firstly because it promises a speedy outcome of our project, but even more because you have hereby proved yourself a true friend, by regarding my letter to you as a mere expression of impulse and over-enthusiasm. Such forbearance leads me to hope that you have imagined yourself in my position and realised how everything must have seemed to me. I am sure you will have guessed the frustration with which I have awaited every post-day, and how this put me in an unpleasant humour. Not being on the spot, I could not guess what was happening, and this uncertainty inevitably aroused a thousand doubts, all the more distressing because I could not in my heart believe that they could have any foundation.

Your letter has stilled every doubt I might have had concerning your conduct, and I should not be worthy of your friendship if I did not unreservedly withdraw anything I may have written which could cast doubt on the honesty of your intentions. I therefore beg you to forget the whole matter as something which can have no influence upon our future friendly relations, and I await an assurance of this in your next letter.

I have no time today to write more—Due asks me to thank you for the guitar, which he looks forward to receiving. I am equally grateful for the trousers—I had forgotten about them and thought they had slipped your memory too, but they are very welcome, as just now I have to save all I can. I have almost finished the first

---

[1] Due, *op. cit.*, pp. 26–27.
[2] See page 179.

act of Olaf Tr. *I think it will turn out really well, and hope this play will cause us less trouble than C.*

Best wishes,

Your affectionate friend,

Henr. Ibsen.

P.S. Do me the favour of consigning my last letter to the flames. I hate to think of you having it.

Olaf Tr. was probably to be about Olaf Tryggvesson, a king of Norway (c.995–1000) who was bred in Russia, became a Viking chieftain, led an invasion of England in 991 and, on the conclusion of peace, became a Christian and had the doubtful honour of being adopted godson by King Ethelred II. He spread Christianity throughout Norway, by force where necessary, and even into Iceland and Greenland, before being killed in a battle against the Danes. He seems a promising subject for a play, and one would like to know what Ibsen would have made of him, especially in view of Ibsen's hostile attitude at this time towards state-established religions; but he never completed the work, and the fragment has not survived.

Twelve weeks later, on 5 January 1850, Ibsen again wrote to Schulerud:

My dear friend!

Your last letter contained news of Catiline's *death sentence—it grieves me, but there is no use losing courage. You are perfectly right when you say this that apparent defeat must not be regarded as such. C. was only intended as a forerunner of the plans we agreed on in this field, and it may yet fulfil its purpose. I am absolutely of your opinion that it is wisest to sell the play, and I think its rejection, to judge from the theatre's reply, may turn out to our advantage rather than to our disadvantage, since it seems that it was not for any integral reason that it was not accepted. You must of course arrange the sale of the play at your own discretion; I would merely observe that it seems to me better to sell the publishing rights rather than have it printed at our own expense, since in the latter event we should have to pay a lot of money to cover the printing and, besides, would only gradually get any return from it, whereas in the former event we would receive an honorarium. However, you must do as circumstances suggest.*

Now a little about my literary activity. As I think I told you, the first act of Olaf T. *is more or less ready; the little one-act play* The Norsemen[1] *has been revised, or rather will be—I am busy with it at the moment—and will in its new form deal with a broader theme than I had originally envisaged. I have used a few stories and descriptions from Telemark to write some short poems, adapted to fit well-known folk melodies, and have thus had a shot at nationalistic writing. I have, too, half-completed*

---

[1] Later adapted into *The Warrior's Barrow.*

a longish, perhaps rather over-dramatic poem entitled Memories of the Ball, *which owed its existence to my supposed infatuation of last summer. But my most important work since you left has been a national-historical* nouvelle *which I have entitled* The Prisoner at Akershus, *and which treats of the sad fate of Christian Lofthuus.* [A long paragraph follows telling Lofthuus's story].[1]

I think we should preface Catiline *with some introductory remarks, and I therefore beg you to copy and insert the following:*

FOREWORD

This play was originally intended for the stage, but the directorate of the theatre found it unsuitable for this purpose. Although the Author has grounds for supposing that the play's rejection does not stem from any integral defects, it is nevertheless not without a certain anxiety that he sets his essay before the public, from whom however he anticipates the forbearance for which a beginner may not unreasonably hope on his maiden appearance.

N.B. Please don't let any printing errors creep in. I should like to have the manuscript back, and should be grateful if you would let me have two copies of the play when it is ready...

Best wishes,
Your affectionate
Henr. Ibsen.

The 'supposed infatuation of last summer' probably refers to a girl of nineteen named Clara Ebbell, to whom he had dedicated a poem that year entitled *To the Star*. Neither it nor the longer *Memories of a Ball* have much to recommend them beyond a technical facility; apart from that, they are conventional adolescent poems of hopeless adoration, which rather suggest that Clara, a religious girl who disapproved of his freethinking, did not reciprocate his feelings, at any rate with much passion. He remained in contact with her, however, sending her poems from Christiania the following year, so that she cannot have rebuffed him completely.

Ibsen seems to have been somewhat timid as a suitor. 'He seldom expressed passion,' records Due. 'It was as though his spiritual life found expression exclusively, or at any rate essentially, through imagination and thought...I got the impression that there was in his nature a deep-seated reluctance to lay bare his feelings. In particular, he had a notable talent for concealing his wants, so that they did not appear to bother him. Thus his acquaintances never found any cause to pity him, the less so since few of them fully comprehended his true circumstances. I, who was for a time his only confidant, sympathised with

---

[1] See page 47.

E

him deeply, and found it difficult to understand how, in his situation, he could be as merry and vital as he was.'[1]

This timidity in relation to physical matters was, as we shall see, to remain a feature of Ibsen's character. One of Reimann's sons who shared a room with him told Eitrem that he well remembered Ibsen going off in a sleigh 'at a spanking pace' to take some kind of apothecary's examination in Arendal. The man who gave him the lift could remember only one thing from the trip— 'the little chap was so scared, so dead scared, that he, the driver, had to laugh. They rode over some water. The ice boomed, as often happens in cold weather. But Ibsen got frightened and jumped out of the sleigh and ran for the shore. He wouldn't get back into the sleigh until it had crossed the ice.'[2]

Occasionally Due seems to have succeeded in persuading Ibsen to indulge in the lighter side of life. 'Now and then,' he tells, 'we arranged dance parties. Grimstad had no adequate locale for such entertainments, but we tackled the problem practically and shamelessly in the following manner. The moving spirits among us young people would approach in turn the good gentlemen who owned the largest houses and bluntly ask if we might hold a dance there. The kindly citizens of Grimstad usually granted permission, and with the assistance of two violins and a flute, home-mixed punch and negus, coffee or tea, and cakes, our ball was ready. Several times I had exhorted Ibsen to partake in these festivities, but important considerations had compelled him to decline. The fact was that he had no evening coat and, what was worse, had never danced and did not dare to make his debut at a ball. The sartorial problem, however, was solved by one of those with 'full wallets and empty heads' giving him credit. This at first amazed Ibsen, but then he decided that this confirmed his judgment of them, and when at the end of the year he was presented with a bill for the garment, he merely regarded this as providing further confirmation, saying in his humorous way: "First he is fool enough to give me credit, then he's fool enough to expect me to pay the bill". I can, though, reveal that this debt of Ibsen's was fully honoured.

'So now he was equipped to play the gallant, but the business of inviting a partner and taking his place among the ranks of dancers he found intimidating...We sought, however, to instil courage into Ibsen, and with the assistance of his lady and other well-wishers succeeded in getting the couple launched into a brisk gallop, not admittedly without its hazards in the early stages, but with no sensational disasters; and soon it went sweepingly, so that the situation was saved. Later he tried his hand at other dances, with fair success.'[3]

---

[1] Due, op. cit., p. 36.
[2] Eitrem, Ibsen og Grimstad, p. 27.
[3] Due op. cit., pp. 42–44.

It is interesting that Ibsen should have pretended that he had never danced, since we know that, as a boy at Skien, he had in fact been a keen dancer.[1] Due adds: 'Ibsen was not musical. When we had a sing-song, he would join in, but incorrectly, since he had no ear.'[2]

Of the projected *nouvelle*, *The Prisoner at Akershus*, referred to in Ibsen's last letter to Schulerud, a little over a chapter has survived; this appears to have been all that he wrote of it. The opening is Dickensian (and may indeed have been influenced by Dickens, some of whose works we know were in the book club to which Reimann and Nielsen had allowed Ibsen access). 'In a corner of Christ Church cemetery in Christiania,' runs the first sentence, 'there is a small area which is used as burial place for criminals who have died at the fortress of Akershus, and which is consequently known as "Criminals' Corner".' Each day a woman in mourning visits this place, briefly and obscurely does something or other to a grave that is marked with a nameless cross, and departs. When the narrator, Brynjolf, tells his uncle Bjarme of this occurrence, the latter replies thoughtfully that it is a pity he didn't know about this thirty years ago when he was occupied with his 'headache'—'a work that unhappily lies uncompleted in my desk, because I lacked the end of the story'. But he promises his nephew that he will show him the manuscript that evening, 'because I think in this story of the woman I have discovered how it all ended'. The narrator then tells us that 'that good soul has now gone to his rest, but he has left me his manuscripts, the only things in my life that I have ever inherited or am likely to inherit'. The contents of this manuscript he will now relate. But unfortunately the second chapter goes no further than the heading: '*Chapter Two. In which the Reader makes the acquaintance of Fru Justitia, as she appeared in the previous Century*', and a description of the Lofthuus farm. "All this is now gone. Only on a small hillock a little way above the house stands an old oak tree, which affords a fine view of the neighbourhood, and was, in consequence, the then owner's favourite spot. The local people still refer to it as Christian Lofthuus's Oak'.

Here, tantalisingly, the fragment ends. Did some rekindled flicker of affection for Else Sofie Jensdatter impel him to begin this work in, we must presume, praise of her grandfather, and did some stronger feeling of guilt and rejected responsibility stay his hand? It seems curious that he should have abandoned so exciting a theme after so promising a beginning. This fragment of *The Prisoner at Akershus* is, in fact, the best thing Ibsen wrote at Grimstad, matched only by perhaps a couple of scenes in *Catiline*. But when a writer

---

[1] See page 37.
[2] Due, *op. cit.*, p. 44.

is twenty-one, poetry often seems a more attractive medium than prose, and a fortnight after he had mentioned *The Prisoner at Akershus* so excitedly to Schulerud ('my most important work'), we find him turning aside to compose an elegy in memory of his admired Adam Oehlenschläger, who had just died at the age of seventy-one. He sent this to Schulerud, explaining that he had composed it 'in melancholy ardour', and asking him to 'arrange to have it inserted in the *Christiania Post* as soon as possible'. It was printed there, rather belatedly, on 16 February.

The time had now come for Ibsen to make the final preparations for his matriculation examination, which would involve spending a term at a crammer's in Christiania. After six and a quarter years of boiling medicines and preparing plasters, he was to devote himself entirely to reading, painting and writing, and that exchange of ideas through discussion and debate which has always been the most valuable part of a University education. On 12 April 1850, at the request of a young lady named Sofie Holst, he wrote his last poem at Grimstad, *Moonlight Wandering after a Ball*.

Hush! How still! No longer echo sounds of music and delight.
Now no voice, no violin breaks the soft silence of the night.

Westwards soon across the earth the moon her last still glance shall throw;
Earth that dreams in white oblivion 'neath the lilies of the snow.

Dance is ended; yet my eyes still see the dancers as they lead,
And are led in their sharp patterns swaying in a light sylphide.

Soon the moon will seek her valley, hands of sleep will close my eyes.
And the sea of dreams my soul will wander, winged with memories.

The same day, he wrote a farewell note in Christopher Due's album:

If friendship depended on constant companionship, ours would cease, but if it consists of mutual sympathy and the soaring of spirits in the same sphere, then our friendship can never die.

Your affectionate friend,
Henrik Ibsen.

It was the custom for anyone leaving a job to burn his name and the date of his departure on some object. Such a branded inscription may be seen today on a cork drawer in the counter of the apothecary's at Grimstad (now the Ibsen Museum); it bears the statement like an epitaph: *Henr. J. Ibsen*, 15–4–50. The fifteenth was the day on which he officially terminated his employment; but it happened to be a Monday, and there is no record of any ship sailing eastwards from Grimstad that day. On Saturday 13 April, however, the *Prins Carl* left Grimstad early in the morning, and among the passengers whom it deposited at Brevik, not far from Skien, at 11.30 a.m. the same day, we find, in the list printed in the local newspaper *Adresse-Tidende for Brevik*, the name 'Ipsen'. He would have reached Skien by road the same afternoon or evening.

Ibsen had originally intended to proceed direct to Christiania from Grimstad without seeing his family, but before leaving he had received a letter from his sister Hedvig begging him to visit them en route. Ibsen at once agreed. 'He says,' Hedvig explained in a letter to her cousin, Hanna Stenersen, 'that he had always very much wanted to come here first, but didn't like to mention it because he didn't know if Father would approve'.[1] What lay behind these last seven words no one has ever been able to explain.

Ibsen stayed a fortnight with his family in the house at Snipetorp. They were one fewer than when he had left; Johan, the second son, had emigrated to California to seek his fortune in the goldfields. His letters home were to cease this year, and no more was ever heard from him; his family presumed him dead. Nicolai, the third son, had been dropped on the floor when a child, and the injury had affected him, making him abnormally shy and withdrawn. He, too, after failing in business, was to emigrate to, and die in, America. Ole, the youngest, was not yet fifteen, and the only member of Ibsen's family with whom he could make any real contact was his sister Hedvig, three years his junior. During this stay, as she was to recall over half a century later, Ibsen took a long walk with her to Bratsberg and told her of his dreams. He wanted, he said, to achieve nothing less than complete fulfilment 'in greatness and in love'. 'And when you have done that?', she asked. 'Then,' he replied, 'I want to die.'

On 27 April he journeyed down to Brevik and sailed thence, with his schoolfriend Boye Ording, for Christiania, again in the *Prins Carl*. Not only did he never see his parents or any of his brothers again; he even ceased to write home. There has been much loose and unnecessary speculation as to the reason for this prolonged schism; Ibsen explained it clearly enough in a letter he wrote to his uncle Christian Paus in 1877 on Knud Ibsen's death. 'To un-comprehending eyes,' he stated, 'I know it looks as though I had voluntarily and deliberately cut myself off from my family, or at any rate permanently set a distance between myself and them; but I think I may say that impossible circumstances from a very early stage were the principal cause...That I so seldom wrote home during those years of struggle was chiefly because I could not be of any assistance or support to my parents. I thought it vain to write when I could do nothing practical to help them; I stood in constant

---

[1] Quoted by O. Mosfjeld in *A-Magazinet*, 9 August 1928. Hedvig refers thrice in her letters to Hanna around this time to letters from Ibsen, so he seems to have been corresponding with them at least fairly regularly up to the time of his departure from Grimstad. The break came later.

hope that my circumstances might improve, but that happened very late and not long ago...I also felt a strong reluctance to come into close contact with certain spiritual trends then prevalent, with which I could feel no sympathy and a collision with which could easily have provoked unpleasantness, or at any rate an atmosphere of discord, which I wished to avoid.'

The 'spiritual trends' were a reference to a priest named G. A. Lammers, who had become pastor at Skien in 1849. Lammers was a fervent evangelist who had become dissatisfied with the established state church, and by the following year he had decided to form a breakaway group. Only three days before Ibsen's arrival in Skien, on 10 April 1850, *Addresse-Tidende for Brevik* carried an announcement that Lammers was gathering money towards the erection of a prayer-house in the vicarage grounds for 'mission meetings and other godly assemblies'. Ibsen's mother, sister and youngest brother, Ole, had all fallen under Lammers's spell and become strict pietists. To the free-thinking disciple of Voltaire such an atmosphere must have seemed peculiarly intolerable. His sister's defection appears particularly to have disturbed him. Nearly seventy years later, she wrote: 'When as a youngish girl I became gripped by the Lammers movement and became a dissenter, he greatly disapproved of this step. I think it was partly because of this that he never came back here.'[1] Although she occasionally wrote to him over the next thirty years, it was only in old age that a close and warm friendship was renewed between them.

But no man can escape the roots of childhood. Skien remained strongly in Ibsen's mind. *Brand*, which he wrote in 1865, is full of memories of his birthplace; in 1869 he was to refer in a letter to Hedvig to 'the old home, to which I still cling fast by so many roots'; and when, in 1875, he sat down to write a preface to the second edition of *Catiline* and began to reminisce about Grimstad, Skien, too, came back to him and for the first time for over a quarter of a century he wrote a letter to his aged father. The letter is lost, but Knud Ibsen's reply has survived, with its pathetic expression of joy at hearing at last from his famous son; 'for I have not heard or seen anything of you, as you yourself say, for twenty-five years.' Unhappy memories have a more lasting influence than happy ones, being less easily dispelled by their opposite, and when Ibsen disembarked at Christiania from the *Prins Carl* on 28 April 1850 it must have been with a very firm resolve to renounce the past. He was not then to know, though it later became part of his philosophy, that whatever you turn your back on gets you in the end.

---

[1] Interview in *Fremskridt*, 19 November 1917. But sectarianism was nothing new in Skien; as early as 1784 B. H. Løvenskiold, in his *Beskrivelse over Bradsbierg Amt*, (p. 226) had noted that the town 'had become famous for the number of its inhabitants who have become addicted to so-called Pietism'. (Mosfjeld, *op. cit.*, p. 57).

THREE

❧ Ibsen at University

(1850-1851)

THE CHRISTIANIA which greeted Ibsen as a twenty-one year's old student in 1850 was a small and, by any but the most humble standards, unimpressive town. Eighty years previously, at the time of the first official census in 1769, it had contained no more than seven and a half thousand inhabitants, and even now they numbered only thirty thousand. Few of the buildings stood higher than two storeys. There were no rail[1] nor telegraphic communications, and no gas lighting in the streets, although pipes for the last-named amenity were just being laid. (London had known street gas-lighting for nearly forty years). As late as 1855 a correspondent to *Morgenbladet* was to complain that the first sight to greet a visitor entering the city over the New Bridge was a vast dunghill, that the sewers were so inefficient that the filth in the streets reached to the edge of his galoshes, and that many gutters lay full, untouched and stinking throughout the summer. Between Piperviksstranden and Munkedamsveien lay a large swamp that, in warm weather, 'polluted the air with its foul water'.[2]

The city contained few buildings of distinction. A handful remained from the eighteenth century, such as the military school, but these did not appeal to contemporary taste, which preferred the neo-classical, with pediments and pilasters—a style new to Norway, and exemplified in the new palace, started in 1823 and completed in 1848 on a hill a quarter of a mile outside the western limits of the city. Near the foot of this hill, the finishing touches were being

---

[1] Except in the public gardens, where, in 1849, so an English traveller tells us, 'a train of imitative railway carriages had been constructed to which a miniature locomotive was attached. These revolved on a platform, something after the fashion of a roundabout at a country fair. But the engine was innocent of fire and smoke, except such as proceeded from the pipes of some of the worthy citizens who selected it as their favourite post, and appeared to perform the functions of stoker and engineer, the train being really propelled by machinery under the platform'. (Thomas Forester, *Norway in 1848 and 1849*, London, 1850), p. 448.

[2] For the information contained in this and the succeeding paragraph, see S. C. Hammer, *Kristianias Historie*, IV (Christiania, 1923) pp. 408-411.

applied to the University, the members of which were still in temporary
housing on Prindsensgade. Fires had been so frequent that, by a recent or-
dinance, new buildings in the centre of the city had to be of brick; only in the
outskirts could wooden houses be erected in the traditional style. But within
the city limits, rebuilding was proceeding apace. Public edifices of varying
degrees of hideousness were beginning to arise: St Olaf's Church, Holy Trinity
Church (Trefoldighedskirken), Oskarshal pleasure palace, a fire station, a
new prison and, ugliest of all, the eagerly awaited Parliament building, though
this last was not to be completed until 1866. Constables had only recently
replaced the old-fashioned watchmen, and foreign travellers were amazed to
see iron-collared convicts from Akershus, where Christian Lofthuus had died,
working in chain-gangs side by side with ordinary labourers.

Socially, the pattern was the same as in Stockholm and Copenhagen.
There was a small aristocratic upper stratum. A German traveller, Theodor
Mügge, writes of wealthy young ladies in feathered hats riding English
thoroughbreds, their houses filled with English carpets and French damask;
and he notes that they spent a good deal of each year abroad.[1] Titles of
nobility had, however, been abolished in 1821, and the rising merchant class
was beginning to marry into the grand families. The poor were very poor
indeed. Eilert Sundt, who in 1858 published the results of investigations he
had carried out in 1855, records that of 285 families he visited in the city that
year, 233 lived in one room, and that among the working-class each room
contained an average of 4.9 people. Barely half the families even had their
own kitchen; and in 1851 and 1852 1,800 people, representing over 6 per cent
of the city's population, received poor relief.[2]

On his arrival in the capital, Ibsen took lodgings with his friend Ole Schulerud in a house owned by an old lady called Mother Sæter at the corner of
Vinkelgaden and Filosofgangen, and enlisted at a well-known crammer's
affectionately known as Heltberg's *studentfabrik*, or student factory. Here he
was to prepare for his matriculation examination, which he was to sit the following August. Many distinguished men passed through the doors of this
remarkable establishment, to have the rough edges rubbed off their knowledge of logarithms and Latin grammar; and great was the variety of its occupants, 'a medley of human beings from all corners of the land and every
stratum of society, from failed merchants and lamed cadets to middle-aged
farmers and seamen whose love of adventure had driven them, first on long

---

[1] Hammer, *op. cit.*, pp. 370–372.
[2] Eilert Sundt, *Om Piperviken og Ruseløkbakken–Undersøgelser om arbeidsklassens kaar og
sæder i Kristiania* (Christiania, 1858), quoted by Hammer, *op. cit.*, pp. 414 ff.

voyages to far-off lands, and then, when they did not find what they sought there, on a new long voyage to the golden shores of knowledge'.[1] Heltberg himself, though by now crippled by gout and strangled by asthma, was a splendidly witty and original teacher in his dogskin breeches and fur boots; he is sympathetically remembered in many novels and books of reminiscences.[2]

Of more immediate importance to Ibsen than his matriculation, however, was the fate of *Catiline*, which, after the various vicissitudes described above, had at length been published on 12 April, the day before Ibsen left Grimstad. This had been entirely due to the generosity of Schulerud who, having received some small legacy, had devoted it, with extraordinary faith, entirely to the publication of his friend's supposed masterpiece. *Catiline* was issued by a book-seller named P. F. Steensballe, on commission; and its appearance should have been something of an event in the Norwegian literary world, for, improbable as it may seem, it was the first Norwegian play to have been published since Henrik Wergeland's *The Venetians* seven years previously. The point underlines a state of affairs that was to dominate the next thirteen years of Ibsen's life, the fact that the Norwegian theatre was, at this time, totally dependent upon foreign plays, mainly Danish, French and German.

On the day after publication, a favourable notice of *Catiline* appeared in the handwritten student magazine *Samfundsbladet*. This review was written by the editor, a lively young man with few pretensions to original creative talent, but an unusually perceptive and widely read critic. His name was Paul Botten Hansen; he was three years older than Ibsen, and was to become a close friend—one of the few, apart from Due and Schulerud, that he was ever to know. Botten Hansen wrote that it was a pleasure to read a young poet who did not seek to pander to fashion. He discovered in the play 'a certain Shakespearean strength and earnestness', and especially praised the author for bringing about his hero's destruction as the result of inward spiritual conflict rather than of external circumstances.

A couple of weeks after Ibsen's arrival in Christiania, on 16 May, was printed the first, and indeed the only review of *Catiline* to appear in any general news-paper: the *Christiania Post*, which had published the two poems *In Autumn* and the *Elegy for Adam Oehlenschläger*. The reviewer was a classical philologist named F. L. Vibe, and he found much to criticise. The poet, he noted with regret, had departed from the historical facts and indulged in forced pathos, too often reminding one of *Love Without Stockings*, that parody of neo-classical French tragedy by J. H. Wessel reference to which recurs with such curious

---

[1] Erik Lindseth in *Ny Illustreret Tidende*, 13 August 1882.
[2] Notably Bjørnson's poem *Gamle Heltberg* and Arne Garborg's novel *Bondestudentar*.

frequency in the articles and reminiscences of the time. However, he found
the work not altogether lacking in merit. 'The author,' he concluded, 'has an
unusual talent for raising himself to a tragic height and power, together
with a rare gift for allowing the passions to emerge in full strength, and his
language is of a purity such as we have seldom encountered.'

These were the only reviews of *Catiline* to appear before October, when the
leading literary periodical, *Norsk Tidsskrift for Videnskab og Litteratur*, noticed it.
Again the reviewer was a classical philologist, a species with which the Scandinavian countries are heavily burdened: Carl Müller. He was much less sym-
pathetic, listing with relish the 'absurd contradictions in the characters'; the
best he could find to say was that there were a few redeeming glimpses of a 'comprehension of formal requirements' which suggested that Herr Bjarme might
some day 'give us something more accomplished'.

Even this tart review was not without an accompanying consolation, for
in the same issue the editor, Professor M. J. Monrad, a brother of the theological student S. C. Monrad who had been one of Ibsen's tutors in Grimstad,
and an important figure in the University as well as in Norwegian cultural
life,[1] added a few words of personal encouragement. While regretting that the
young author had so little grasp of form (a criticism which, whatever may
be the other shortcomings of *Catiline*, seems curiously unjustified), he rejoiced
that the play was firmly based on a central idea, and that this idea was 'both
clear and beautiful', namely, the conflict between the instinct for good and
duty and 'the individual's dark longing for independence'. He concluded by
expressing the opinion that a poet with so striking an imagination must ultimately succeed in finding the form he required.

All this was considerably encouraging. Unfortunately, not only did the play
remain unperformed; hardly anyone bothered to buy it. Of the edition of two
hundred and fifty copies, only forty had been sold by the end of the year.
Eventually, Ibsen and Schulerud resigned themselves to the book's failure.
'I remember,' wrote Ibsen in his preface to the second edition 'that one
evening, when our mutual household finances posed seemingly insuperable
problems, we degraded this pile of print to the category of waste paper, and
were fortunate enough to dispose of it to a pedlar. For the next few days we
lacked none of the primary necessities of life.'

The failure of the play is not surprising. However much *Catiline* may have
been in tune with the spirit of Europe in 1850, it was out of tune with the
prevailing spirit in Norway. 'Norwegian spiritual life,' comments a literary

---

[1] He was Professor of Philosophy at Christiania for fifty-two years, from 1845 until
his death in 1897.

historian of that country, 'underwent an idyllic period during the eighteen-forties. Contemporary life was poor and lacking in impulse, all was peace, no danger threatened, people buried themselves in memories, and began for the first time to study their own history, their folk traditions, their national origins. Literature was a quiet lake, cut off from the oceans of the world, barely touched by the storms that raged outside. Welhaven, the leading poet of the age, has only tired and peevish words for the Paris rebels of 1848 who disturbed him in his contemplation, and Andreas Munch rubs his hands in bourgeois glee at our country escaping the upheavals of Europe. *Catiline* is the only Norwegian work through whose pages there glows something of the tumultuous unrest and spirit of rebellion that gripped the world outside Norway in 1848.'[2]

Meanwhile Ibsen was, for the first time in his life, meeting people of his own age who knew more about literature than he did and who were, them-selves, writers. One such was Paul Botten Hansen, who had written the sym-pathetic review of *Catiline*. A gifted linguist with an immense range of reading, he was already beginning to acquire what was, during the next decade, to become one of the largest private libraries in the country. He had an extensive knowledge of European culture, and the following year was to write a long thesis on *The Young Germany*. What Coleridge was to Wordsworth, Botten Hansen was to Ibsen, opening up new horizons of thought and literature for him. Ibsen was to recall him affectionately as 'a man whose appreciation has always been precious and important to me, and to whom I hereby express my renewed gratitude'.[3]

Another stimulating companion was a farmer's son from Telemark whom he met at Heltberg's student factory, Åasmund Vinje. Ten years older than Ibsen, and as heavily bearded, Vinje had a sharply satirical turn of mind and was a brilliant talker. Gerhard Gran has described him as 'a conversationalist such as we have never had [in Norway] before or since'—and Norway is a country where good conversation is as common as in Ireland. At this early stage in his career, Vinje's powers were far from fully developed; he was inhibited by having to write in *riksmaal*, the formal language used for writing which was based on Danish and was far removed from Norwegian conversa-tional rhythms. *Landsmaal*. the language spoken by country people such as himself, was not yet accepted as a written form, though, as we shall see, Vinje was to do much during the next few years to champion its use.[4] This gap be-

[1] Gerhard Gran, *Henrik Ibsen*, I (Christiania, 1918), pp. 20–21.
[2] Preface to *Catiline* (1875).
[3] Gran, op. cit., p. 28.
[4] See Appendix B.

tween the spoken and written tongues was a handicap to Norwegian writers which few foreigners can appreciate; to comprehend it, one must imagine a J. M. Synge or a Sean O'Casey forced to write in the language of Disraeli or Oscar Wilde. If one compares the characters of Walter Scott who speak English with those, so incomparably more alive and richer, who talk in Scots, one may, likewise, perceive the dilemma.

Vinje was full of undigested knowledge, but he was a lively and exciting companion for Ibsen, whose radical opinions he shared to an even stronger degree. Another yet more radical young man happened by chance to be living at Mother Sæter's, under the same roof as Ibsen: Theodor Abildgaard. Abildgaard was closely and vigorously associated with the workers' movement which Marcus Thrane had recently founded. Thrane, following a visit to Paris (where he had been imprisoned for two months as 'having no visible means of support') and to the London of the Chartist manifesto, had been infected by the English Christian Socialists' enthusiasm for the co-operative movement, and in eighteen months he had established no fewer than 273 workers' associations in Norway, with 20,854 members, demanding amongst other things shorter hours of labour, the abolition of trade monopolies and the provision of small-holdings to reduce the competition for employment. Abildgaard found a ready disciple in Ibsen, and only a month after the latter's arrival in Christiania, on 29 May 1850, he and Vinje persuaded Ibsen to join them in a political demonstration.

A German from Schleswig named Harro Harring, who had fought for both the Greeks in their war of liberation against the Turks, and the Poles in their rebellion against the Russians, had come to Norway in 1849 to seek refuge in his old age. There he founded and edited a radical paper, *The Voice of the People*, and at the beginning of 1850 he had published a play entitled *The American Testament* which the authorities decided outstepped the limits of the freedom of the press. An order was issued for his deportation, and on the morning of 29 May the police entered his house and escorted him on board a ship, where he was held prisoner until it sailed. The news of this spread rapidly through the town, and a protest was drawn up, signed by a hundred and forty names, of which Ibsen's was one. This document having been presented to the senior member of the cabinet, the assembly made its way to the quay, where a deputation went on board the steamer and addressed a few words to Harring, who then appeared on deck and was hailed with three times three cheers, followed by a cheer for Norway and freedom. Ibsen, we are told, 'was from first to last an eager participator in this affair'.[1] It was the only political demonstration in which he was ever to take part.

---

[1] Jæger, op. cit., p. 67.

In addition to Botten Hansen, Vinje and Abildgaard, there was a fourth
student whom Ibsen met during these first weeks in Christiania and who was,
in the future, to have a more important impact on his life than any of them:
Bjørnstjerne Bjørnson. Bjørnson was younger than the others, only eighteen,
the son of a country clergyman; but he attended Heltberg's only occasionally
that spring, and it was some little time before he and Ibsen became closely
acquainted (though he was among those who signed the Harring protest).
In his poem *Old Heltberg* (1873), Bjørnson remembered his young fellow-
pupil:

> Thin and intense, with a face pale as gypsum
> Behind an immense coal-black beard, *Henrik Ibsen*.

Some remembered his hair and beard as brown, some as black; presumably
it was of that very dark shade of brown which is often mistaken for black;
but all are agreed as to its bushiness.

It was important for Ibsen that he should have come thus early into contact
with people of his own generation whose horizons were European and who
were, moreover, of a critical and satirical turn of mind instead of, like so
many of their contemporaries, being carried along on the popular wave of
national romanticism. Where others, such as Andreas Munch and Welhaven,
dwelt on the past, Botten Hansen, Vinje and Abildgaard were absorbed with
the present. Vinje was much influenced by the Danish writer and journalist
Meïr Aron Goldschmidt, who had founded a provocative magazine in Copenhagen named *The Corsair*; he learned from Goldschmidt to think of the age as
one of doubt and contradiction, as 'a hovering between yes and no, or rather a
combination of the two', so that 'behind the most serious truth one glimpses
the parody peeping through her curtain, and beneath a light jest one hears
the bell-note of seriousness'.[1] This dual vision, this satirical touch, was something that Bjørnson, the patriot and romanticist *par excellence*, was never to
acquire, any more than he was to escape the narrowness of nationalism.

During the Whitsun vacation Ibsen settled down to re-work the one-act
play *The Norsemen* which he had begun at Grimstad. Botten Hansen, in his
favourable review of *Catiline*, had expressed regret that Ibsen had not chosen
a national-historical theme instead of setting his play in Ancient Rome.
Ibsen himself appears to have had divided feelings at this time on the question
of nationalistic literature. On the one hand, it was less than a year since he had
written the passionate *Sonnets to King Oscar* and *Awake, Scandinavians*! But in
his subsequent *Elegy for Adam Oehlenschläger*, while declaring that by the latter's
death the Norse gods had lost their spokesman on earth, he at the same time

---

[1] Gran, *op. cit.*, I, p. 29.

expressed the hope that literature would now strike out on new roads, since poetry that sings of 'the enshrined past' could not answer the demands of the new age. None the less, *The Norsemen*, or, as he now re-entitled it, *The Warrior's Barrow*, turned out to be a dramatic poem very much in the mould Of Oehlenschläger's historical tragedies such as *Earl Haakon the Mighty* or *The Vikings in Byzantium*.

The action of *The Warrior's Barrow* takes place on the coast of Normandy 'shortly before the introduction of Christianity into the North'. An old Norse warrior, Bernhard, and his foster-daughter, Blanka, live there; she tends the burial mound, or barrow, of a warrior who has been killed in the past by marauding Vikings. Both she and Bernhard are Christians. Norsemen now arrive, worshippers of the old gods, led by their king, Gandalf, and bent on avenging the death of his father Audun who had been killed on a raid here. He meets Blanka; they fall in love at first sight; she tries to persuade him to turn from paganism to Christianity (as, coincidentally or not, Clara Ebbell at Grimstad had tried to convert Ibsen from atheism). Bernhard now tells Gandalf that the burial mound is in fact Audun's and that he, Bernhard, killed him. The Vikings demand that Gandalf carry out his oath either to kill his father's murderer or to die himself. Rather than kill Blanka's foster-father, he decides to kill himself. She tries to persuade him that an oath to the Norse gods need not, and should not, be obeyed. At this crisis Bernhard reveals himself as Audun; wounded in the battle, he had been found and tended by Blanka, and had become a Christian; the mound contains only, symbolically, his Viking sword and armour. Gandalf, converted, takes Blanka back to the North to be his bride; Audun and the Vikings' bard, Hemming, remain behind.

Such is the banal plot of this short play, and there is no pretending that, dramatically, it has any but the most meagre merits. Even the idea of the Viking who turns Christian to end his days in peace on a southern shore is a blatant crib from *The Vikings in Byzantium*, where an ancient Syrian hermit is revealed to be the great warrior Olaf Trygvesson (about whom Ibsen had begun a play while at Grimstad). Bernhard-Audun's conduct, in particular, is quite inadequately motivated, and none of the characters have any real individuality. Such virtues as the play possesses are poetic rather than dramatic; like *Catiline*, it moves with considerable skill from rhymed to unrhymed verse, and contains several fine passages, notably those in which Gandalf proclaims his faith in the heathen gods.

It often happens, however, that a dramatist's inferior second play is accepted where his more original first effort has been rejected, and so it was with Ibsen. Although patently less good than *Catiline*, *The Warrior's Barrow* was more in tune with the current fashion of romantic nationalism, and the

Christiania Theatre, which had turned down the earlier play, accepted this one for production that autumn. Ibsen had submitted it under the same pseudonym as before, Brynjolf Bjarme.

Encouraged by this, he started work almost immediately on a third play, in blank verse, again with a romantic-nationalistic theme, entitled *The Ptarmigan of Justedal*. In Andreas Faye's *Norwegian Tales* he must have read the story about a little girl who had been the only person in her valley to survive the Black Death; when, years later, people discovered her, she had become 'shy and wild as a bird', so that she came to be called the Ptarmigan of Justedal. In Ibsen's dramatisation of the story, a young farmer's son, Bjørn, and an old hunter, Paal, are walking in the mountains. They begin to speak of the 'little people'; Paal tells how, recently, he took aim at a ptarmigan

> But in a trice the bird was gone
> And in its place a sprite crouched on the bough.

He asks Bjørn where he has been lately, and Bjørn replies that he has been exploring in Justedal. 'God forgive you!' cries Paal.

> No man has set foot there for many a year.
> It has lain desolate since the Black Death.
> Men say ghosts walk there, and the unburied dead
> Haunt its harsh hillsides.

Paal goes into the hut, and Bjørn, left alone, recalls sadly how

> She called me from her bough, winding her horn,
> Since when I have felt drawn towards that valley
> By some invisible power.

As he speaks, he hears the ptarmigan girl, Alfhild, singing.

Scene Two is in Bjørn's home. His father, a fierce old farmer named Bengt, has autocratically decided that Bjørn shall marry his foster-daughter, Mereta, though neither loves the other. To settle the matter he has summoned Mogens, a bibulous and pedantic priest, the forerunner of those other un-sympathetic clerics whom Ibsen was to create: Pastor Strawman in *Love's Comedy*, the Provost in *Brand*, Pastor Manders in *Ghosts* and the drunken Molvik in *The Wild Duck*. An old minstrel, Knud, appears, but Bengt drives him irritably away; when he tells Paal and Bjørn they are alarmed, for this Knud is a famous bard:

> He brings good luck to those who hearken to him.
> But if a man should drive him from his gate,
> His house is cursed.

Bjørn hears that his father plans to match him with Mereta, but will have none of it. He can only think of the ptarmigan who has bewitched him, and creeps secretly off to the unlucky valley of Justedal to find her.

In Act Two he meets her. Meanwhile, in Bengt's house, Mereta and a young friend of Bjørn's, Einar, pledge their love to each other. Old Bengt surprises them and warns Einar off.

At this point, halfway through the second act (the title-page tells us that it was to consist of four), Ibsen abandoned the play; though he was to take it up again six years later and rewrite it as *Olaf Liljekrans*. The *Ptarmigan of Justedal* (like *Olaf Liljekrans*) has been over-readily dismissed by such few critics as have bothered to consider it; as far as it goes, in characterisation and plot development, it was patently the best thing that Ibsen had yet done. The old people especially, Bengt the farmer, Paal the hunter, Mogens the priest and Knud the minstrel, are splendidly drawn in brief, swift strokes, as is the atmosphere of sick enchantment. Why Ibsen stopped writing it we do not know; it may have been simply that, with his examination approaching, he felt he could no longer afford to spend any more time away from his studies.

Some time during the summer, Ibsen and Schulerud moved from Mother Sæter's to a Fru Holt on Møllergaden. Living mainly on Schulerud's small allowance, they at first managed almost luxuriously, for it seems they were able to afford not merely dinners provided by their landlady, but even a servant. The latter, however, did not last long; and soon they had to drop the dinners too. Since it would have damaged their reputation, to say nothing of their credit, for it to be known that they could not afford a square meal, they made a habit of going out around dinner time and returning an hour or so later so that the other lodgers and the servants would imagine they were eating in town. They would then make do with coffee and sandwiches of cheese and sausage-meat. Botten Hansen tells that, although he saw Ibsen almost daily at this period, he had no inkling of the extreme poverty in which the latter lived;[1] as at Grimstad, Ibsen's pride forbade him to reveal his circumstances to his friends. It was presumably during this summer or autumn that Ibsen and Schulerud took the desperate measure of selling their remaining copies of *Catiline* as waste paper.

Ole Schulerud's young brother Johan (the boy to whom Ibsen had, in Grimstad, been stingy with the liquorice) was staying with them now. The three inhabited a tiny room with space for only two beds, one of which the Schuleruds had to share. Johan remembered the three of them, Ole's tiny legacy having been exhausted on the publication of *Catiline*, as being 'permanently

[1] *Illustreret Nyhedsblad*, 19 July 1863.

poor', and Ibsen as 'dark and unapproachable. I didn't like him, and I could see no evidence that he liked me. Small of stature, with an unattractive, square face'. Occasionally, Johan recalled, they would have parties with boston[1] and toddy, at which Botten Hansen and Abildgaard were frequent guests, and on these occasions Ibsen would be 'much more talkative and agreeable than at other times'.[2]

However, a young man's first year at University is often spent in circumstances of comparative want, and that summer of 1850 must, in the main, have been a happy one for Ibsen, rejoicing in his new friends, the liberating atmosphere of University life and the knowledge that a work of his was to be presented at the country's leading theatre. Not many youthful playwrights can have been able to claim the honour of seeing their first play printed and their second accepted for production shortly after their twenty-second birthday. Admittedly there came a slight setback in August, for that month he failed his matriculation. His tutor at the crammer's, Theodor J. Lie, wrote him a good reference, saying that he had a '*right faithful and retentive memory, assisted by happy natural gifts*', but in no subject did he get the maximum mark of 1, and in only one, German, did he even succeed in achieving 2, or 'Very Good'. In most subjects, including Norwegian composition, he scored a moderate 3; on the three Latin papers he got 3, 4 and 5 respectively; and in both Greek and mathematics he failed with 6, so that his average over the whole examination was no more than 3.67. But his creative writing must already have seemed to him more important than his University studies, for he never bothered to attempt the Greek or mathematics papers again, although in view of the papers which he had passed he was entitled to style himself *Student* Ibsen. He continued to attend lectures, but medicine, which he had originally intended to follow, had apparently lost its interest for him; he now studied only literature and aesthetics. He joined the student literary club which had been founded the previous year, and made the required inaugural speech, prefacing it with a recital of seven of his own sonnets.

One would like to know what Ibsen was reading at this time, but unfortunately neither he nor his friends have left any record of this. He may, as many have assumed, have continued to read Kierkegaard, to whom old Miss Crawfurd at Grimstad had introduced him, but it is by no means certain that he did. Such evidence as there is of Kierkegaard's possible influence on Ibsen's writing does not appear until over ten years later. It has, similarly, been asserted that Ibsen probably studied Hegel at this time, because Hegelian philosophy

---

[1] A kind of whist.
[2] Interview with Johan Schulerud in *Verdens Gang*, 23 and 24 June 1910.

F

was now sweeping Europe and the new professor of philosophy at the University, M. J. Monrad (the author of the kind editorial note about *Catiline*) was a disciple of Hegel; but we have no evidence that Ibsen ever read a line of Hegel, and if he did, he may well, like Kierkegaard (cf. the latter's journal for 1843) have found Hegel 'merely comic' with his 'eternal hinting and deceiving'. One author who did make an impact on him, however was the Danish poet, philosopher, critic and dramatist Johan Ludvig Heiberg (1791–1860), whom Ibsen was to meet in Copenhagen the following year and who was one of the very few writers from whom Ibsen, in later life, confessed to having learned something. Heiberg's influence was at its height in Scandinavia in 1850, and he was much discussed in the circles in which Ibsen moved; moreover, there is clear evidence in the drama criticisms which Ibsen was shortly to write that he was well acquainted at any rate with Heiberg's little book *On Vaudeville*.[1] But, like so many young men who find themselves, during their first year at University, in stimulating company after years of forced reading, Ibsen may not have devoted overmuch time to books, and in any case he seems, in common with many dramatists and novelists, not greatly to have enjoyed or comprehended the abstractions of philosophy.

That summer and autumn he also wrote a number of poems. Twelve of these he copied neatly on to light blue paper in the scratchy, difficult, sharply slanted handwriting which we find in his early letters and manuscripts (and which contrasts so remarkably with the lucid bold copperplate of his maturity), and posted to Clara Ebbell at Grimstad. 'In sending you the enclosed writings', he wrote stiffly in the short note which accompanied them, and which suggests that she can hardly have reciprocated his feelings with much warmth, 'it is my hope that the mood which evoked these poems may serve as an excuse for the observations expressed therein, which might partly be misinterpreted by others and by you. I beg you to forgive me for not being able to refrain from adding these words, probably the last that I shall ever address to you'.[2]

The poems included the sonnet sequence which Ibsen had read as a preface to his inaugural speech at the Students' Union, and three romantic trifles entitled *In the Night* (which dates from Grimstad), *Youthful Dreams* and *Among the Ruins*. Of these, *In the Night* and *Among the Ruins* are conventional lyrics, and *Youthful Dreams*, although skilfully composed in rhymed stanzas, contains no original thought or idea. The sonnets, however, were much the best and most complex poems that Ibsen had written up to that time. On the lake of

---

[1] Heiberg's probable influence on Ibsen's dramatic criticisms has been well analysed by Professor Sigmund Skard in *A. O. Vinje og antikken* (Oslo, 1938), pp. 124–125.

[2] In fact he wrote to her once more, the following February, enclosing a poem *To a Troubadour*. Shortly afterwards she married a wealthy man twice her age.

life, he says, there glide two ships, sailing in opposite directions. One, a merchantman laden to the waterline, rows slowly but safely in the lee of the shore; the other, all sails set, entrusts itself to the winds and tosses perilously upon the waves. Each of us must choose to which ship he will entrust his life. If we choose the second, the ideal instead of the material, our voyage will be hard and uncertain, and our reward will probably come late; but it is better to be like the swan, which discovers the joy of song only in its last moments, than to find those joys early and then lose our way, 'and wander lost across life's burning sands'. Over the next fifty years, Ibsen was to return again and again in his work to this theme, of the choice that faces man between idealism and compromise.[1]

Of still greater interest, though, are the two other poems which Ibsen sent to Clara Ebbell: *The Miner* and *The Bird and the Trapper*. They were the only two poems of this group which Ibsen retained for inclusion in the volume of collected verse that he published as his farewell to that medium in 1871. With the sonnets, they represent an important departure for Ibsen as a poet. Hitherto, his poems had been lyrical—save only for the inferior, Kiplingesque exhortations inspired by the political events of 1848. But the sonnets, *The Miner* and *The Bird and the Trapper* are all dramatic poems, in the sense that the poet, instead of merely recording his emotions, dramatises them, as one dramatises an idea for a play; unlike his earlier, lyrical poems, they create strong visual images. The English poet whom Ibsen, in his shorter pieces, most closely resembles, though the resemblance is far from complete, is Thomas Hardy (a writer with whom he had, of course, much in common when he turned to prose). Like Hardy, Ibsen was an accomplished lyricist but at his best as a poet when writing dramatic verse, whether in the form of dramatic monologues or of sharply told anecdotes. *The Miner* is an example of the first category, *The Bird and the Trapper* of the second. Lyrical poetry is scarcely translatable (what has anyone ever made of Heine in English?), but dramatic poetry can retain something of its effect when simply rendered into free verse; the content comes over, if not the form.

Barely half a mile from Ibsen's childhood home at Venstøp was an iron mine, only just below ground surface. The noise from it must, when the wind was right, have been audible at the house, and as a child he must surely have gone and watched the men working there. The subject of the miner had attracted other poets; Oehlenschläger had written a poem on the theme, and so, in 1811, had the Swedish poet Erik Gustaf Geijer; but where Oehlen-

---

[1] The subject for debate at the Students' Union on the evening when Ibsen read these sonnets was 'Realism v Idealism'.

schläger had been attracted by the mystery of the darkness, and Geijer by the peace, Ibsen had been fascinated by the hard and remorseless toil. All of us who write poems, however badly, write at least one in adolescence or early manhood which foretells our future, and with Ibsen that poem was *The Miner*:

Groan and thunder, mountain wall,
Before my heavy hammer blow.
Downwards I must carve my way
Till I hear the iron ore sing.

Deep in the mountain's lonely night
The rich treasure beckons me.
Diamonds and precious stones
Among the red branches of the gold.

Here in the darkness there is peace,
Peace and rest for eternity.
Heavy hammer, break me the way
To the heart-chamber of what lies hidden there...

When I first entered here
I thought in my innocence:
'The spirits of the dark will solve for me
Life's obscure riddles.'

No spirit has yet taught me that strange answer.
No sun shines from the depths.

Was I wrong? Does this path
Not lead to the light?
But the light blinds my eyes
If I seek it in the mountains.

No, I must go down into the dark.
Eternal peace lies there.
Heavy hammer, break me the way
To the heart-chamber of what lies hidden there.

So blow follows blow
Till he sinks weak and tired.
No ray of morning shines.
No sun of hope rises.

The Bird and the Trapper anticipates, to English ears, the manner of a poet with whom, again, Ibsen had more in common than might at first appear: D. H. Lawrence:

Once when I was little
I was running in my father's garden.
The bird was singing its morning song
From its high branch and picket fence.

And I cut from the pine-branch
An ingenious bird-trap.
Before I can count ten
The bird sits there inside it!

And I carried with cruel delight,
Quickly, the trap into the house.
Frightened the bird with my angry
Glance, with my cries and threats.

When I had thus amused myself
And sated my cruelty,
I put the cage on the table;
Cautiously opened the door.

O, how it uses its wings!
It is offered life and freedom.
It would soar high to the light
But—crushes itself against the window pane.

You are revenged, cruelly revenged.
Now a power has trapped me
In a cage, where I can only flutter crazily.

And an eye stares at me
Coldly and scornfully through the bars.
This glance confuses my soul.
Fear makes my body shake.

And when I think I see
The path that leads to freedom,
I sink with broken wings
From my dreamed soaring.

Henrik Jæger tells that Ibsen planned during this first year in Christiania to publish a volume of verse, but gradually rejected poem after poem from his Grimstad days until there was hardly anything left.[1] He no longer wanted to

---

[1] Jæger, *op. cit.*, p. 239. J. B. Halvorsen (*op. cit.*, p. 8 footnote) denies on Ibsen's authority that such a volume was contemplated; but Ibsen's memory, where his early years are concerned, frequently proved false, and Jæger's statement at least deserves to remain on record.

write poems of mood, but poems of ideas; and it was upon the latter kind, beginning with those quoted above, that he was to concentrate during the remainder of his time in Christiania.

On 26 September 1850 came the eagerly awaited production at the Christiania Theatre of *The Warrior's Barrow*. The part of Blanka was performed by a young actress named Laura Svendsen; later, under her married name of Laura Gundersen, she was to become one of Norway's most famous actresses and was to create several of Ibsen's greatest roles, including Ellida in *The Lady from the Sea* and Gunhild Borkman. Ibsen, extremely nervous, hid himself, we are told, in the darkest corner of the theatre; but the play, surprisingly, was well received, and was repeated twice that autumn.

Ibsen's enthusiastic friend, Ole Schulerud, whether from altruistic motives or in the faint hope of retrieving a little of his lost legacy, at once set about trying to get *The Warrior's Barrow* published. He approached Steensballe, the bookseller who had issued *Catiline* on commission, and a contract was signed under which Ibsen was actually to receive an advance of twenty-five specie-dollars (about £6):

I, The undersigned Bookseller Steensballe, hereby acknowledge that I have contracted with Student Schulerud regarding the purchase of Brynjolf Bjarme's manuscript of *The Warrior's Barrow*, dramatic poem in one act, and *The Gold Harp*, epic poem, on the following terms:

1. Steensballe shall have the right to print 1, one, edition of 4-500 copies.

2. Steensballe shall pay, in return for the rights of this 1st edition, 25, twenty-five, specie-dollars, of which 10, ten, specie-dollars shall be paid forthwith, the remainder when 250, two hundred and fifty, copies have been sold.

Christiania 19 December 1850.

I hereby acknowledge receipt from Herr Steensballe of 10, ten, specie-dollars as instalment on the above sum.

Ole Schulerud.

For some unknown reason, however, the play was not printed, and this, the original version of *The Warrior's Barrow*, was not published until 1902 (though a revised version, on the occasion of its performance at Bergen in 1854, was serialised in four parts in a local newspaper). Ibsen quickly recognised the play's limitations, and it was one of the only two plays of his which, when a collected edition of his works was planned towards the end of his life, he decided to omit. (The other was *St John's Night*.) No trace has ever been discovered of the planned 'epic poem', *The Gold Harp*, and it is not known whether Ibsen ever began it.

1850, then, had been a year of poetry. 1851 was to be primarily a year of journalism. Ibsen continued, naturally, to write poetry, as an undergraduate should; but he needed another medium as outlet for the combativeness which was so important a part of his character. An opportunity arose when, in the New Year, he found himself chosen by the Students' Union to become editor of their handwritten magazine, *Samfundsbladet*, in succession to Paul Botten Hansen, probably through the latter's influence.

Ibsen edited *Samfundsbladet* for nine months, but with decreasing assiduousness; in the first quarter of the year he produced three numbers, in the second quarter only one, and in the third quarter none at all. The reason for this was that his energies gradually became absorbed in a more exciting project which Botten Hansen and Vinje had just started, a new, independent literary and political weekly of their own. Their inspiration and model for this was the Danish magazine *The Corsair*, which, as stated, Meïr Aron Goldschmidt had founded in Copenhagen; Vinje was a great admirer of that neurotic, battling controversialist who, like Vinje himself, despised all party ties and smote around at everyone and everything (among his targets had been such respected figures as Heiberg and Kierkegaard). An advertisement issued in Christiania on 5 March 1851 announced that the new magazine would contain, among other delights, 'Poems by Brynjolf Bjarme'; and since, following the production of *The Warrior's Barrow*, Ibsen was now allowed free tickets to the Christiania Theatre, he was also to write the drama criticisms. The magazine had no name. In place of a title, it carried on the front page of the first issue a picture of the main square of Christiania, Stortorvet, with a man in several grotesque postures, on foot and on horseback, eyeing the world satirically. Subsequently the same man was shown in the Storthing gallery alertly listening to the Parliamentary debates and taking notes. As a result the magazine came to be known as *Manden, The Man*.

For the next nine months, therefore, Ibsen busied himself with drama criticism and political and topical commentaries, as well as with editorial and sub-editorial work and an occasional, and by no means unskilful, caricature. His first drama criticism to be published, on 12 January in *Samfundsbladet*, was a brief and rather flat notice of a production of Holberg's comedy *The Political Tinker*; and on 15 February he contributed a dutiful and dullish survey of the history of the Students' Union. The same issue, however, included a lively piece by him on the old question of the desirability of the country having a Norwegian theatre. The Christiania Theatre had refused to let the Students' Union give a public performance there instead of in their own inadequate premises, and Ibsen took up the cudgels. 'It has often been stated in the Students' Union,' he declared, 'that it is from us that any Norwegian Theatre must originate...The preparatory work is up to us, it is we who must accustom the people to hearing Norwegian spoken from the stage; but the theatre-going public of the capital is not the people. To travel the country preaching theatrical reform is hardly practicable; so why not seize the opportunity to scatter the good seed as widely as possible, and Fair Week is ideally suited to this.' (At Fair Week the capital was filled with people from the countryside).

On 1 March he reviewed, again in *Samfundsbladet*, a student vaudeville in one act entitled *The Asylum in Greenland*, defending the decision to give it a second performance after the first one had been ill received. The review tells us nothing interesting except, by implication, that Ibsen had read J. L. Heiberg's short book *On Vaudeville*, several undigested gobbets of which may be found floating in Ibsen's prose. Then, on 23 March, in *The Man*, he took the bold step of publicly criticising his own professor's lectures. J. S. Welhaven was not only professor of aesthetics but also the leading Norwegian poet now that Henrik Wergeland was dead. Unlike the gifted but naïve Wergeland, Welhaven was a scholarly, elegant and dignified versifier somewhat in the Matthew Arnold mould. Welhaven had attacked the fashion which had arisen in the eighteenth century of re-telling ancient Greek and Roman myths; taking his text from Holberg, who had satirised this cult, he condemned the contemporary Danish poet Frederik Paludan-Müller for indulging in similar re-tellings, as in his poem *Tithonus* (a subject which Tennyson was to treat more memorably ten years later). Ibsen, with some percipience, suggested that Welhaven was wrong in identifying Paludan-Müller's efforts with those of the previous century. Although Paludan-Müller might have failed in this particular instance, Ibsen asserted, 'it in no way follows that the Myth is unsuited to be used in our time as the basis for a poem of ideas...In myth, the content of popular consciousness is a blending of history and imagination...Since the subject-matter of myth is timeless, its validity in time can never be so limited as to disqualify an author from laying another stone upon that mythical foundation. We no longer voyage the seas like Columbus to discover a new country, but rather to study the nature of that country whose existence we accept. So it is with mythical poetry...To draw it up from its resting-place on the ocean bed and consider it anew from a fresh and imaginative standpoint is no violation of the sacredness of myth, nor any perversion of its quintessential nature, but rather a necessary step in its logical development'. That last sentence might almost serve as a preface to *Peer Gynt*.

Ibsen was now finding his feet as a journalist, and on 13 April *The Man* printed a review by him of a modern German play, Karl Gutzkow's *Zopf und Schwert*, which is interesting on two grounds. Firstly, it underlines how in-adequate he found even at this early stage in his career, the trivia of Eugène

Scribe, the most popular and esteemed playwright of the day;[1] and secondly, it shows that he was already aware of the possibilities of drama written to be read rather than staged, the genre of which Alfred de Musset was the contemporary master. Fifteen years later Ibsen, like de Musset, was temporarily to abandon stageable drama for the drama of the study and in so doing was to write what many people regard as his two greatest and most theatrically exciting plays. The review, for all its occasional *longueurs*, is worth quoting *in extenso*, if only because it reveals the perplexities amongst which the young dramatist was groping:

'Our theatrical repertory having long been recruited exclusively from France and Copenhagen, a play of the new German school was recently shown. The public seemed not to find this modification of their normal diet much to their taste. Far be it from me to seek the cause of this in the public's fastidiousness, for God knows if there is one thing our audiences are not, it is fastidious. The true reason is not hard to find. When a public has grown accustomed, as ours has, year in and year out to the dramatic candy-floss (*slikkerier*) of Scribe & Co., cautiously seasoned with a suitable admixture of various poetical substitutes, it is very understandable that the solider German fare must strike even the ostrich stomachs of our theatre-goers as somewhat indigestible.

'Between modern French and modern German drama there are essential differences. The French drama (using the word drama in its true sense, as covering spectacles in general) makes contact with life only through the medium of actors; only thus is it born into existence. For drama, as it leaves the hand of a French playwright, is still embryonic, and only answers to its name when it achieves reality through actual performance. For a Frenchman, the new drama has no title to be regarded as literature for reading, any more than our mountain peasants would regard a sheet of music as such. The German dramatist, on the other hand, writes his play without specifically envisaging it in performance. If it can be staged in the form in which it leaves his pen, well and good; if not, it can be read, and he regards it as thus equally satisfying the requirements of drama, for in Germany the claim of drama to be regarded as reading literature is one with its claim to be regarded as dramatic literature.

'From this it naturally follows that the German, when he writes a play for the stage, has other considerations in mind than when writing without

---

[1] Ibsen told Henrik Jæger in 1887 that 'he of course saw much Scribe in his youth, but that, dramatically, he then rated the elder Dumas higher'. Jæger's notes for his biography, first printed in H. Midbøe's *Streiflys over Ibsen*, Oslo, 1960, p. 162).

thought of performance. But this conflict between his general view of drama, and the demands which he has to face on such isolated occasions, reveals itself in his work and destroys the unity without which art cannot exist. In order, as he supposes, to achieve reality, he paints characters and situations with a broad brush, but thereby defeats his purpose, since he thus oversteps the boundaries of drama. Thus the German drama is to the French as a *tableau vivant* is to a painting; in the former, figures exist in their natural dimensions and colours, in the latter they merely *appear* thus...

'This is not to say that the French drama has no advantages over the German; it is a question of how far it meets the demands which it has set itself. If literal reality has no place in art, neither does a work that does not contain the germ of reality within it; and herein lies the weakness of the French drama. In it characters too often appear as pure abstractions; to portray contrast (the hobby-horse of French drama) they are usually painted as either angels or devils, seldom as people. Whereas when the German aims at reality, which is not in general his hunting-ground, he does it with a vengeance, portraying not just human beings as such but only the most trivial kind of everyday people as we daily see and hear them. Yet the character of an everyday person is, from an artist's standpoint, by no means trivial; it is as interesting to him as any other.

'The play under review is as typically German in its faults as in its virtues. It is essentially a play of situations, for it is the situation that develops; the characters do not.'

After outlining the absurd plot, which takes place at the Prussian court, and delivering himself of some comments on the characters ('Sir Hotham is the complete Englishman, ready to help his friend without ever losing sight of his country's material interests'), the dramatic faults of the play ('When the Princess is arrested she addresses a thunderous speech to the Dragoons, stopping at frequent intervals to let her lady-in-waiting have her say, which strikes us as unnatural'), and the performances, which he praises rather uncritically, Ibsen continues:

'But now a little about our public's reaction to the play. Were it not the fashion just now to attack the theatre and the 'Danish' players, this might have seemed a good opportunity for them to express their indebtedness to both without imperilling their artistic conscience. But by no means! The play was greeted with scarcely any applause, except for those moments when the author moves into burlesque, as when the Dragoons march in with the soup tureen and the woollen stockings, and the King appears without coat or trousers. And what was it, in the last-named instance, that pleased our ingenuous public? Not the fact of the King of Prussia receiving the Prince of Bayreuth in his underpants, though the situation is artistically comic, but the joy of seeing Herr Jørgensen appear thus clad upon the stage—that was the great joke...And this is the public that clamours for a National Theatre! In truth, should this and other demands currently being made by this public be met, then "Goodnight, ye Muses!" But with our prospects of a National Theatre we shall deal more closely in a later article.'

After a dutiful piece in *Samfundsbladet* later the same month on the inadequacies of the Union library, we find Ibsen, on 4 May, trying his hand at opera criticism. The subject was Rossini's *William Tell*, and he had sharp words to say about the libretto. 'It is regrettable that this splendid music should be shackled with so moderate a text. It consists merely of loose fragments torn from Schiller's tragedy of the same name and lumped together without the librettist achieving any real unity or coherence. The effect of the music is unquestionably much reduced in consequence.' In the same article, Ibsen noticed revivals of two plays by Scribe, *La Famille Riquebourg* and *Une Chaumière et sa Coeur*, the latter being a collaboration with Robert Alphonse. In view of the hoary myth, which one may still hear repeated, that Ibsen was a disciple of Scribe, it is worth noting that he described these efforts as 'two old plays that ought long ago to have been regarded as dead and buried'.

The following week, again in *The Man*, we find Ibsen attacking an anonymous French vaudeville, *Un Homme Blasé*, for its complete lack of realism and structural incompetence:

'One naturally expects that the hero's character will reveal itself through dramatic action; but our author is of another opinion. Instead of letting his hero do things, he makes him *tell* the audience about his *ennui*, how life has lost its sparkle and everything seems an interminable misery. That this lengthy narrative should interest the good friends to whom he addresses it seems scarcely likely; for he says nothing that they cannot already know. What the cause of all this boredom is we are not informed; the hero merely assures us that he is bored, and we must take him at his word... At last one of his friends has an idea. He must get married. It seems curious that this not impossibly out of the way notion has not occurred to him before; however, our author will have it so, and we must accept it. But this idea comes to nothing, and so the first act ends. But then the blasé gentleman meets a young peasant girl and is soon head over heels in love with her. Unfortunately all this takes place behind the curtain during the interval between acts one and two, so that we have to be satisfied with an account of the affair which the hero is kind enough to give us...

'The fact that the public whistled must be taken as a happy sign that there are, after all, a few among us who can distinguish truth from falsehood. The few who clapped we must bear with; their demonstration can hardly have been on behalf of the play, and if it was aimed at the acting it was fully justified...The directors of the theatre can, however, scarcely be censured for presenting this piece. The public is always complaining that it is offered nothing but warmed-up left-overs, so something new must be offered. We ourselves write nothing, neither do the Danes, Scribe has been done to death, and what is there left? Besides, it is good for us now and then to be given a really clear picture of what a play ought not to be.'

From May until August, Vinje was away on holiday, and in his absence Ibsen took over the political commentary of *The Man*, which the editors now decided to re-name *Andhrimner*, after the cook who prepared the food for the gods in Valhalla. On 18 May he reported a debate in the Storthing on the repeal of the usury law, which allowed money-lenders to fix their own rates of interest for short-term loans without security. Ibsen singled out for especial scorn A. B. Stabell, the member for Akershus and editor of the then liberal newspaper[1] *Morgenbladet*, who that year had left the opposition party and joined the government, and had delivered himself of the unfortunate remark that 'it would be improper for educated men to listen to the clamour of the rabble and allow themselves to be influenced by it'. 'These words', commented Ibsen, 'were uttered in this year of grace 1851 by Herr Stabell, that same Stabell who for so many years has reiterated his faith in the infallibility of popular opinion; who has set himself up as the standard-bearer of 'the nine-tenths', and has delivered resounding assurances of the political authority wielded by the common man, listening for his opinions like a conscientious actor cocking an attentive ear towards the prompter's box...Stabell's conduct reminds one of that resilient English priest who set his mind on dying, as he had lived, the guardian of his parishioners' souls, forswearing Catholicism under Henry VIII, re-embracing it under Mary, re-forswearing it under Elizabeth, re-embracing it yet again under James, and thus achieving his ambition.' Ibsen accompanied this article with an excellent caricature showing an unfortunate debtor being relieved of his clothes by two smiling usurers.

The next week, on 25 May, he contributed to *Andhrimner* a general theatrical

---

[1] It was to go Conservative in 1859, largely because of the foundation that year of a 'Reform Club' which it feared might be used for revolutionary ends.

article on a theme he had already touched upon in his review of Rossini's *William Tell*, the tendency to underrate the importance of libretti in opera. Ibsen never had much ear for or appreciation of music except in its simplest forms, such as folk song, and liked opera mainly for its dramatic quality, so that a bad libretto offended him more than it would musically-minded spectators—'who regard opera as a combination of two separate entities, music and text, of which, in their view, the one can make its effect even if the other is less successful...The most complete harmony must exist between the music and the text; the music is the soul of the opera, the text the concrete form holding it...When music lovers declare that they prefer to close their eyes during a performance so as not to be disturbed in their enjoyment of the music, this is either an affectation or else is grounded on a total misunderstanding of the purpose of opera music. In a concert hall, it is permissible, since there the words are inessential and the music is everything and sufficient unto itself; but this is not the case in opera, where the music is a content first perceptible through the plastic form that is its setting'.

The occasion of these observations was Bellini's opera *Norma*, about a Roman pro-consul, Severus, who, after seducing a priestess, Norma, and giving her two sons, deceives her with a temple maiden named Adalgisa. Ibsen saw it performed on 20 May, and within ten days wrote a parody, also entitled *Norma*, in which the characters were members of the Norwegian Storthing. Some ten pages long, it was published anonymously in *Andhrimner* in two instalments, on 1 and 8 June, with the following prefatory explanation:

'The other day I found myself in the Parliamentary gallery. The subject under discussion was of the usual kind, and I cannot, therefore, remember what it was about. When Schytz rose to speak, and I consequently had nothing upon which to fix my attention, I allowed my imagination to roam, and reasoned thus. In these 106 heads, some wigged, some not, may be found the essence of all the finest talents that old Norway has to offer... wisdom, eloquence, patriotism, liberalism...I let my thoughts wander thus for some hours until Schytz stopped speaking and the peace of my reflections was abruptly disturbed. The same evening I saw *Norma*, and suddenly the revelation struck me: 'Our Storthing is really a gifted company of actors!...The more I considered the matter, the clearer it became. Holmboe is the noble and respected father in the comedy, Motzfeldt, Lange and Harris are the peevish old uncle who has lost his feeling for the poetry of life but is useful to have around in the background, however much his prosaic worldly wisdom may seem to throw water on the fiery plans, and castles in the air, of the young lovers. The opposition is a kind of corporate coquette, whom every young hothead eagerly courts but, in the end, decides not to marry (especially when her rival in his affections dangles a tempting dowry). Stabell is of course the hero of the play. He is one of those genuinely dramatic characters of whom Heiberg says 'one must guess at rather than fully comprehend their nature,' and at the end of the play they are in the situation in which, at the beginning, one would least have expected to see them.

'Such were the reflections that moved me to pen this opera, *Norma, or a Politician's Love*, the text of which follows, and which I hereby offer to our Storthing for performance on any festive occasion of their choice. The music they must find themselves, but since they have at their command virtuosos on every thinkable instrument from trumpet to bassoon and drum, I think they will find no difficulty there.'

Ibsen's parody opens with a chorus of Druids (members of Parliament) worshipping at the shrine of Freedom, which they have sworn to guard. Severus (Stabell) enters as they leave, and begins an eloquent speech in praise of Freedom; then he finds he is alone, and says he could have spared all that rubbish. Adalgisa his present love (the Government) enters, and accuses him of still secretly loving Norma (the Opposition). Severus replies that she was merely a youthful passion, a foolish dream, of whom he is now well cured. Norma now enters with her two children by Severus (votes of 'no confidence'[1] in the Government); abandoned by their father, she laments, they seem certain to die. Severus enters to her; she upbraids him, and he begs the stage manager, for decency's sake, to lower the curtain. When it rises again, the Druids are asleep, although the day is well advanced, 'since, as is well known' (the stage direction informs us) 'they are always somewhat behind the time'. Norma raises her dagger to kill Severus, but the Prime Minister 'appears in the form of an angel and transforms Severus into a demi-god, or, as the modern term is, a minister of the crown'. So all ends happily.

Norma was not intended to be performed, nor does it ever appear to have been; yet it is not without significance in any study of Ibsen's work. Written in brilliantly rhymed verse, rather reminiscent, to an English reader, of the best of R. H. Barham's *Ingoldsby Legends*, it was, if we except the Grimstad lampoons, Ibsen's first essay at satirical verse, and was a pointer to what was to come. Of his next ten plays, four (*St John's Night, Love's Comedy, Peer Gynt*

---

[1] Alarmed by the growing strength of the workers' movement under Marcus Thrane, Stabell had, when in opposition, dropped the vote of no confidence which he had been generally expected to move, and which would almost certainly have been carried. Ibsen believed, probably correctly, that Stabell was putting personal ambition before political integrity.

and *The League of Youth*) were conceived as satires, and a fifth, *Brand*, was primarily regarded as such when it first appeared, although to modern readers (as with *Peer Gynt*) the satire has dwindled and the tragedy remains.

On 8 June, in the issue that contained the final instalment of *Norma*, Ibsen contributed two further parliamentary commentaries, the second of which he illustrated with another admirable caricature, of a man trying to push a pig towards its trough while the pig resists indignantly complaining: 'Leave me alone, I can find my own way!' These commentaries, like his theatre articles, are uncommonly lively and pungent pieces, and leave one to reflect how fortunate it was that no newspaper editor had the imagination to offer the young writer a position on his staff. The delights of journalism often seem more attractive to an undergraduate than those of creative writing, especially when he is near the starvation line, and, as we shall see, Ibsen was to snatch eagerly at the first salaried post that was offered to him. But *The Man* and its successor, *Andhrimner*, aroused an astonishing lack of interest among the students and citizens of Christiania (they never achieved even a hundred subscribers), so that it is quite possible that no newspaper editor in Christiania even read it; and subordinate journalists in a small town have their own mouths to think of without recommending lively young fellows who might jump ahead of them. In any event, journalism was poorly developed in Norway at this time; even the Christiania dailies such as *Morgenbladet* contained only four pages, including one of advertisements, and read like the more unprepossessing kind of provincial news-sheet.

Later that month the thorny problem of nationalistic drama raised its head again, when *The Goblin's Home*, an 'original play in three acts with music and chorus' by P. A. Jensen, was performed. This seems to have been a particularly unhappy example of rustic whimsy, and Ibsen, after a blistering summary of the plot, concluded his notice:

'Such is the basic content of this national drama, *The Goblin's Home*. One does not need to dig deeply to find that such nationalism as it contains is merely a tacked-on embellishment and has no organic connection with the play. Amongst such tinsel we may enumerate a quarterstaff duel, a country dance, a few rustic swear-words and some fragments of *patois* which may dazzle the ignorant but which, critically investigated, reveal themselves in all their hollowness and triviality. What does this shell contain? A theme which is anything but national; or is it a feature of our national life that old hunters wander around farmyards leaving behind infant daughters who, after a lapse of sixteen or seventeen years, are then reclaimed by their rightful guardian? (I use the word 'guardian' because the parson says that Astrid is his niece, but with every respect for the worthy cleric I must add that I strongly suspect him to have been something of a bounder in his youth, and to be more closely related to the young lady than he is prepared to admit.) Nor can the secret wedding be described as typically national, nor the parson's efforts to test and strengthen Gutorm's Christian faith. In other words, our national dramatic literature is no better off than it was before the performance of The Goblin's Home. Nor can it be as long as our authors fail to distinguish between the demands of reality and the demands of art, and lack the taste to polish the rough surface of reality so that it may qualify to be admitted into the realm of art. Then they may realise that nationalism in art does not consist merely of the trivial copying of scenes from everyday life, and will see that a national author is one who understands how to give his work those undertones which call to us from mountain and valley, from meadow and shore, but above all from within our own soul.'

How could Ibsen know that he would, in nine years, find himself compelled to stage this wretched piece himself at the theatre of which he was, at least nominally, artistic director?

All these articles were unsigned; but before June was out, the name of Henrik Ibsen appeared in print for the first time, beneath two songs written for the gathering of students from the various Scandinavian countries which took place in Christiania that month. They are lively and agreeable lyrics of an undemanding kind, which stood up well to those composed for the occasion by established poets such as Welhaven, Munch and Jørgen Moe, and attracted favourable attention. The following month, July 1851, the pseudonym Brynjolf Bjarme was printed for the last time, over a long ballad (of a hundred and seventeen verses!) entitled Helge Hundingsbane, published in Andhrimner. From now on, Ibsen was to use his own name.

Helge Hundingsbane appeared in three parts, on 6, 13 and 20 July, and the day after the publication of the first instalment (though the events were unconnected) Ibsen found himself in trouble. In addition to his work for The Man, Andhrimner and Samfundsbladet, Ibsen had been contributing to the radical newspaper Arbejderforeningernes Blad, which had been edited since the beginning of the year by his friend Theodor Abildgaard. Unfortunately we do not know which of the articles in this newspaper were written by Ibsen, since all contributions were unsigned and no manuscripts have survived.[1] He had also been

---

[1] Ibsen told J. B. Halvorsen (op. cit., p. 8 footnote) that his contributions to Arbejderforeningernes Blad were 'merely insignificant'; but he may have been referring to their quality rather than their frequency.

helping Abildgaard with a local workers' Sunday school, presumably, since he was a freethinker, in general rather than religious subjects. On 7 July the police raided the newspaper office, arrested Abildgaard and Marcus Thrane, the workers' leader, and took away as many manuscript articles as they could lay hands on in order to identify and act against the authors. Ibsen was only saved by the quick thinking of the compositor, who crumpled up a number of manuscripts and threw them on the floor, where the police rather indolently took them to be waste paper. These included all of Ibsen's unprinted contributions and, whether for lack of evidence or because they were only interested in the big fish, the authorities took no action against him. Thrane and Abildgaard spent three years in prison awaiting trial, and then served four year sentences; by the time they were released, in 1858, their movement lay in ruins. Thrane's downfall bears a resemblance to that of his predecessor among Norwegian champions of liberty, Christian Lofthuus, and it is ironical that Ibsen, who was himself to become a famous champion of liberty, should have had such humiliating connection with them, fathering an illegitimate child on to the grand-daughter of the one and, as it were, denying the other. A bolder spirit than Ibsen might have declared himself and accompanied his friends to prison; but Ibsen's courage, throughout his life, was limited to the written word. He was, as the man who gave him the lift from Grimstad across the ice had noticed, timid of physical danger.

The Sunday school closed, as a rather pathetic announcement informed the pupils, 'since Stud. Ibsen does not feel able to conduct it unassisted'. When it re-started in October, Ibsen was turning to other fields of activity, and Vinje took his place. Thus ended Ibsen's brief career as a Sunday school teacher.

During July and August the theatre was closed for the summer, and Ibsen, despite the fright he had been given, concentrated on political commentaries. The most forceful of these pieces was an attack on the servility of the Swedish press. The Swedish newspaper *Morgonbladet* (not to be confused with Stabell's *Morgenbladet*) had complained that Sweden was being insulted by 'the little people of Norway, a small country that has for centuries been nothing more than a province of Denmark'. Ibsen retorted: 'It would be sad indeed if this yelp were to be taken as an expression of the feelings of the Swedish people. Whence does it arise? Not from the Swedish people, but from the mildewed Swedish aristocracy...Norway, with its liberal institutions, has always been a thorn in the flesh of these anachronistic relics; their party has always feared lest the Swedes might learn from Norway how a people that has matured towards independence roots out such obsolete institutionsas have ceased to justify their existence...The Swedish people is too clear-sighted, too enlightened, to let itself be blinded, and *Morgonbladet* must not hope that it can arouse nation-

G

alistic hatred as a barrier to divide Norwegian from Swede, any more than it can close the eyes of the Swedish nation to the inexorable necessity of certain reforms within their own frontiers.'

On 28 September 1851 *Andhrimner* folded, after thirty-nine issues. Despite the vigour and vitality of its contributions, it had steadily lost money, and eventually the publisher, Axelsen, decided that he could not afford to continue. Ibsen, who had a long memory, was to caricature him unkindly in *The League of Youth* in 1869, thinly disguised as Printer Aslaksen, a figure whom he also introduced into *An Enemy of the People* in 1881. The little magazine reads excellently, even at this distance of time, and it is a sad comment on the apathy of the Christiania students that it should never have succeeded in mustering even a hundred regular subscribers.

Ibsen now found himself at a period in life when three or four careers seemed to beckon to him, none of them very enticingly. He had given up his early ideas of becoming a doctor or a painter. He had completed two plays, but although one had been published and the other performed, neither had achieved any real success. The theatre as such does not appear particularly to have excited him. It is noteworthy that his dramatic reviews of 1851 hardly ever say anything interesting or constructive about the actual staging or performances, which usually receive only a short paragraph of conventional and uncritical praise. In the ordinary course of events he would probably have continued with his studies for another three, four or even five years in the leisurely Scandinavian manner, or perhaps, if he could not make the necessary money on the side, have sought a job in journalism. He had written few poems during the nine months he had been working on *Samfundsbladet*, *The Man*, *Andhrimner* and *Arbejderforeningernes Blad;* only half a dozen are known to have come from his hand during this time, most of those that appeared in print dating from the previous year. He had left *Olaf Tryggvesson* and *The Ptarmigan of Justedal* both uncompleted. Playwriting can hardly have seemed to hold out any possibilities of a livelihood in a country where nearly all the actors were Danish, and where the capital itself was so small that even a successful serious play could hardly hope to achieve more than half a dozen performances. It was chance, not inner compulsion, that at this particular juncture determined that Ibsen's career was to be in the theatre.

The man singled out by fate to be her instrument in this operation was a forty-one year old composer and violinist named Ole Bull. Born in Bergen in 1810, Bull had attended university at Christiania, ostensibly to study theology, but had devoted most of his time there to music and political agitation. Then, during a visit to Paris, he heard Paganini play, and immediately, with the impulsiveness which characterised his whole life, conceived the ambition of becoming a great violinist. He could afford little in the way of tuition, far less the expense of studying in a foreign conservatoire; nevertheless, despite being virtually self-taught, he developed a brilliant technique and, while still a young man, achieved international fame, not least through performances of his own works and arrangements. From 1843 to 1845 he spent two years in the United States, where his talents were particularly admired.

In the summer of 1849 Bull returned to his native Bergen and gave a series of concerts there. During this visit he learned that the citizens, infected by the widespread desire in Norway to develop a specifically national culture, were considering the project of founding a Norwegian National Theatre in their town; and they asked Bull, as their most famous living citizen, to lend his support. Bull, an erratic, attractive, ebullient character with a passion for idealistic causes (in 1848 he had waited on Alphonse Lamartine, with a Norwegian flag in his hand, to express the sympathy of the Norwegian people with the new Republic), at once agreed. The town already possessed a charming theatre, built in 1799 by the then flourishing local amateur dramatic society[1] on a patch of raised ground overlooking the water, and capable of holding eight to nine hundred people. Bull, acting on behalf of his sponsors, leased it for the winter of 1849–1850, and on 23 July 1849 he inserted an advertisement in the local newspaper Bergenske Blade inviting applications from anyone who wished to join as an actor, or to contribute in any other way. 'Those Ladies and Gentlemen,' the advertisement stated, 'who number among their accomplishments singing, instrumental music, acting or national dancing, will be considered for engagement. Original dramatic and musical works are invited, and will be rewarded as circumstances permit.'

Lorentz Dietrichson, later to become a close friend, and also an enemy, of Ibsen, was a boy in Bergen at the time, and has described the response. 'From crofts and respectable villas, from factories and from the street itself, they came milling forth, labourers, kitchen-maids, errand-boys and crones...Every scullery girl who could sing a note, every artisan who could recite a poem, sang, declaimed or acted, each convinced that he or she was destined to become a classical stage lover or a prima donna.'[2] Even an old aunt of Dietrichson's applied, and was accepted, despite the fact that the absence of a front tooth

---

[1] In 1800, the year the theatre was opened, this Society numbered no less than 600 members, of whom, astonishingly, 400 were women. They presented six or seven plays a year until the Society was wound up in 1828. In 1835 they reconstituted themselves and hired a permanent Danish company to give performances to its members; but as this company was free to hold public performances also, and in fact mainly subsisted on these, the Dramatic Society had, by 1849, lost all real importance. (See T. H. Blanc, Norges først nationale scene, Christiania, 1884, pp. 8-10).

[2] L. Dietrichson, Svundne tider, I (Christiania, 1894), pp. 147-148.

rendered her speech somewhat indistinct; the theatre generously acquired a tooth for her and, when her engagement was terminated, less generously demanded the tooth back. The enthusiasm for the new project was tremendous. Dietrichson recalled how he and his fellow schoolboys would wait for Bull outside the theatre and follow him cheering to his home where, never the man to miss an opportunity for a speech, he would address them from a first-floor window, promising 'to offer everything he possessed for the Norwegian Theatre, and vowing that as long as he had a farthing in his pocket and a drop of blood in his heart, he would consecrate them to the Theatre and to Old Norway—speeches full of bombast and rant, but, at the time, most assuredly uttered from the heart. That a short while later he declared himself prepared to consecrate his last farthing and drop of blood to Oleana on the other side of the globe did not abate our enthusiasm for him.'[1]

From all these applicants Bull selected a company whose inexperience was matched only by their willingness to learn, and on 21 November 1849 they gave their first performance before an invited audience. The bill, a lengthy and varied one typical of the theatrical fare of those days in any European country, comprised five items. The curtain rose, appropriately, on a play by Ludvig Holberg, the most famous author (in fact, the only internationally famous author) whom Norway had yet produced, and a native of Bergen; the piece chosen was his charming comedy *Henrik and Pernilla* (1724). There followed Mozart's Jupiter Symphony, now heard for the first time in Bergen; a mono-logue, *The Man from Paradise;* then, eagerly awaited, a performance by Bull of his own composition *Et Sætersbesøg (Visit to a Mountain Farm);* and, finally, a comic sketch in the Bergen dialect entitled *The Shoemaker*. Bull described the reception in a letter to his wife (30 November 1849): 'During the past week I have tested public reaction by inviting the theatre's patrons and some other people to attend a trial performance. The result was astounding! Even our opponents declared themselves not merely dumbfounded, but even convinced that here are talents of so superior a kind that their like has never previously been seen in Bergen...I am having a Machine constructed which will heat the whole Theatre.' This last was an important innovation, for previously there had been no heating of any kind, and spectators had been accustomed to watch performances in their overcoats, 'which', T. H. Blanc, the historian of the Bergen Theatre, records, 'were not always of the most distinguished quality.'[2]

---

[1] Dietrichson, *op. cit.*, I, p. 151. On the subject of Oleana, see pp. 106–7.

[2] Blanc, *op. cit.*, p. 22, footnote. A member of the company recalled that on the rise of the curtain the players were commonly greeted with an overwhelming odour of drying clothes and *gammelost*, an excellent but pungent Norwegian cheese with which the citizens of Bergen sustained themselves during the long performances. (Marie Bull, *Minder fra Bergens første nationale scene*, Bergen, 1905, pp. 91-2.)

Bergenske Blade complimented Bull on the 'pure language, good diction, rounded gestures and fluid movement' to which he had trained his company.

On 2 January 1850, the Norske Theater held its first public performance (it had been planned for Boxing Day, but they had been compelled to postpone it). The main item was another Holberg comedy, *The Woman of Whims*, supported by various musical items. During the next five months, before the theatre closed for the summer on 2 June, twenty-seven performances were given, comprising sixteen different plays, eight of one act and eight of two or more acts. The enthusiasm in the town remained great; as early as 22 December 1849, before the season had even opened, Bull wrote to his wife that all seats had been taken for the twenty performances so far planned.

However, as was so inevitable in so small a town (Bergen then contained only 25,000 inhabitants) no bill could be played for more than two or at the most three performances, and the income from the sale of seats proved insufficient to cover expenses. In September 1851, accordingly, Ole Bull went to Christiania to petition the Storthing to give the National Theatre in Bergen a monetary grant. His request was turned down. This refusal sparked off a violent debate throughout the country, and nowhere were the pros and cons of the matter more hotly argued than among the students of Christiania. The last issue of *Andhrimner* to appear, on 28 September, included a violent indictment of the Government's parsimony by Paul Botten Hansen, and Vinje wrote an open verse letter to Bull which was printed in *Morgenbladet*.

More importantly for posterity, the matter was the subject of a particularly vehement debate in the University Literary Society. It must not be supposed that even intelligent opinion was unanimously behind Bull. While it was agreed that Norway ought to have a national drama of its own and not be dependent on Danish, French and German plays, it was not generally accepted that Norwegian plays ought necessarily to be written in the vernacular *landsmaal* instead of in the (virtually Danish) *riksmaal* used for formal writing. Ibsen himself, as we have seen from the dramatic criticisms he wrote earlier in the year, had clearly seen the dangers inherent in too chauvinistic an approach to the problem.

But when the University Literary Society debated the issue, a poet named Andreas Borchgrevink read a scornful paper on 'A Visit to the National Theatre at Bergen' in which he poked fun at the limitations and inexperience of Bull's company. When he had concluded, Ibsen rose and delivered an eloquent speech in Bull's defence. His words are unfortunately not recorded, but an eye-witness has stated that 'his countenance spoke the unmistakable language of anger'. It was almost certainly this speech that first brought the young Ibsen to Ole Bull's notice. The student supporters of the Norwegian

Theatre promptly took further action. As a protest against the Storthing's decision, a motion was put before the Students' Union that a 'musical evening' be arranged to raise funds for the new enterprise. After a fiery debate the proposal was carried by a large majority.

On 15 October 1851, accordingly, a grand concert was held in Christiania. The house was full, over a thousand people somehow managing to fight their way in; many had to be turned away. Ole Bull, naturally, performed, and songs were sung by Emma Dahl, a famous operatic artiste of the day, and by the three choral societies of the capital, representing the students, the mercantile class and the manual workers respectively. Ibsen contributed two pieces, a prologue in nicely rhymed pentameters, read, according to *Morgenbladet*, 'with deep feeling and natural freshness' by Laura Svendsen, the young actress who had played Blanka in *The Warrior's Barrow*, and a choral piece, which the three choirs sang together to 'a powerful and impressive setting by Ole Bull'. Both of Ibsen's compositions were praised in the press, and down in Telemark the *Skien Correspondent* proudly reported the success of the local boy, not forgetting to add that 'Herr Ibsen is a son of Knud Ibsen, merchant of this town'.

The tickets were evidently very cheap, for the net takings amounted to no more than 300 specie-dollars (£75); but even that was an appreciable contribution to the Norwegian Theatre's resources. The occasion was, though, to have a much further-reaching effect. Bull met Ibsen, was impressed by him, and offered him a job. The salary was humble indeed: five pounds a month. But the prospect of being able to abandon Greek and mathematics (the two subjects which he still had to pass in order to matriculate), and of actually being paid to write, must have seemed irresistible. Barely a week after the concert, he said goodbye to Botten Hansen and Vinje, packed his few belongings and departed by steamer for Bergen. On 26 October *Bergenske Blade* listed, under the heading NEW ARRIVALS IN THE CITY, the name of 'Stud. H. Ibsen, c/o Sontum'. The minute book of the Bergen Theatre takes up the tale:

'On 6 November, Student Henrik Ibsen was engaged, having signified his willingness, to assist the Theatre as dramatic author, for which a monthly honorarium of twenty specie-dollars is to be paid him as from 1 October'.

He was to spend six years there, years of poverty, bitterness and failure, learning the alphabet of his craft.

FOUR

The Unholy Trade

(1850-1854)

'It is a most unholy trade'
(*Henry James, on the theatre, to William Heinemann*)

BERGEN IS, TODAY, a much more attractive city than Oslo, and it must have been so then, perhaps to an even greater degree. Despite the great fire of 1830 it was, as contemporary photographs show, still essentially of the eighteenth century, with 'whitewashed wooden houses with pantiled red roofs, steep steps leading from the front doors to the street and, outside every house, the traditional water-butt and bench where the whole family would sit in the mild and humid summer evenings...receiving visits from friends and neighbours, the father in his dressing-gown, nightcap and slippers, with a long pipe in his mouth, the mother with her knitting and her sons and daughters about her'. Thus Lorentz Dietrichson,[1] who was a schoolboy when Ibsen arrived in Bergen and other witnesses amplify the picture. 'The number of streets is very limited', observed a Professor of German from London University, 'and they are so narrow that there is hardly space sufficient to admit of the passage of two vehicles...The houses are huddled together, but they have about their exterior an air of cleanliness and comfort, and the interior is commodiously arranged, though not much embellished...The quantity of butcher's meat consumed in the town is but small, as the middle and lower classes live almost exclusively on fish, which is very abundant...The greatest inconvenience the inhabitants are subject to is the want of timber, and even of firewood, which two articles must be brought from great distances, and are consequently very dear.' The harbour, he noted, 'very rarely freezes, although nearly half a degree nearer to the Pole than St Petersburg, whose harbour is closed up by ice for four months and longer every winter'; and the inhabitants struck him as being more cosmopolitan than those of other Norwegian towns.[2]

The climate was (and is) very rainy. Every baby in Bergen was popularly

---

[1] Dietrichson, *op. cit.*, I, pp. 16-17.
[2] Wilhelm Wittich, *A Visit to the Western Coast of Norway* (London, 1848), pp. 89-93.

supposed to be born with an umbrella; but the setting on the fjord, with its seven surrounding hills, was idyllic, even when as was usually the case, the peaks of these were shrouded in cloud. 'Delectable, merry, earnest and peaceful,' Dietrichson apostrophised his birthplace, 'with all your strangeness, your rain and mist, your fresh beauty and your eternal youth.'[1]

Fishing was the principal industry, and the principal topic of conversation; Bergen was not a place where the arts or any intellectual interest flourished. 'The habit of buying books', Dietrichson tells us, 'had not yet become widespread, and only four or five houses boasted anything that could be called a library...Apart from its theatre, the town possessed few sources of public entertainment.'[2] These he enumerates. A Madame Davidsen challenged all-comers, of whichever sex, to foot-races on Sunday afternoons; Rippo performed feats of strength, juggled and walked a tightrope; there was a ventriloquist named Professor Bill, and a magician named Olivo who showed 'Cosmoramas'; and occasional visits were paid by a troupe of horseback artists. Café life was virtually unknown, and a billiards saloon which had been opened in the late forties was regarded with suspicion. Two music societies existed, and an art society; and on Saturday afternoons in the summer one might see 'countless groups of both sexes, belonging to the lower middle class, singing their way into the countryside, with their baskets of food and drink...always with a fiddler or a clarinettist at their head, the melody of whose instruments would last long into the bright summer night'.[3] The citizens, Dietrichson concludes, were 'a curious mixture of calculation and idealism, provincialism and poetry'.[4]

Ibsen was fortunate in his first landlady in Bergen—though landlady, to judge from the account of an English traveller who lodged with her a couple of years before Ibsen, is scarcely a dignified enough description. 'There are besides the hotels', wrote Thomas Forester,[5] 'several private establishments at Bergen where travellers are entertained with the advantages of more quiet and comfort than at the hotels. We considered ourselves fortunate in having been directed to that of Mrs Sontum. Well connected, and allied to persons of great consideration, circumstances having induced her to embark in her present undertaking, she is indefatigable in her endeavours to promote the comfort of her guests. Her house is the favourite resort of English travellers, and abundantly merits the preference given to it...Nor must I omit the daughters

---

[1] Dietrichson, op. cit., I, p. 21.
[2] ibid., p. 125.
[3] ibid., p. 128.
[4] ibid., p. 144.
[5] T. Forester, Norway, in 1848 and 1849 (London, 1850), pp. 232–234.

of our hostess...Two sorts of fish (trout and fried cod), besides lobsters and cutlets, with dishes of strawberries, wild and cultivated, were served for break-fast. The dinners were excellent. We had salmon, and more varieties of fish than I can name; and some national dishes which we thought admirable...We had good Bordeaux wine at one and eightpence a bottle...But the evening reunion was the most agreeable part of the day, when we assembled round the supper-table, spread with cold meat, lobsters, tarts and cakes, tea being served *à l'Anglaise.*'

Nor was Fru Helene Sontum (as some might infer from the above account) a snob; on the contrary, all reports of her agree that she was a kindly lady who mothered her guests.[1] Even if Ibsen did not get the full treatment accorded to Mr Forester, things must have seemed an extraordinary improvement on conditions at Mother Sæter's or Fru Holt's. Within five days of his arrival, he was writing an epithalamium for the wedding of Fru Sontum's son, Nicolai, a conventional but agreeable and deftly turned poem, which we must assume earned him, if he had not already received it, an invitation to the marriage feast.

During the six years he was to spend in Bergen, Ibsen performed practically every task associated with theatrical production except that of acting; he is one of the very few playwrights who seems never to have performed on any stage, not even as an amateur. But, in addition to writing plays and prologues to other people's plays, he directed, coached in movement and speech, designed sets and costumes, ran the business side and saw to the accounts. Evidence of all this activity is to be found in the archives of the theatre, now in Bergen University Library: the account books, most neatly kept (his experience at the apothecary's must have served him well here); and, an endless source of fas-cination, his prompt books, with his stage plots for various plays, the move-ments of the characters carefully traced in dotted lines, and his set and costume designs, extremely detailed (as one would expect, remembering his early interest in dress), and coloured with paint or crayon. His handwriting in these prompt books, as in his manuscripts and correspondence of this period, is small and crabbed; as he grew older and more famous his handwriting became, in contrast to the general rule, neater, not only in his correspondence but even, blessedly for his editors, in his rough drafts.

Ibsen's first official assignment at Bergen, appropriately enough, was to write a prologue for an entertainment which the theatre, in return for the support which the Christiania Students had given, performed on 17 November in aid

---

[1] e. g., Victor Smith's interview with Fru Henrikke Holst-Tresselt (Rikke Holst) in *Lørdagskvelden,* 22 December 1923.

of the Students' Union Building Fund. It was spoken by the most talented of
the theatre's young actesses, Louise Brun; Ibsen's name, surprisingly considering that he was now a member of the company, is not mentioned in the programme. His next task, was one which he must particularly have relished. The
policy and performance of the Bergen theatre had been attacked in one of the
two town newspapers, *Bergenske Blade*, by a local worthy boasting the unfortunate name of Poul Stub, who, by coincidence, had acted as one of Ibsen's
correspondence tutors when Ibsen was preparing in Grimstad for his matriculation. Stub had corrected Ibsen's Norwegian essays. Apparently the newspaper
had received no free tickets since the opening performance, presumably
because the entire season had been over-subscribed by the public, and this
neglect seems to have influenced Stub's attitude, for he poked fun at the inexperienced actors in a pedantically spiteful and unnecessary way. Ibsen replied
to Stub's remarks point by point in the rival paper, *Bergens Stiftstidende*, on 30
November, attacking Stub particularly for the negativeness of his criticisms.
'If a critic is to pose as an actor's mentor,' suggested Ibsen, 'he must explain to
him how a role *should* be played, never mind how it should *not*'—a remark that
might profitably be pinned up above many a critic's desk. He continued the
assault on Stub in three further articles on 4, 18 and 21 December, with a zest
that makes one wonder whether he had not perhaps personally experienced
the sharpness of Stub's pen at the expense of his Norwegian compositions.
Like Ibsen's dramatic and political articles in Christiania, these essays are excellent examples of polemical writing, clearly reasoned and precisely worded,
and reading them a century later one is again grateful for the fate that allowed
him no opportunity at this period of his life of taking up journalism as a career.

Ole Bull had by now left Bergen; it had never been the intention that he
should do more than launch the theatre. He had given two years to the schemes
and the financial sacrifice to himself, in loss of earnings, must have been considerable. He had in fact planned to leave at the end of October 1851, but had
stayed a few weeks longer; now, in November, he returned to the United
States, there to embrace an even more idealistic and improbable cause. Bull
was an admirer of the Welsh philanthropist Robert Owen, who at the beginning of the century had set up a model factory at New Lanark in Scotland, in
which he refused to employ young children, provided further education for
the older children whom he did employ, limited the working hours of his
adult workers and established a co-operative store. In describing his experi-
ment Owen had, in 1817, been the first recorded man in Britain to use the word
'socialist', and between 1825 and 1829 he had tried, vainly, to found a socialistic
community in America at New Harmony, Indiana. Bull, seeking to succeed
where Owen had failed, bought 125,000 acres in Potter County, Penn-

sylvania, to start a socialistic Norwegian community which, immodestly, was
to be named Oleana; but his title to the land turned out to be faulty, and the
scheme ended in disaster. (Ibsen was later to commemorate this unfortunate
project in *Peer Gynt*, where Peer speaks of founding a new community to be
called Gyntiana).

From the time of Bull's departure, things began to go less well for the Bergen
Theatre. The first play of the new year, 1852, a Norwegian work entitled
The Christmas Guest, by C. P. Riis, was a fiasco; on the second night there was
so thin a house that the reviewer of *Theatervennen* commented: 'We can hardly
remember having seen so few spectators in a theatre'. They had better luck
with Ponsard's *Charlotte Corday*, in which the young Louise Brun created an
excellent impression in the title role and a new actor, Andreas Isachsen (with
whom Ibsen was to have a long running feud, extending beyond his stay at
Bergen) gave a fine performance as Marat. Isachsen was the first *student* to join
the company (i.e., the first to have passed his matriculation, then, as now, an
important status symbol in Scandinavia), and the advent of so qualified an
intellectual into the theatrical profession created something of a sensation in
the town. *Charlotte Corday* opened on 1 February, and five days later a topical
new play, entitled *The First Jew*, also proved successful. The entry of Jews
into Norway for residential purposes had been forbidden until 1851, and the
play dealt with the problems encountered by an early immigrant. The author's
name was kept secret, but it was generally supposed to be the local Recorder,
a lawyer of literary leanings named C. R. Hansson.

Although Ibsen's contract had specified that he was to 'assist the theatre as
dramatic author', it was also intended that he should help with the work of
instructing the actors and the rest of what would nowadays be called production. The theatre, however, already possessed an artistic instructor, a local
schoolmaster named Herman Laading. Laading, at thirty-eight, was fifteen
years older than Ibsen, and was quite a considerable person in Bergen. Peter
Blytt, a timber merchant and board member of the theatre, shortly to become
its chairman, describes Laading as 'a cultured and educated man with a natural
elegance of manner...and a vast and encyclopaedic knowledge'.[1] At Christiania University the subjects which he had read included law, medicine,
theology and even mineralogy, all, apparently, to some effect. He was also a
fine fencer and an excellent shot, and knew several languages. Blytt further
describes him as amiable but very quick-tempered, and a 'master-conversa-
tionalist', adding that he was often, but wrongly, thought to be affected.
Laading had started his own school in Bergen in 1837, and continued to run

---

[1] Peter Blytt, *Minder fra den første norske scene i Bergen* (Bergen, 1894) pp. 13–14.

it while working at the theatre; indeed, he ran it for fifty years, until his retirement in 1887. The Scandinavian theatres have always displayed what to other countries sometimes seems an exaggerated respect for the academic mind; however, in this instance the choice may have been justified, since the members of the company had, for the most part, scarcely any education at all, and in the performance of historical plays especially some kind of general background knowledge was plainly desirable.

The board soon realised that the precise duties of Laading and Ibsen must be clarified, and on 10 February 1852 wrote to them suggesting that the instructional work be divided into two: 'either, the one instructor to study roles with the actors and the other to take charge of the scenic arrangements, or the one to instruct the actors and the other to instruct and educate the pupils'.[1] The former arrangement seems to have been agreed upon as the less unworkable of the two. Meanwhile, both Laading and Ibsen were given a formal three months notice, that they might then be appointed to their new posts.

The directors of the theatre were finding considerable difficulty in choosing plays that lay within the capabilities of their company and were suited to the taste of their audience. The French conversation pieces popular in Christiania made demands which the untrained actors of Bergen, unlike the Danish players of the capital, could not meet. (By one of the more chauvinistic of the Bergen theatre's regulations not only the actors and instructors, but even the prompter, had to be of Norwegian birth.) The great classics were even more obiously outside the company's range; attempts that season to stage Calderon's El Alcade de Zalamea, Oehlenschläger's tragedy Axel and Valborg and Garrick and Colman's The Jealous Wife all failed completely, none of the plays surviving more than two performances. In an enterprising effort to meet the situation, therefore, the board decided to send their new 'dramatic author', together with the two most talented younger members of the company, Johannes and Louise Brun, abroad, to study foreign theatrical methods and obtain new and suitable plays; and on 13 April 1852 Ibsen was given a new contract which included a travel grant of two hundred specie-dollars (£50) 'to visit, over a period of three months, certain foreign theatres, notably in Copenhagen, Berlin, Dresden and Hamburg, in order to acquire such knowledge and experience as may equip him to fill a position at the theatre as instructor, the work to include, in addition to the instruction of the actors, responsibility for everything pertaining to the furnishing, equipment and decoration of the stage, the actors' costumes, etc.'[2] On return, he was to occupy this post for five years at an annual

---

[1] A. M. Wiesener, Henrik Ibsen og det norske theater i Bergen, 1851–1857, (Bergen, 1928), p. 9–10.

[2] Bergen theatre archives quoted by Wiesener, op. cit., p. 11–12.

salary of three hundred specie-dollars (£75). This, small though it sounds, was not bad by the Norwegian standards of those days; it was the same as the older and more experienced Laading was to receive, and represented an increase of 25 per cent on Ibsen's original salary. The board must have felt satisfied with and confident in their new recruit. Paris was not included in the itinerary, presumably because neither Ibsen nor the Bruns knew French.

On 15 April 1852, accordingly, Ibsen sailed from Bergen to see, for the first time, what the world looked like outside Norway. There was no direct route by ship to Copenhagen, so they travelled via Hamburg, which was linked with Bergen by a regular fortnightly service. Ibsen's companions were even younger than he was; Johannes Brun was twenty, his wife, whom he had married the previous year, twenty-one. They were two deeply contrasted characters. Johannes Brun, Blytt tells us,[1] was merry and spontaneous and, like Ibsen, extremely clothes-conscious and elegant in appearance. Louise, on the other hand, was rather reserved and formal, and 'not handsome', and was careless in her dress 'almost to the point of slovenliness'. Both were destined to reach the heights of their profession and to die while still in their prime, she at thirty-five, he at fifty-eight. Johannes Brun, indeed, was to become perhaps the most famous of all of Norway's actors, and to create several of Ibsen's most famous character roles, including the Old Man of the Mountains in *Peer Gynt*, Daniel Hejre in *The League of Youth*, and Ulric Brendel in *Rosmersholm*. His statue stands outside the National Theatre in Oslo only a few yards from that of Ibsen.

After a brief pause in Hamburg, of which Ibsen vexatiously records no impression, they reached Copenhagen on 20 April. The Danish capital still had oil lighting in the streets and watchmen shouting the hours, but its cosmopolitanism and elegance, and architectural pleasures, must, to the young provincial from Norway, have been a revelation. It possessed, moreover, in the Royal Theatre, Det Kongelige, one of the great theatres of Europe, with a fully international repertoire and actors and actresses comparable to the best of France and Germany, and better than those of England, where Macready had finished his career the previous year (though he was to live for another twenty-two, surely the longest time that any great actor has spent in unenforced retirement), and Irving was a boy of fourteen. Ibsen's first task was to look for a room, and he found what he wanted, central and agreeable. An advertisement in the newspaper *Adresseavisen* on the day of his arrival, which presumably led him to it, gives us details. 'For a polite gentleman (*en galant Herre*), a large, bright, handsomely decorated room, with three windows to the street in a genteel house, to be let, immediately or from the 1st, at Reverentsgaden 205, 2nd floor, adjacent

[1] Blytt, *op. cit.*, pp. 23–24.

to Kongens Nytorv.' It sounds much better than what he had been used to in Norway, but he must have wanted to live a little more grandly if possible, as official representative of Norway's first national theatre.

C. R. Hansson, the literary-minded Recorder of Bergen, had given Ibsen a letter of introduction to the director of the Royal theatre, Johan Ludvig Heiberg, and this proved of great value. Heiberg, besides being a scholar, was a considerable poet and dramatist, and one of the very few authors whom Ibsen, in his maturity, admitted to admiring. Born in 1791, the son of a woman who later, as the Baroness Gyllembourg-Ehrensvard, was to achieve fame as a kind of Danish Mrs Gaskell, Heiberg had been elected to a lectureship in Danish at Kiel University at the age of thirty-one; but creative writing attracted him more than academic life, and three years later he returned to Copenhagen with the expressed intention of introducing vaudeville to the Danish stage. Vaudeville then meant not, as now, music hall, but comedies with music, with the characters, at climactic moments, breaking into songs consisting of new lyrics set to familiar tunes.[1] Heiberg wrote a great many of these, based on French models but with Danish settings and topical Danish themes; Ibsen was to stage several of them in both Bergen and Christiania. The author of a number of comedies and straight plays, of which the best are perhaps *The Day of the Seven Sleepers* and *A Soul After Death*, Heiberg was also, as stated, a poet, and a vigorous critic; and in 1847, five years before Ibsen met him, he had been appointed to his present position as Director of the Royal Theatre. Since Oehlenschläger's death two years previously he was regarded as the most eminent man of letters not merely in Denmark, but in Scandinavia, more so than his juniors Hans Andersen and Søren Kierkegaard. In many ways he must have seemed a pattern of what the young Ibsen might have hoped to become; his fields of activity, and his critical, nonconformist standpoint were very much Ibsen's own.

Heiberg had now virtually retired from authorship and had become a formidable pundit. 'Standing in the centre of his office in the Royal Theatre,' we are told, 'he would hold audience with his hands clasped behind his back, his legs parted, the upper half of his body swaying from side to side, as he fastened his stare, as cold as water, upon his unfortunate visitor, who as often as not would become confused and lose the thread of his discourse under the impact of that superior and ironic smile.'[2] Hansson had, however, with lawyer's cunning, couched his introductory letter in terms highly flattering to Heiberg, describing Ibsen as 'a bright and gifted young man of more than

---

[1] See Appendix C.
[2] O. Zinck and W. Kolling, reported by Robert Neiiendam in *Mennesker bag masker* (Copenhagen, 1931), p. 117.

common poetical talent'. whom he had come to like, since he had 'found in him the same passionate admiration of you that formed one of the worthiest emotions of my youth'.[1]

Hansson's letter seems to have had the required effect, for Heiberg immediately granted Ibsen and the Bruns free entry to the theatre each evening; disappointingly, however, he advised them not to bother to attend any rehearsals since, the season being so far advanced, nothing of interest was in preparation. He commanded his chief instructor, Thomas Overskou, who was also a playwright and translator of some repute, to show Ibsen round the theatre, drawing his attention in particular to the stage machinery, which was far in advance of anything that Ibsen had seen in Christiania or Bergen. Overskou, writing to his daughter at this time, described Ibsen as 'a little clenched (*sammenbidt*) Norwegian with alert eyes'.[2]

Overskou was not, as a stage instructor, the best of models for a young man; even by the standards of those days, he was coming to be regarded as somewhat old-fashioned. However, he proved a friendly and helpful guide, as Ibsen's letters to his directors in Bergen (the first we have from his hand since those which he had written to Schulerud from Grimstad) show.

'*I am happy to be able to tell you* [he wrote on 25 April 1852] *that...both Heiberg and Herr Overskou have received us with exceptional kindness, and through the latter I shall easily obtain all the information I require concerning the internal organisation of the theatre. As regards the other matters you have instructed me to investigate, such as the procuring of a dancing teacher for Brun and his wife, etc., I have not yet managed to arrange this, but hope to do so within the course of the next week.*'

Three weeks later, on 16 May, he wrote his employers a long and informative letter; he had a good deal to report.

As dancing teacher for H. Nielsen [another actor from Bergen who had joined them in Copenhagen], *and for Brun and his wife, I have engaged Herr Hoppe, solo dancer at the Royal Theatre, reckoned to be the best they have and, a point on which I assured myself before approaching him, their most experienced instructor. The main subject of instruction is to be the Minuet, and anything else that will assist in the learning of elegance of movement upon the stage*'.

The man who could have told Ibsen most about dancing he had, alas, met only briefly.

As regards the projected engagement of a dancer to instruct the other members of the company in Bergen, I have the following to report. Balletmeister Bournonville

---

[1] Neiiendam, *op. cit.*, p. 118.
[2] *ibid.*, p. 118.

left for Christiania soon after my arrival here, and I was able to discuss the subject with him only in general terms the evening before his departure; at the end of the month, most of the other dancers here will go up to join him. Herr Gade, another leading dancer, who will be remaining here, might possibly not be averse to sailing to Bergen this summer, but you would in such an event have to provide a guarantee that he would be able to undertake the journey without sustaining any financial loss...As regards the internal appointments of the Theatre, Herr Overskou has undertaken to acquaint me with them, as also with the methods of stage management, machinery, etc. Books on costume I have not been able to obtain, but Herr Overskou is going to let me know what there is and where I may get hold of them; so I shall be able to purchase these before my journey is finished...I have bought only one play, Ten Years Ago, *by Carl Bernhard;*[1] *but for this item of expenditure, too, I must crave a small extra allowance, since I shall probably happen in Germany upon something which might be worth buying...Regarding my grant for this journey, I greatly fear that it will not suffice. During my stay in Hamburg I had a foretaste of what it means to be a tourist in Germany; and Brun, too, would have been considerably embarrassed if our fellow-traveller, Dr Hofmann, had not helped him and made it possible for him to continue to Copenhagen. I therefore beg that I may be advanced the sum of 48 specie-dollars [£12] from my salary, which, together with the 12 specie-dollars which I applied for as I left, and which I hope you have approved, could be subtracted from my salary at the rate of 5 specie-dollars per month.*

Ibsen goes on to report on the plays he has seen.

We have been very fortunate with the repertory, We have seen Hamlet, *and several other plays by Shakespeare, and by Holberg—also* La Bataille des Dames, A Sunday at Amager, The Kinsmen, *etc.*[2] *I need hardly add that we acquainted ourselves with everything that might be of artistic interest. The Danes have in all respects shown us the utmost courtesy and good-will and, so far from feeling any annoyance at our seeking to liberate ourselves from their influence upon our theatre, they only wonder that this has not happened long ago. I have made the acquaintance of H. C. Andersen; he advises me strongly, when I have finished in Dresden, to go on to Vienna to see the Burg Theatre; he may be there himself then, in which case he will act as my guide; if not, I hope Professor Dahl may be able to assist me.*

Hans Andersen was then forty-seven, and five years previously had paid a famous visit to Charles Dickens in London; but unfortunately, the directors

---

[1] This comedy was not in fact by Bernhard (the pseudonym of A. N. de Saint Aubin) but by his nephew Andreas Buntzen. It was performed at Bergen in October 1852.

[2] *La Bataille des Dames* was a comedy by Scribe and Legouvé; *A Sunday at Amager* a vaudeville by Heiberg's wife, Johanne Luise Heiberg; and *The Kinsmen* a vaudeville by Henriette Nielsen. All three were subsequently performed at Bergen.

of the Bergen Theatre decided that they could not afford to extend their young apprentice's tour beyond Dresden, so that the fascinating prospect of Hans Andersen showing Ibsen around Vienna never materialised. 'We feel,' wrote the Bergen board on 28 May, 'that it will be much more rewarding for you to stay longer at a place such as Dresden than to move on from town to town.' They also warned him that 'we know from experience that living in Germany is very cheap, so that if you do not manage on your 200 specie-dollars we shall be forced to conclude that you have not arranged your economy wisely', and at first refused to refund him the 24 specie-dollars he had paid to Hoppe for dancing lessons, telling him that he and the Bruns were expected to pay for this out of their grants. Since neither he nor they could afford this, Ibsen had to write another begging letter to his board; not the last example he was to encounter of the parsimony of committees.

But these irritations must have been more than compensated for by the new horizons that were being opened for him theatrically and aesthetically. He was indeed, as he had told his board, 'very fortunate with the repertory'. During his six weeks in Copenhagen that spring he, who had never previously seen a Shakespeare play on the stage, saw four—*Hamlet*, *King Lear*, *Romeo and Juliet* and *As You Like It*. He also saw four of Holberg's best comedies, *The Lying-In Room*, *Henrik and Pernilla*, *Pernilla's Brief Mistress-ship* and *The Woman of Whims*; three Oehlenschläger tragedies, *Queen Margareta*, *The Vikings at Byzantium* and *Earl Haakon the Mighty*; Mozart's opera *Don Juan*; two of Heiberg's own works; including his best and most famous vaudeville, *No*; and two plays by a popular second-rate Danish dramatist named Henrik Hertz, *Sheikh Hassan* and *King René's Daughter*, the latter of which had already been translated into English no less than thrice and become popular throughout the English theatre (sufficient proof, the English theatre being what it then was, of its, and the author's, mediocrity). The actors, too, were far superior to any he had seen in Norway. The great tragedian Michael Wiehe was then at his peak, and a generation later Ibsen was to name him as still the finest actor he had seen. 'When I recall his performances,' he said, 'it is as though I were walking through a gallery filled with ancient statues. Pure *plastik*! Pure beauty!' He was also fortunate enough to witness, for the first time, a major actress demonstrating her art: Johanne Louise Heiberg, whom he saw in one of her most famous parts as Lucretia (the title role) in Holberg's *The Woman of Whims*, a lady so moody and changeable that her two lovers, ecstatically describing their mistresses to each other, do not realize that they are speaking of the same person. Fru Heiberg was to become a close friend of Ibsen in later years, and he was to address to her one of his most delicate poems.

In contrast to Wiehe, there was the young Fredrik Høedt, who was to be the

H

founder of a new school of acting, more realistic and analytical, less inclined to the grand manner and subtler in his appreciation of psychological nuances. Ibsen saw Høedt as *Hamlet*, but admired him more as the young lover, Grignon, in Scribe's *La Bataille des Dames*.[1] When one remembers the wretched plays that Ibsen had seen in Christiania and, reading between the lines of his dramatic criticisms, the moderate talents of the actors there (to say nothing of Bergen, where even the Bruns were still raw beginners), one realizes what a revelation to him these evenings in the theatre at Copenhagen must have been. The actors, he reported wonderingly to his directors in Bergen, knew their parts before rehearsals of a play began.

His experiences in Copenhagen were not limited to the Royal Theatre. He also visited the Casino Theatre on Amaliegade (which twenty-five years later was to stage the first performance of Strindberg's *The Father*), and the Royal Court Theatre at Christiansborg (now the Theatre Museum). At the latter, he watched a performance by the University Drama Society attended by King Frederik the Seventh. At the former he saw a romantic comedy by Jens Christian Hostrup called *Master and Pupil* which interested him enough to make him call on Hostrup at the latter's home to discuss the play, which he subsequently directed at Bergen. Hostrup later remembered Ibsen from this visit as 'a quiet, withdrawn personality'.

Finally, and by no means least, it was probably during his stay in Copenhagen that Ibsen happened upon a short book written by a young German Professor at Jena and published only that year which was to have a considerable influence upon his writing. It has rather glibly been assumed that Ibsen discovered Herman Hettner's *Das Moderne Drama* after his arrival in Dresden; but as avid a reader of advertisements as Ibsen always was can hardly have missed noticing, in the columns of the leading Danish magazine of the day, *Fædrelandet*, a large advertisement drawing the attention of the public to a newly opened 'Newspaper Salon' on the corner of Kjøbmagergade and Silkegade where books and papers might be perused on payment of an entrance fee of eight skillings (about two pence), 'including refreshments'. Considering that Ibsen's purpose in Copenhagen was to study modern trends in European drama, it seems likely that he would have availed himself of this inexpensive means of reading a book that, we know, was much discussed in the city that spring.

Two aspects in particular of Hettner's book must have interested him: the sections dealing with historical drama and with *Märchenlustspiel*, or romantic fairy-tale comedy. Hettner asserted that historical plays should be written so as to be psychologically relevant to modern times; human character had not

---

[1] Midbøe, *op. cit.*, p. 163.

changed fundamentally over the centuries, nor, *mutatis mutandis*, had the issues of human conflict. Historical drama, in other words, should be written as psychological character-conflicts, and not, like Oehlenschläger's plays, as grand opera without music. Nor was there any place in serious drama, whether historical or modern, for the paraphernalia of coincidence with which (as in Scribe's plays) it was commonly cluttered: overheard conversations, intercepted letters, mistaken identities and the like. Such things were all very well in comedy; but in serious drama, what mattered (Hettner asserted) was conflict of, and development of, character. The lesson of Shakespeare had been largely forgotten; Hettner held up *Coriolanus* as a model.

As regards *Märchenlustspiel*, the important thing about this genre, it seemed to Hettner, was the fact that it dealt with two opposite worlds, that of everyday reality and that of fantasy; in the best plays of this kind, these two worlds are constantly being juxtaposed in such a way that the world of dreams is shown as a source of truth and wisdom, while that of everyday reality is made to seem comic and unrealistic. As a prime example of this type of play, Hettner instances Shakespeare's *A Midsummer Night's Dream*. It is a genre that has always seemed to hold an especial appeal for Scandinavians—Oehlenschläger, Heiberg and Hostrup had all experimented in it, and so, in plays as well as in stories, had Hans Andersen. Ibsen's next five plays were to be either historical dramas or *Märchenlustspiel*, and in each of them he was to follow, or try to follow, Hettner's precepts—though here again, as with Kierkegaard, we must beware of assuming that Hettner did more than crystallize ideas that were already present in Ibsen's mind. Another demand which Hettner made, that dramatists should stick closely to historical facts, Ibsen was, like Shakespeare, to ignore.

Hettner also drew Ibsen's attention to a recent play by a young German dramatist, Friedrich Hebbel's *Maria Magdalena*, written nine years previously in 1843. Hettner thought this powerful melodrama, written in high-flown prose about ordinary village people, worthy to stand beside Sophocles's *Electra* and Goethe's *Faust* as an outstanding specimen of the tragedy of ideas, and as an example of how *bürgerliche Tragödie* need not be trivial, but may be both profound and poetic. Several witnesses, such as John Paulsen and Gunnar Heiberg, have testified to Ibsen's later admiration of *Maria Magdalena*[1], and it seems probable that it stemmed from this period; after reading Hettner's

---

[1] 'The best evidence of how unforgettable an impression *Maria Magdalena* made on him is the meticulous *précis* he dramatically gave us of the plot. I saw the various scenes come alive before me, and heard not without emotion the old father's last, despairing cry: *Ich verstehe die Welt nicht mer!* [I understand the world no longer!]—a sentence which had long haunted Ibsen. (John Paulsen, *Mine Erindringer*, Copenhagen, 1900, pp. 162–3). Gunnar Heiberg also records that Ibsen advised him to read Hebbel (*Salt og Sukker*, Christiania, 1924, p. 44).

praise, he is hardly likely to have missed the chance of studying it. Hettner did not know of Alexander Ostrovsky's experiments in the same field (his play *The Bankrupt*, though written in 1849, had been banned, and although he was to become known in Russia in 1853 through *The Poor Bride*, it was to be many years before his fame spread to western Europe). Nor did Hettner know of Gogol or Turgenev, both of whom, like Ostrovsky, would have supported his faith in the potentialities of *bürgerliche Tragödie*. Their examples would have been useful to Ibsen; in the event, ignorant of their experiments, he was, in his own good time, to follow the path that they had trod, and go far beyond them.

Shortly before Ibsen left Copenhagen, Heiberg honoured him with an invitation to dinner at his house; but the occasion proved something of an anticlimax. To Ibsen's disappointment, the great man discoursed on neither literature, the theatre nor even politics, but solely on questions of gastronomic interest; and he never saw Heiberg again before the latter died in 1860, embittered at the constant sniping he had had to undergo from his fellow-countrymen during his last years. Ibsen (although Heiberg had by then rejected *The Vikings at Helgeland*), wrote a handsome elegy in his honour. 'He lit a torch in the land. You used it to burn his brow. He taught you to wield a sword. You pressed it against his heart. Boldly he fought the trolls of his day. You crushed him between your shields.' The situation of the prophet who is without honour in his own country had, by 1860, already become familiar to Ibsen.

On 6 June, the Bruns having returned to Norway, Ibsen departed alone for Dresden. Here he found a helpful guide in a celebrated fellow-countryman, the old Norwegian painter J. C. Dahl, to whom (Dahl noted in his diary) Ibsen handed his letter of introduction on 11 June, having settled in an apartment at Topfergasse 13. He was not able to obtain free tickets to the theatre, as he had done at Copenhagen, but he was lucky enough to see, and compare, two exciting actors of contrasting styles. One was Emil Devrient, a fine performer in the traditional classical manner, (and son of the mighty Ludwig Devrient, who frequently collapsed in an epileptic fit while playing Lear); the other was an exciting young Polish actor, Boguwil Dawison, whose more modern approach, with its realism and subtlety of characterisation, resembled that of Fredrik Høedt. Ibsen saw Dawison play Hamlet, and much preferred it to Høedt's performance in the role which he had seen in Copenhagen the previous month.[1]

[1] H. Midbøe, *op. cit.*, p. 163. The repertory also included, while he was there, *A Midsummer Night's Dream*, *Richard III*, Goethe's *Egmont* and Lessing's *Emilia Galotti*, but we do not know how many of these he saw; probably, as will appear, at least the first-named.

He studied the stage machinery at the Hofoper, and spent many hours in the Dresden art galleries and museums. In those days photography was in its infancy, and until one saw the original works of a painter one knew of them, if at all, only by engravings or verbal description; the effect of the great galleries of Dresden on one who still cherished ambitions of his own in the field of painting can be imagined. (When, a dozen years later, he visited Italy, it was the paintings and sculptures, more than anything else, that excited him.) Remembering that one of his tasks on this trip was to obtain books of costume design to assist the Bergen theatre in its staging of foreign plays, he reported to his directors on 24 June the discovery of two such volumes which impressed him: 'Bonnard's *Costumes from the 13th to 18th Centuries*, and a *Collection of Spanish Folk Costumes* which has recently been published here.' Unfortunately, the theatre informed him that they had already ordered some costume books from Paris, and refused him authority to buy them.

Ibsen stayed in Dresden for about a month, returning to Norway some time in July. Ships sailed from Hamburg to Bergen on 15 and 29 July that year, and Dahl noted in his diary that Ibsen took leave of him on 2 July, which suggests that he travelled by the earlier ship. Paul Botten Hansen, in his short biography of Ibsen printed in *Illustreret Nyhedsblad* in 1863, writes, presumably with Ibsen as his source, that Dahl 'despite certain outbursts of his customary harshness, on the whole treated him [i.e., Ibsen] with much kindness and courtesy'. He had hoped to see Berlin on his way home, and also to spend a short while in Hamburg, both cities with an old tradition of fine theatre. His biographers have generally assumed that he did neither, on no evidence that I can discover; if, as we may assume, he left Dresden shortly after saying goodbye to Dahl on 2 July, how else did he spend his time until the boat sailed on, at the earliest, 15 July?.But if he visited either Berlin or Hamburg, or anywhere else, he left no record of it.

During his three months abroad, probably while he was in Dresden, Ibsen completed a play which he may perhaps have begun at Bergen in the spring: *Sancthansnatten, St John's Night* (i.e. Midsummer Night). This is unique among Ibsen's plays in being the only one which he refused to allow to be printed in his lifetime. When, in 1897, his German editor (and, later, executor) Julius Elias asked permission to include it in the German collected edition of his works, Ibsen angrily replied (19 September 1897): 'I neither will nor *can* permit the play *St John's Night* to appear in any collection of *my* works. The play is a miserable thing which is not really by *my* hand. It is founded on a rough mess of a draft which I was given by a student acquaintance, re-worked, and put my name to, but which I cannot now possibly acknowledge as being mine... Far from illuminating the rest of my work it stands totally outside of and unconnected with it; I have therefore for many years regarded it as unwritten and non-existent.'

This statement may be true; but ten years earlier he had told Henrik Jæger, his first biographer,[1] that, after agreeing to co-operate with this student acquaintance (one Theodor Bernhoft, the nineteen-year-old son of a poet and bookseller) he had himself written a draft and sent it to Bernhoft, who replied that he was now otherwise occupied and no longer interested. Certainly when *St John's Night* came to be performed at Bergen the following year, and again when he applied for a civil list pension eleven years later, Ibsen felt no qualms about naming it as his own unaided work. However, in accordance with his wishes, it was not printed until after his death, in 1909, and has been dismissed by most commentators as negligible. It is in fact a curiously engaging work, considerably superior to *The Warrior's Barrow* and *The Feast at Solhaug*, both of which he allowed to be printed, and one imagines that his rejection of it stemmed not from any lack of merit so much as from the almost pathological horror which he showed throughout his life at any suggestion that anything he had written owed anything to any other author, living or dead. He was, indeed, probably less influenced by other writers than any other great dramatist, but not as little as he made out.

He called the play an *eventyrkomedie*. *Eventyr* means, roughly, fairy tale, so that *eventyrkomedie* is the Norwegian equivalent of *Märchenlustspiel*, that genre of which Hettner had written with such feeling in *Das Moderne Drama*. Four young people are gathered in a house on Midsummer Night: Johannes and Juliane, who are engaged but do not love each other; Julian Poulsen, a student friend of Johannes; and Anne, Juliane's step-sister, whose freshness and innocence contrast with the sophisticated artificiality of the other three, and whom they regard as 'fey'. A *nisse*, or goblin, lives in the loft; Anne accepts his presence, sensing no difference between natural and supernatural things; only she can see him. This goblin, a kind of Puck, puts a potion into the bowl of punch which the young people are about to drink; then, in a charming scene, they go up to the hilltop where the midsummer pyre is dying, and catch a glimpse of the other-world of the supernatural. But only those with poetic souls, Anne and Johannes, see and understand; to the two blinded by intellect, Julian and Juliane, it is an obscure and incomprehensible vision. Under the influence of the magic night, all four declare themselves to the ones they truly love, Johannes to Anne and Julian to Juliane. Next morning, they realise they

---

[1] If we exclude the 2,500-word 'profile' which Paul Botten Hansen wrote for *Illustreret Nyhedsblad* in 1863. For the information about the authorship of *St John's Night*, see Jæger's notes on his conversations with Ibsen in 1887 (Midbøe, *op. cit.*, p. 143).

are betrothed to the wrong people. At first, they resign themselves fatalistically to the apparently unavoidable; in the end, however, each gets his or her true partner.

St John's Night is written mainly in prose, with occasional excursions (as when the goblin speaks) into rhymed verse. It is very much in the romantic fairy-tale tradition which was popular in Scandinavia then—Oehlenschläger had written a comedy entitled *A Midsummer Night's Play*, and Heiberg a similar one, *The Day of the Seven Sleepers;* Hans Andersen had exercised himself in the genre, and, as stated, Ibsen had seen Jens Christian Hostrup's *Master and Pupil* while in Copenhagen.[1] Ibsen's *St John's Night*, however, like Strindberg's later and remarkable essay in the same genre, *The Virgin Crown*, has a wit and individuality which lift it far above the rest of its kind; in this, his first essay in prose drama, he shows himself already able to write excellent colloquial dialogue, to create satirical characters, and to keep a complicated structure of plot and sub-plot continuously ticking. Julian Poulsen, quoting undigested gobbets of Heiberg and Kierkegaard, is the first of those pretentious charmers, vain, romanticising and self-pitying, who were to become a feature of Ibsen's work, the forerunner of Falk in *Love's Comedy*, Peer Gynt, Stensgaard in *The League of Youth*, Hilmar Tønnesen in *The Pillars of Society*, Hjalmar Ekdal in *The Wild Duck* and Ulric Brendel in *Rosmersholm*. Through Julian, Ibsen ridiculed that exaggerated passion for all things national which had made it fashionable to admire everything rustic simply because it was, or seemed to be, untainted by Danish or Swedish influence, just as later, in other countries, it was to become fashionable to admire any literary work that was, or appeared to be, working-class. The attempt to create a new language (*landsmaal*) based on the country dialects became the subject of a questioning eyebrow, not for the last time in Ibsen's work; so, too, did the kind of bogus aestheticism which W. S. Gilbert was to caricature a generation later in *Patience*. *St John's Night* is too topical in its allusions, and too reminiscent of *A Midsummer Night's Dream* in certain phases of its plot, to stand much chance of proving more than an interesting curiosity if it were staged today; but the ridiculer of contemporary poses who was to hold an unflattering mirror up to his countrymen in *Love's Comedy*, *Brand*, *Peer Gynt*, *The League of Youth* and *An Enemy of the People* is more clearly distinguishable in *St John's Night* than in any of the other plays of Ibsen's immaturity. And Julian, towards the end of the play, makes a point which Ibsen was to stress more sharply in *Love's Comedy*, and which was

---

[1] The action of these three plays by Oehlenschläger, Heiberg and Hostrup takes place, as does *St John's Night*, on a summer night when the supernatural world reveals its secrets: and Heiberg, like Ibsen, suggests that only those whose souls are genuinely poetic can see that world.

especially to enrage contemporary opinion: the necessity of qualifying one's ideal of love when one gets married.

On Ibsen's return to Bergen, the board got down to the problem of defining his duties in his new post of instructor and distinguishing them from those of Laading. On 30 August 1852, these were finally clarified. Laading was to be *rolleinstruktør*, Ibsen *sceneinstruktør*. Laading was 'to be at the theatre every day from 9 to 12 to direct reading rehearsals, using the rest of the time for special study of the roles and general education of the actors'. Amongst other things, it was specified that he was to pay especial attention to 'giving the actors the necessary historical information and ensuring correct interpretation of the roles, seeing that their diction is correct, and stressing that they memorise their roles painstakingly and accurately, so that they can attend the opening rehearsals without books or papers'. Ibsen, as *sceneinstruktør*, was 'to be present at the theatre for as many hours each day, holidays included, as may be required for complete and painstaking instruction on the stage, that each play may be ready for public performance at the time laid down by the Board. In other words, he is, when he has found the players sufficiently prepared, to continue the instruction from the point reached at the last reading rehearsals... He may, if necessary, send the players back for further reading rehearsals. The *sceneinstruktør* shall also be responsible for (1) supervising the scenic arrangements for each play (costumes and decor included), and for the general staging (groupings, entries, exits, etc.). (2) supervising in detail each actor's gestures and mine, so that all physical expressions shall fit the words of the character represented. (3) ensuring that the players play together, and indicating to each of them the role that he or she has to play in the plot as the situation changes'. It was further laid down that the two instructors should, before any new play went into rehearsal, confer so as to reach agreement on the interpretation of the various characters, 'the Board to decide, in the event of disagreement' on this or any other point.

The duties of the two instructors were thus inconveniently divided; the equivalent in a modern production would be as though a new director were to take over halfway. Amazingly enough, the theatre archives, which record evidence of disagreements and complaints, suggest that there was in fact little serious conflict between the two. On 30 November 1852 Laading asked to be relieved of his post, but this appears not to have been the result of dissatisfaction with his working conditions but merely because he found it difficult to combine so responsible a duty with that of running his own school. In the event, he was persuaded to stay. This lack of disagreement between Laading and Ibsen is the more surprising in that their attitudes towards acting seem to have been almost diametrically opposed. Whereas Ibsen liked his players to be naturalistic,

Laading, according to an actress who worked under him, 'was of the old school, and liked the conventional French style of acting with all its affectations. He wanted us to *act*, not to be natural'.[1]

A letter which Ibsen wrote to Laading twenty years later suggests that it was the difference between the two men in age and maturity, coupled with Ibsen's shyness, which prevented them from quarrelling. 'Yes,' wrote Ibsen (10 March 1875), 'those years in Bergen were certainly my years of schooling! I found myself at that time in a state of fermentation, which did not permit me to open myself completely to anyone. I did not really understand myself, and this must explain, if not excuse, many follies and so forth that I committed. You, on the other hand, were already a mature man, and this created a distance between us. But you often showed me a friendliness which closed the gap, and I was grateful to you for this, without being able to give this feeling proper expression.'

One of Ibsen's jobs at Bergen was to provide a new play to be performed each year on the anniversary of the opening of the theatre, 2 January, and that autumn of 1852 he offered as his contribution for the coming anniversary *St John's Night*. It was accepted, and thus became the second of Ibsen's plays to appear on the stage. Anticipation in the little town was great; the theatre-goers of Bergen were eager to see what their young 'dramatic author' could do. New decor, a luxury that the theatre could scarcely afford, was prepared, so that the play would not be seen in the familiar standard sets; it would not be quite true to say that no expense was spared to make the evening a success, but at least the few pennies that the theatre could disburse were freely given. The opening performance was sold out in advance, and many people were turned away without tickets. Alas, the occasion turned out a fearful failure. The first night audience so disliked the play that they whistled and hissed it; and at the second performance not merely seats but whole rows were empty. Word spread fast in a town that size. *Bergenske Blade* dismissed it as 'a somewhat unfortunate piece, though it contains some pretty fancies'. The management accepted the verdict of the public and withdrew the play, replacing it, ironically, with P. A. Jensen's *The Goblin's Home*, that tedious essay in rustic romanticism which Ibsen had condemned so severely in Christiania, and exactly the kind of play for which *St John's Night* had been intended to ring the death knell.

Why was it such a failure? Was it because of integral defects in the play, inadequacy of performance—or did the subject matter offend? Did the public dislike seeing a nationalistic ideal held up to ridicule? Did the chauvinistic extravagances of Julian Poulsen suggest an implied criticism of the affectionately

---

[1] Sophie Monsen, interviewed in *Bergens Tidende*, 13 January 1913.

remembered utterances of the town's idol, Ole Bull? We do not know. Perhaps Peter Blytt, of the theatre board, reflects the general reaction when he says in his memoirs that the play struck him as 'a curious, rather obscure mixture of romance and reality.'[1] Time and again in Bergen, and later in Christiania, Ibsen was to find that his audiences disliked any play that did not fit into an established and recognisable category. Whatever the reason, St John's Night died and remained forgotten for over half a century until its post-humous publication.

This failure must have been a bitter disappointment to the young dramatist, not merely in itself but in its implications. The Bergen public had shown that it preferred banal melodramas, superficial comedies and mock-rustic folk-tales to anything critical, novel and unusual. Seldom can the prospects for experi-ment have seemed as unpromising to any writer as to the young Ibsen in Bergen. Even at this early stage of his career we find him challenging and experimenting; but he had neither the actors to carry out his wishes nor the public to appreciate them. It is not hard to imagine with what feelings he must have turned to the direction of the plays that formed the rest of the season, a list that makes the programme of the humblest modern provincial theatre or stock company appear almost astral by comparison. The best of the bunch that winter and spring, apart from a solitary Holberg, Jacob von Thyboe (the first Holberg that Ibsen was to direct) were Henrik Hertz's King René's Daughter, the elder Dumas' Katharine Howard and Scribe's Babiol et Jablot, and even these, though reasonably competent in their stagecraft, were trumpery and meretricious rubbish.

It was an exceptionally bad period for the drama throughout Europe. During the half-century that had elapsed since the death of Schiller in 1805, a gap had opened between the theatre and the serious playwright. A number of interesting plays had been written, but most of them remained unperformed even in their own countries, let alone in so theatrically backward a land as Norway. The two most exciting, Georg Büchner's Danton's Death and Wozzeck, both composed in the eighteen-thirties before Büchner died of typhoid at the age of twenty-three, were to remain for many years unknown to anyone. Neither play was staged anywhere before the twentieth century; nor, in Norway, was anything to be seen before 1900 of either of those other brilliant but tragically-fated young German dramatists of the period, Friedrich Hebbel,[2] whose Maria Magdalena Ibsen had discovered through Hettner, or

---

[1] Blytt, op. cit., p. 11.
[2] Though Hebbel was slightly known in Denmark, where Adam Oehlenschläger had looked after him in Copenhagen in 1842, the winter before he wrote Maria Magdalena.

Christian Dietrich-Grabbe (1801–1836), the author of that eccentric but re-
markable play, *Comedy, Satire, Irony and Deeper Meaning;* nor anything by
Heinrich von Kleist, who had committed suicide in 1811 at the age of thirty-
four, except *Kätchen von Heilbronn,* and that not until 1868. The Russian realists,
Gogol, Turgenev and Ostrovsky, had equally long to wait. Neither *The
Government Inspector* (1836), nor *A Month in the Country* (1850) reached Norway
before 1890, nor anything by Ostrovsky until the present century. Alfred de
Musset's comedies of the eighteen-thirties were unperformed in Norway until
the sixties, when Ibsen himself directed *Un Caprice.* It is a commentary on the
theatrical taste of the period that the only contemporary plays in the general
European repertoire which have survived are the farces of Eugène Labiche, such
as *An Italian Straw Hat* (1851). Zola was not to start writing for the stage until
the seventies, nor Becque till the eighties.

Nor, in Bergen, did Ibsen have the opportunity, which he would have found
in, say, Copenhagen or Stockholm, to work on classical plays. No Greeks, no
Shakespeare, no Molière; even the few English Restoration playwrights who
reached him, and there were not many, did so in botched adaptations hideously
translated, and shorn of the elegance of their prose they must have seemed
pretty poor stuff. Only Holberg and Heiberg can have had anything to teach
him that he did not already know about construction and characterisation.
From Scribe he could have learned no virtue that was not better exemplified
in both these writers; and whatever Ibsen's admiration for Oehlenschläger as a
poet, he can hardly have been blind to his limitations as a dramatist.

Neither could the circumstances under which Ibsen worked as a director
have been much less fortunately arranged. As already stated, his duties in this
field were confined to deciding the decor and costumes and arranging the
movements; the interpretation of the roles, and the speaking of the lines, were
Laading's business. Not that this was an uncommon arrangement in those
days. Even at the Royal Theatre in Copenhagen, Thomas Overskou limited his
advice to visual matters, not bothering about the psychology of the characters,
their relationships, or the way the actors spoke their lines. Such subtleties were
not then regarded as necessary to a theatrical performance, any more than until
very recently they were regarded as necessary in opera. Tragedy was, to repeat,
a kind of grand opera without music, interesting only in so far as it afforded
opportunities for sonorous declamations, spectacular outbursts and striking
visual effects; comedy was merely an excuse for individual inventiveness.
Nobody except a very few innovators, such as Fredrik Høedt and Boguwil
Dawison, expected a play to reflect real life, any more than they would have
expected an opera to do so; what people wanted to see on the stage, in tragedy
as in opera or musical comedy, was a world of fantasy. There was no such thing

as what we today would call a straight play; there was tragedy, comedy, farce and melodrama, with or without music. Comedy might be in prose, but tragedy had to be in verse; the idea that a tragedy could be written in prose, or could be about people of humble birth and of ordinary human dimensions like the lower-paying members of the audience, would have struck both actor and public as absurd. (Even a play such as Hebbel's *Maria Magdalena* was in a high-flown prose, to modern ears uncomfortably close to the language of *Maria Marten*). Such few attempts as there had been to break this rule, had failed; which seemed to confirm its general validity. Büchner had succeeded, but nobody knew about Büchner; *Danton's Death* had been published in 1835, but in a version vulgarised almost beyond recognition, and the confused manuscript of *Wozzeck* was not to be discovered until 1879, the year in which, by a strange coincidence, Ibsen achieved international fame with *A Doll's House*, achieving, in his own way, what Büchner had sought to achieve forty years earlier—the writing of a major serious play in simple prose, employing characters who were not Kings and Princesses, nor even Capulets and Montagues, but ordinary people called Mr and Mrs, such as might live next door.

The actual stage conditions under which Ibsen operated at Bergen were some fifty years behind the times, and resembled those commonly to be found on the Continent and in England during the eighteenth century. The sets had no side walls, but a painted backcloth and a sequence of painted wings, with borders (i.e., hanging strips of cloth) overhead. The wings were mounted on wheels which rested in a kind of tramline, and were moved by a cranking device beneath the stage. Spectators sitting in the side seats could see through the gaps between the wings. The backcloth had to be rolled up like a home cinema screen before being hoisted into the flies to make way for another. The lighting consisted of chandeliers above the stage and auditorium, footlights, and lamps vertically arranged behind the various wings to give a primitive kind of side illumination. Gas was not introduced at the Bergen Theatre until 1856, the year before Ibsen left; until then, chandeliers, footlights and wing lamps worked on candles or petroleum. Little variation was possible, and such as there was was obtained by the use of movable coloured shades. Light and shadow were often painted on the decor. The front of the stage received the most light, thanks to the footlights and the extra illumination from the lamps and candles in the auditorium, and all dialogue scenes (as opposed to crowd scenes, mime, dances, etc.) were accordingly played downstage. In any case, words spoken upstage tended to get lost in the wings. The smoke, melted wax and spilt oil inevitably gave the decor, and especially the wing cloths, a soiled appearance. When, in 1848, the management had tried winching the main auditorium chandelier up to the roof, so as to give more effect to the stage lights, spectators complained that it was no longer possible to 'enjoy the diversion of looking at the audience when the plays or the performance were such that a broader field of view might prove less exhausting to the limbs and spirit than if eye and mind should be directed uninterruptedly towards the stage'.[1]

New decor, when the theatre could afford it, which was not often, and then only in the case of a new Norwegian play such as St John's Night, usually consisted simply of one or more new backcloths. The wing sets were seldom changed, and included standard representations of 'a street', 'a park', 'a church', 'winter', 'a grotto', 'a pillared hall', etc. A French visitor to Bergen in 1841 had satirically enquired why the theatre's painter employed his talents on the faces of the actresses instead of on the scenery.

Doors, windows, furniture, vases of flowers, mirrors and so on were, as in other countries, normally painted on the wings and backcloth. Even in England and on the Continent it was not until well into the second half of the century that real furniture was used; as late as 1888 we find Strindberg, in his preface to Miss Julie, complaining that 'stage doors are made of canvas and flap at the slightest touch', and pleading that 'even if the walls have to be made of canvas it is surely time to stop painting them with shelves and kitchen utensils.'[2]

The normal number of rehearsals judged necessary for a production when Ibsen was at Bergen was three to five. Such properties as could not be painted on the decor (chairs, tankards, etc.) were borrowed from well-wishers in the town; these even included eighteenth-century clothes, of which the citizens of Bergen, already famous for their thrift, had a surprising number in their family wardrobes. These were especially welcome when, as occurred once or twice a season, a play by Holberg entered the repertory.

---

[1] Bergens Stiftstidende, 31 January 1848. An excellent study of stage conditions at Bergen in the eighteen-fifties has been made by Roderick Rudler: see his Scenebilledkunsten i Norge for 100 år siden in Kunstkultur, 1961, and his Ibsens teatertid i Bergen in Bergens Tidende, 7 November 1864.

[2] Nor were things much better in Christiania. When Schiller's Mary Stuart received its premiere there in 1841, a critic complained that 'Queen Elizabeth's residence consisted of the Pompeian room which is familiar to us from every performance that we have been offered of the new French drama, and which is now almost worn out', and when Macbeth was performed for the first time in Norway in 1844, the same periodical (Den Constitutionelle) remarked that 'the room in Macbeth's castle into which Duncan enters was the inevitable Pillared Hall, the backcloth of which is by now completely indistinguishable'. Things were different in Germany, where the scenic designer was so highly regarded that his name was printed on the bills together with those of the actors, and he would be called on to the stage during a performance to take a bow whenever his handiwork elicited the plaudits of the public. (cf. Rudler, op. cit.)

The normal placing of actors at Bergen was in a horizontal bow, with its tips in the downstage corners and everyone facing the audience, even when they were meant to be speaking to each other. Ibsen's sketches in his prompt books show that he tried to get away from this convention; and when the company visited Trondhjem in 1856, his direction elicited some interesting praise from local critics. 'It deserves to be remarked,' wrote one, 'that the actors have abandoned the stiff and unnatural old-fashioned custom of running right down to the footlights or turning to the audience whenever they have anything to say.' It was also noticed that 'the actors keep quite far upstage' and, amazingly, 'turn towards each other when conversing'. This was eye-opening stuff indeed for the provincial theatre-goers of Norway, and one assumes that it was one of the fruits of Ibsen's study trip to Copenhagen and Dresden.

But although Ibsen was a visually imaginative director, as befitted one whose early ambition had been to become a painter, and although he was in advance of his time in his meticulous attention (when the theatre could afford it) to costume detail, all reports agree that he was not a good instructor of actors. He was far too timid. Peter Blytt relates: 'There was not much about him to suggest the creative genius which he was later to display. This quiet, reticent, not very prepossessing, unassuming young man, with a glance that was usually half-veiled and seldom lit up, and then only briefly, rather gave the impression of being an exceedingly withdrawn and shy person. One knew he had a quick and fertile poetic talent...but no one would have guessed that this pale, fully bearded face, with its tightly closed lips, concealed a mind of such quality...He moved quietly, almost soundlessly, about the wings at rehearsals...He not infrequently manifested a certain helplessness, and appeared embarrassed when forced directly to address any actor or, worse still, actress, in order to rebuke or even to correct them...He carried the director's books without in the true sense of the word being a *director*...He struck me as a naturally withdrawn personality who had difficulty, and even reluctance, in forming a close and intimate relationship with anyone. He preferred to wander around alone and unnoticed...

'It became repeatedly evident,' Blytt continues, 'that economic calculations and estimates, which were naturally an essential part of his work, lay somewhat outside his range. But no one doubted his good will. Undemanding and retiring, he aroused in that easily emotional and often passionate theatrical world no enmity—though one might now and then perceive in him a certain indolence, doubtless the consequence of his quickly fermenting talent...He was regarded with a certain shy veneration, and when, as stated, he moved soundlessly or, as the company sometimes put it, mooched (*tussede*) around in the wings in his curious, capacious and somewhat worn cloak, he was respected but won little sympathy. He scarcely made any intimate friends...but he made no enemies either. He preferred to go his own way, taciturn, enclosed, little understood...He did not often interrupt with instructions at rehearsals, and delivered no harangues, but when he did intervene his comments were perceptive, illuminating and to the point. His suggestions were brief, clear, precise and helpful.'[1]

H. Wiers-Jenssen, the author of the play *Anne Pedersdotter* (known in England as *The Witch*, and brilliantly filmed by Carl Dreyer as *Day of Wrath*) records that an actress who had worked with Ibsen at Bergen, and whom he does not name, told him how Ibsen would rehearse his actors either mooching sound-lessly in the wings (she uses the same word as Blytt) or sitting far back in the auditorium 'pulling at his beard and edging back if anyone came near. He would sometimes approach some young and as yet unintimidating beginner who happened to be sitting near him and, referring to the actress speaking on the stage, would say: "Don't you hear how falsely she said that line? And how untrue and unnecessary that movement was?" "But, Herr Ibsen, why don't you tell her?" "No, *you* tell her, Frøken Nielsen".' They thought of him, she told Wiers-Jenssen, as someone who 'wouldn't frighten a cat'.[2]

Another actress, Lucie Wolf, who worked under Ibsen in both Bergen and Christiania, recalled in her memoirs: 'I remember him as a silent, surprisingly shy man, who I always found kept himself very remote from us, and whose personality in no way encouraged one to speak privately or confidentially with him. He was always amiable and courteous, but in a way that made me get very quickly through whatever it was I needed to ask him. There was no question of his ever giving us instruction as Bjørnson did. I, at any rate, was afraid of him. He always went around wrapped in a great cloak, and if one approached him he shrank back and hid himself like a snail in its shell. I remember someone once asked me to speak to him about a rehearsal we were going to have. "No, thank you!" I said. "Go and ask him yourself! Don't you see how he creeps back into his cloak? And how it bristles all over? That's all the great thoughts he's pregnant with; they're sitting in there ready to burst his cloak and fly out into the world!" His great brain was boiling and seething; his powerful spirit could find no place among us and all the pettinesses we had to battle with when everything was just beginning. That mighty world-shaker could not but feel crushed and bound by the monotonous daily routine of narrow Bergen.'[3]

During the spring of 1853 Ibsen left Fru Sontum's and moved into an apart-

---

[1] Blytt, *op. cit.*, p. 10.
[2] *Aftenposten*, 24 December 1912.
[3] Lucie Wolf, *Mine livserindringer* (Christiania, 1898), pp. 182-3.

ment in the rear annexe of the theatre, where, the theatre archives tell us, he
was provided with 'a complete [!] bed and such furniture as may be necessary
for the two rooms which have been placed at Ibsen's disposal'. An inventory is
given of this furniture: '1 bedstead plus necessary bedclothes, including 4 sheets,
4 pillow-cases and 2 blankets, also mattresses and bolsters, 8 curtains and 8
curtain-holders, 6 birch chairs with covers, 1 birch table and 1 smaller ditto, 1
japanned washstand with mug and bowl'. He was looked after by the theatre's
'restauratrice', an old lady named Frøken l'Abbée 'with a red face and grey
curls beneath her cap',[1] who cooked him two meals a day. Many years later,
Ibsen, remembered the excellence of her cooking. 'Her fried cod,' he told John
Paulsen, 'was a masterpiece.'[2] Sophie Monsen recalled that he 'always ate his
meals by himself in his rooms in the rear annexe—and when he needed anything
he would go across the courtyard to the woman who cooked for him rather
than ring for and disturb the servant, who would then be eating himself. He
was very thoughtful'.[3]

The winter of 1852–1853 had been a depressing one for Ibsen, with the failure
of St John's Night and the dull and dismal list of plays. Spring, however,
occasionally brings consolations to the professionally unsuccessful, and it did for
Ibsen in 1853. He fell in love. At Fru Sontum's, shortly before he moved into
the theatre annexe, he met a young girl named Rikke (i.e., Henrikke) Holst.
She was only fifteen, ten years younger than Ibsen, and not yet confirmed, the
niece, indeed, of that Sofie Holst for whom he had written his last Grimstad
poem, Moonlight Wandering after a Ball. Rikke is reputed to have drawn his
attention to her by pertly throwing a posy of flowers in his face. Ibsen bought
her cakes, sent her flowers and went for walks with her; she was a merry,
extrovert girl and seems to have enjoyed his company. He wrote her several
charming poems, including one entitled Earth Flowers and Potted Plants, in
which he contrasts her freshness with the sophistication of other young ladies,
as a wild flower contrasts with a cultivated plant in a window.

Rikke seems to have reciprocated his love, and he spent a happy spring. On
Whit Sunday, 15 May, he climbed with a group of young people up to
Ulrikken, and declaimed a poem in two parts which he had written for the
occasion. It began with a lyric:

---

[1] John Paulsen, Samliv med Ibsen (Copenhagen and Christiania, 1906), p. 100.

[2] ibid., p. 100. Let no one whose experience of cod is confined to England sneer. The
cod of Bergen, properly prepared, is a masterpiece.

[3] Interview in Bergens Tidende, 13 January 1913. Sophie Monsen had begun as an actress
at Bergen, at the age of fifteen, at a salary of 12 specie-dollars a month, i.e. fifteen shillings
a week. She emigrated to America, and played Margit in The Feast at Solhaug in San
Francisco shortly before the great earthquake there.

SKIEN. Stockmannsgaarden, where Ibsen was born, is the last house on the right, facing the church. Photograph, *c.* 1870.
'My nursemaid carried me one day up into the tower.'

GRIMSTAD. The interior of the apothecary's where Ibsen worked from 1847 to 1850.
'I have actually seen Ibsen in the kitchen over an open fireplace . . . busy preparing medicine next to Mme. Geelmuyden's cooking-pots.'

GRIMSTAD. Water colour by Ibsen of the town and harbour, 1849.
'Everyone who had any savings . . . bought shares in a ship.'

CHRISTIANIA. Lithograph by S. Loos, *c.* 1850. Carl Johansgade, approaching the palace.
'O great and little city!'

THE NORWEGIAN THEATRE IN MØLLERGADEN, CHRISTIANIA. Engraving by L. Kleiser, c. 1860. 'An ugly and dirty street, full of doubtful inns . . . The audience comes in working clothes.'

BERGEN. Oil painting by Frederik Collett, c. 1875. 'Every baby in Bergen was popularly supposed to be born with an umbrella.'

LUDVIG HOLBERG. Copy of an oil painting by J. Roselius. (The original was burnt in 1813.)

ADAM OEHLENSCHLÄGER. Oil painting by J. Gertner, 1846.

JOHAN LUDVIG HEIBERG, c. 1850.
'In many ways he must have seemed a pattern of what the young Ibsen might have hoped to become.'

PAUL BOTTEN HANSEN, c. 1860.
'What Coleridge was to Wordsworth, Botten Hansen was to Ibsen.'

CHRISTOPHER DUE
'A close bond sprang up between the two.'

OLE SCHULERUD
'He was the friend I needed.'

A. O. VINJE, 1868
'A conversationalist such as we have never had in Norway before or since.'

BJØRNSTJERNE BJØRNSON, c. 1860
'For half a century a violent and extraordinary love-hatred relationship was to exist between them.'

SILHOUETTE BELIEVED TO BE OF IBSEN'S MOTHER
AS A GIRL
'In the end she became like a changeling.'

MAGDALENE THORESEN, *c.* 1866.
*'Her attitude towards Ibsen remained, throughout her
long life, curiously ambivalent.'*

RIKKE HOLST, *c.* 1860.
'What proof have I that once I saw the spring?'

SUZANNAH IBSEN, 1872.
'An almost violent hatred of all things petty.'

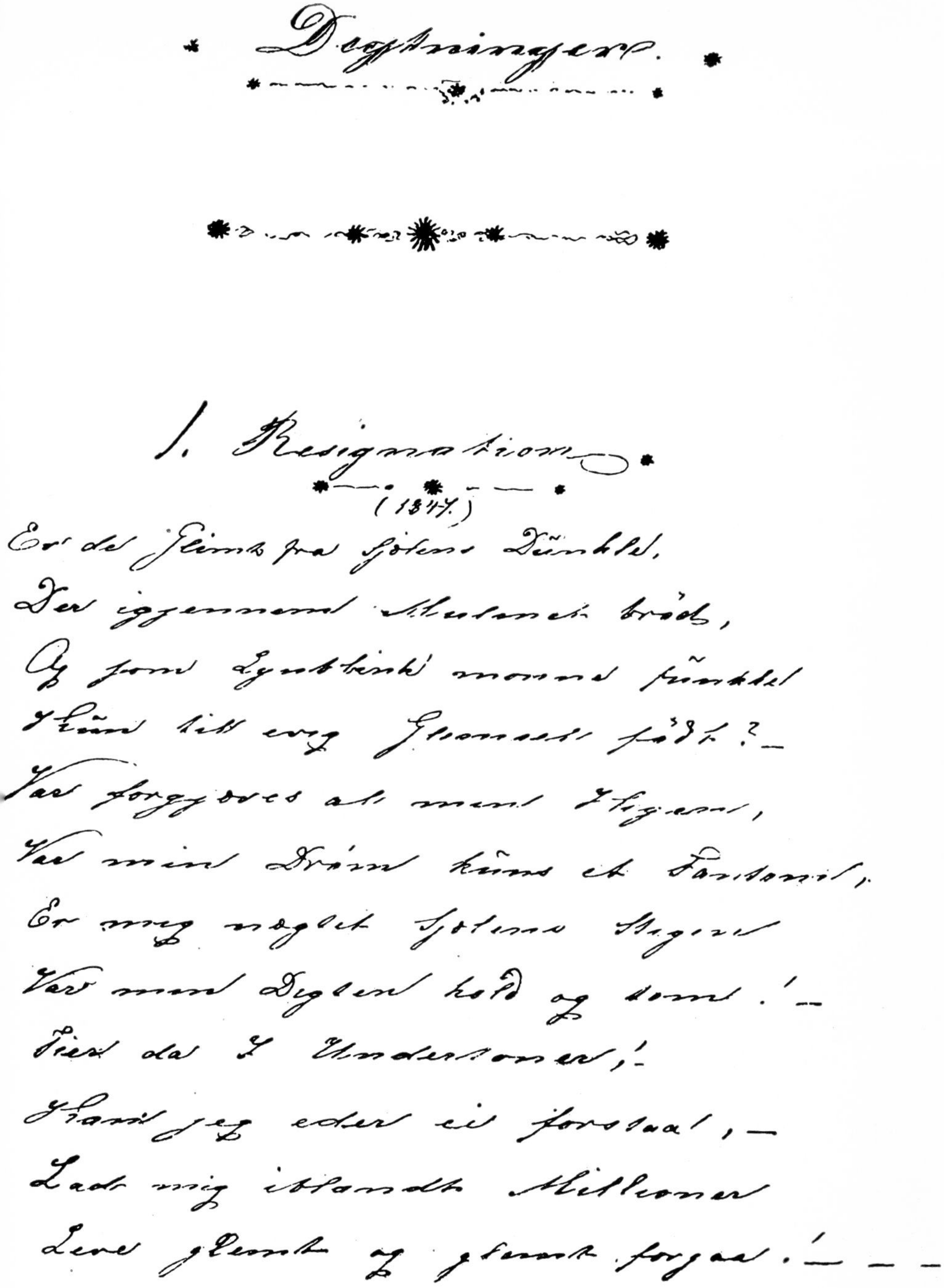

Digtninger.

1. Resignation.

(1847.)

Er det Glimt fra Sjælens Dunkel,
Der igjennem Mulmet brød,
Og som Lynblink monne funkle
Kun til evig Glemsel født? —
Var forgjeves al min Higen,
Var min Drøm kun et Fantom,
Er mig nøgtet Sjælens Stigen
Var min Digten kold og tom! —
Tier da I Undertoner! —
Kan jeg eder ei forstaa, —
Lad mig iblandt Millioner
Leve glemt og glemt forgaa! — —

bsen's earliest known poem, *Resignation* (1847), copied in his own hand 'neatly on to light blue paper', and sent to Clara Ebbell in 1850.

Catilina,

Drama i tre Acter,

af

Brynjolf Bjarme.

Christiania.

I Kommission hos P. J. Steensballe.

J. Steens Bogtrykkeri.

1850

Title page of the first edition of *Catiline*, Ibsen's first play, published in 1850 under the pseudonym of Brynjolf Bjarme.

Three caricatures by Ibsen published in *Andhrimner* in 1851.

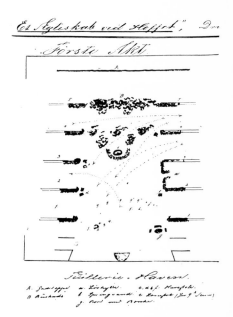

Page from Ibsen's Bergen prompt-book. His
sketch plan for Act One of *Un Mariage sous
Louis XV*, by Dumas *père*, Adolphe Leuven and
L. L. Brunswick.

Costume design in water colour by Ibsen, probably for the character of Olaf Liljekrans.

TORMOD KNUDSEN, c. 1860.
'Ibsen . . . said there were irregularities connected with his birth and bluntly named Tormod Knudsen.'

MARCUS THRANE
'Three years in prison awaiting trial, and then a four year sentence.'

OLE BULL, c. 1850
'Erratic, ebullient . . . with a passion for idealistic causes.'

KNUD KNUDSEN. Treated Ibsen 'like a truant schoolboy'.

JOHANNE LUISE HEIBERG. After an oil painting by Louis Aumont, 1831.
'*A major actress demonstrating her art.*'

H. Ø. BLOM, 1842
'. . I am H. Ø. Blom,
And you are Henrik Ibsen, nothing more.'

KAROLINE BJØRNSON, 1875
'*Everyone who has ever done me any wrong is immediately and for ever her most implacable enemy.*'
(Bjørnstjerne Bjørnson)

The earliest known photograph of Ibsen, 1861 (aged 33).
'Slack and lethargical.'

As swans that long for the south
Soar into the white clouds,
So our desires took joyful wing.
Our spring dreams rose and flew.

and was followed by a *Prospect of Bergen*, in which he affectionately apostrophised the city. Rikke recalled the occasion thirty-six years later: how, when they had reached the top, they unpacked their picnic baskets, the musicians began to play, and Ibsen suddenly leaped to his feet and, standing there on the mountainside, declaimed an apparently spontaneous *Ode to Joy*. 'He could be like that sometimes,' she remembered. 'But there were other times when he did not wish to be seen even by his friends, but would hide himself away completely...When anything annoyed him,' she continued, 'he could leap up suddenly and in swift and bitter outbursts tell his hostess all the truths he had guessed. And that didn't win him friends...When he was alone with you he could suddenly start to talk in a frenzied, ruthless torrent of words—paradoxes and wild truths, so that one walked bewitched beside the little man as he exploded savagely against all conventions. He sometimes said that he was a lonely person, and would always be a lonely person, whom no one believed in and no one, no one in the world, cared about. But there were other times when he would be quite silent and spend long periods shut up like a book. He was usually melancholy.'[1]

Two days after the Whit Sunday excursion, he joined in the 17th of May celebrations, when the young actors of the theatre (the ladies were not allowed to partake in this ceremony) walked in procession through the town wearing the Hungarian *luva* of grey-green cloth with a tassel, to demonstrate their support of Kossuth's new uprising. Rikke remembered how he 'descended from the mountain...and delivered an eloquent speech about how Norway still lay in her swaddling-clothes; but development was near, and must surely come. This aroused great enthusiasm and he was greeted with joyful demonstrations...It made him happy in those days occasionally to stand face to face with a crowd and feel that he had tamed it and was able to control it... Even his friends sometimes felt it was embarrassing to walk with him across the street, for there was something strange about him, even the way he dressed. But once he began to talk, you forgot everything and were caught up by the fire that burned in him.'[2]

On 6 June he wrote a new poem to her, entitled simply *To R. H.*, as romantic

---

[1] Fru Henrikke Holst-Tresselt interviewed by Herman Bang in *Af Dagens Krønike*, a Danish monthly magazine (Copenhagen, 1889), pp. 340–344.
[2] *ibid.*

I

and adolescent as anything he had composed at Grimstad: 'O, I know a fair
land, Distant as the stars of night...There I whisper many a song To the goddess
of my soul.' He ends, like any lovestruck youth, by asking: 'Must my love be
but a memory, and I lost and without hope, or shall I find my richest treasure
in life's reality?' Better than this was a charming poem which he addressed to
a rose that he sent her, asking its pardon for ending its life. When the theatre
season ended, and some of the company went on a walking tour to Voss and
Hardanger, he wrote a buoyant song for them to sing as they walked and
climbed. Whether he accompanied them, we do not know; he loved walking
tours,[1] but may have chosen to remain in Bergen to be near Rikke.

Early that June he asked her to marry him. But her father refused to countenance any engagement before she was confirmed; furthermore, he forbade
her to continue seeing this young poet, who was poor, of uncertain prospects,
had failed his matriculation, held radical political views and must altogether
have seemed, to any respectable citizen, a singularly unpromising match.
Despite this edict, they continued to meet, with her five-year-old brother as
chaperon and a girl friend of hers as look-out, and plighted their troth in a
time-honoured and romantic manner by joining their rings on a key-ring and
throwing them linked into the fjord. Thus, according to an ancient tradition,
the sea had joined them as surely as any priest. Unhappily, one day her father
surprised them together. Many years later Rikke's little brother, then an old
man, remembered the occasion: a clenched fist raised threateningly in the long
avenue of trees, and his father's face 'green with anger'. A bolder lover might
have braved it out; but Ibsen turned tail and fled. That was the end of things
between Ibsen and Rikke Holst. Thirty years afterwards, when revisiting
Bergen, he called on her; she was by now a comfortably married *hausfrau* with
many children. The old warmth, we are told, rose again in him, and he asked
wonderingly: 'I wonder why nothing ever came of our relationship?' She
laughed as in the old days, and said: 'But, my dear Ibsen, don't you remember? You ran away!' 'Yes, yes,' he replied. 'I never was a brave man face to
face.'[2]

It is tempting to exaggerate the effect of the Rikke Holst affair on Ibsen's
life. Most of us have loved and lost in our early twenties; it is an essential part
of any artist's education; and at least his love had been reciprocated. He wrote
a sad little lyric mourning his loss:

---

[1] Marcus Grønvold recalls Ibsen telling him that as a young man at Bergen he had taken
great walks in the countryside, once hiking with Andreas Isachsen to Hardanger. On the
way, he took a plunge in water that had melted from the snow, and then, in the Russian
manner, rolled in the snow. 'It didn't feel especially cold,' he commented. (*Fra Ulrikken
til Alperne*, Oslo, 1925, p. 140.)

[2] Koht, *Henrik Ibsen, Eit diktarliv*, I, p. 980.

One fine spring day
We walked the avenue.
Enticing as a riddle
Was the forbidden place.

And the west wind whispered
And the sky was blue.
A bird sat in the lime tree
And sang to her young.

I painted poems for you
In darting colour-play.
Two brown eyes shone
And laughed and listened.

Above us we can hear
Whispering and laughter.
But we, we said a soft farewell
And never met again.

Now when alone I wander
Along the avenue
Those little feathered dwarfs
Give me no peace.

That sparrow sat and listened
As we walked hand in hand,
And made a song about us
And set it to a tune.

Now every bird has learned it,
And in the leafy eaves
Each tiny beak sings crooningly
Of that fair day, now gone.

It was probably at this time, too, that he wrote at any rate the first draft of
the long, brilliant and bitter poem, *In the Picture Gallery*:

There dwells an ugly demon in my breast
Who sometimes visits me in evil hours;
In loneliness, or when life's joys are best,
As when I dream, or, rhyming, sense my powers...

'Will you not realise,' it whispers, gloating,
'How meaningless it is, your life's short span?
Have you not lost your faith in God and man?

Can you not understand, your hopes are nothing?
Your ideals but a distant candle are;
Your goal a meteor, and not a star?'...

Outside my window stood an apple tree,
Its branches filled with flowers and with fragrance.
There a small bird sang for my ear alone,
Singing of life's great glory and abundance.

Now those bright flowers rot black against the roots.
The once-green leaf rustles against the stone.
A tempest snatched them from the stage of life,
And the sweet singer of the spring has flown.

Now autumn reigns within me and without.
I press my forehead to the window, where
The frost makes foolish patterns on the pane.

What proof have I that once I saw the spring?
A withered leaf, a stump of memory;
That is the sum and total of life's gain!

Not surprisingly, his work at the theatre suffered, and on 30 July the board felt constrained to send him a letter demanding that he apply himself more actively to his duties:

It has come to the notice of the Board that some of the responsibil'ties connected with your work have been postponed and subsequently overlooked, while others have not always been carried out in the most desirable manner...It would be to the advantage of all parties if you could be more active in the theatre, both as regissør and as instruktør. The Board believes, however, that this neglect of duty stems rather from lack of experience than from any want of ability or willingness to perform your duties.

The kindly tone of this rebuke suggests that Ibsen's directors liked and appreciated him, an impression that is reinforced by Peter Blytt in his memoirs. On 4 August, Ibsen replied somewhat plaintively to the above letter: 'That there is much in the matter of scenic arrangements, decor, etc., that could be otherwise, there can be no doubt. The question is whether the Board is willing to agree to the outlay required to supplement the grievous deficiencies now existing...I most readily admit that my work as *regissør* is still not all that it might be, but I assumed that it would be obvious to anyone with knowledge of the theatre that what a *regissør* requires above all else is experience, and I know only too well that it has not been possible for me adequately to achieve this when limited to a mere three to five rehearsals per play.' This excuse, plausibly as it reads, did not strike the Board as sufficient; they acknowledged his letter, but did 'not feel required to retract anything that they had written in their communication of 30 July'.[1]

Ibsen should have written a new play that autumn for the coming anniversary of the theatre's opening but, although he wrote to Paul Botten Hansen on 5 August that he was 'pretty productive, as you will discover before the winter is out', he in fact did no more than revise *The Warrior's Barrow*, individualising the characters more sharply, improving the motivation, reducing the mythological apparatus (rather to the play's detriment), and generally polishing the verse. In this new form *The Warrior's Barrow* accordingly received its second production, at the Bergen Theatre on 2 January 1854. Perhaps it was not unreasonable of Ibsen to wish it to be performed again; after all, it had been sympathetically received in Christiania. But at Bergen it failed, even more calamitously than *St John's Night*, for it was dropped after only a single performance. The local press did not notice it at all. Coming on top of the break-up of his affair with Rikke, this must have been a particularly painful disappointment to him; though there was some faint consolation in that *Bergenske Blade* decided to serialise it, in four instalments. *The Warrior's Barrow* thus became the second of Ibsen's plays to appear in print; though it was not published in book form until over forty years later, when Ibsen allowed it to be included in the German collected edition of his works published in 1898 to celebrate his seventieth birthday. 'I find, on reading it through,' he wrote to Julius Elias, on 7 September 1897, 'that there is, after all, some merit in this youthful trifle, and am very grateful to you for making me include it'; but it is difficult to see what merit so austerely self-critical a writer as Ibsen could have discovered there. It seems blatantly inferior to *St John's Night*, which he refused to allow to be printed in his lifetime. *The Warrior's Barrow* is nearer to being worthless than any other play he wrote.

---

[1] Wiesener, *op. cit.*, pp. 36–39.

FIVE

🔖 Kid Gloves in Bergen

(1854-1857)

THE EFFECT OF THE FAILURE of *The Warrior's Barrow* upon Ibsen's self-confidence can be measured by the fact that he offered his next play to the Bergen theatre anonymously. In September 1854 Peter Blytt became chairman of the Board; at thirty-one, he was only five years older than Ibsen. In his memoirs he records that a few weeks after his appointment to this post, Ibsen came to see him with a quarto notebook under his arm. 'I was immediately struck,' notes Blytt, 'by the fact that he seemed more than usually ill at ease that day. After a few confused preliminary remarks he handed me the book, saying that it was a manuscript that had been sent him by a friend in Christiania, a historical drama or, if one preferred, a tragedy, which the author in question, who wished to remain anonymous, would like to be performed at the Bergen Theatre, should it be deemed worthy of acceptance. But before submitting it to the board he—Ibsen—desired me to read it through and give him my opinion.'[1]

The play was entitled *Lady Inger of Østraat*. Blytt guessed from Ibsen's demeanour that he was probably the author; he read the play, liked it, and quickly put it into rehearsal. It was only a few days before the opening performance that Ibsen admitted to its authorship. Blytt tells us that at a rehearssl Ibsen, in his capacity as *sceneinstruktør*, suddenly rushed on to the stage, interrupted one of the actors in the middle of a long speech, and showed him with unusual feeling how it ought to be spoken. The actors noticed that Ibsen did this without referring to the prompt book, and this confirmed what, one imagines, they must in any case have suspected. Nevertheless, he remained adamant in refusing to allow his name to appear as the author on either the posters or the programme.

H. Wiers-Jenssen, quoting an actress who was in the company at the time, confirms this story with some interesting additional details. The speech about which Ibsen felt so strongly was the one in Act Three in which Nils Lykke says to Lady Inger's daughter, Eline: 'How often have you not sat here at Østraat, alone, your brain in a whirl...longing to get away, to flee far away, you

---

[1] Blytt, *op. cit.*, p. 11.

134

know not whither? How often have you not wandered alone along the fjord, and a gilded ship with knights and ladies aboard, with harps and singers, has glided by, far from the shore; a faint echo of mighty deeds has floated to your ear; and you have felt a longing in your breast, an irresistible longing to know what exists on the other side of the sea?...When you dreamed of the many-coloured life out there in the wide world—when you dreamed of tourneys and merry feastings—did you never see in your dreams a knight standing with a smile on his lips and grief in his heart in the midst of the tumult—a knight who had once dreamed, as fairly as you, of a woman, noble and virtuous, and whom he had sought in vain among all those who surrounded him?'

When (Wiers-Jenssen tells) Ibsen had sprung on to the stage and delivered this speech with a passion which astonished the actors standing silently around, he fell silent for a moment and then said to the actor who was playing the part: 'Well—you know—something along those lines—I think the speech will sound best if you say it that way—But if you don't feel—of course—then—it's you who are acting it—yes.' And he shuffled back into the wings.[1]

Lady Inger of Østraat is set in Norway in 1528. Like *The Warrior's Barrow* and *St John's Night* (and, for that matter, his next two plays, *The Feast at Solhaug* and *Olaf Liljekrans*), it conforms to Aristotle's demand for unity of time, place and action, for the entire story takes place during a single night in Lady Inger's castle. The plot is extremely complicated. Lady Inger, a rich and powerful noblewoman, is under persuasion to lead a Norwegian uprising against the Danish overlords. A Norwegian patriot, Olaf Skaktavl, tells her that a stranger will come to her castle that night; he is the son of a Swedish rebel murdered by the Danes, Sten Sture, and is preparing a rebellion which Olaf begs Lady Inger to support. Sure enough, a stranger arrives; but he is not Sten Sturesson, but a Danish intriguer, Nils Lykke, who has got wind of Sten Sturesson's plans and has come to intercept and kill him. Lady Inger, however, supposes him to be Sturesson. A sub-plot, beautifully worked into the main action, is that Lady Inger's eldest daughter Lucia had, some years before, been seduced by Nils Lykke, and had killed herself; but Lady Inger has never seen Lykke, and does not recognise him. She has a surviving daughter, Eline, whose ambition is to discover and revenge herself upon her sister's seducer; but she knows his face no more than her mother does, and she, like her sister, is seduced by him that night. Then a second stranger arrives at the castle, so late that everyone has gone to bed except Nils Lykke, who is waiting to murder him. But this second stranger is not, as he had expected, Sten Sturesson, but his half-brother Sten Steensson, an illegitimate son of Sten Sture born to him

---

[1] *Aftenposten*, 24 December 1912.

long before by Lady Inger herself. Lady Inger, who has not seen him since childhood, supposes him to be his legitimate half-brother and thinks that if she can kill him she may pave the way for her own son to be King; herself unable to rule because of her sex, she has cherished a secret ambition to become the mother of a King. She has him killed, only to discover that he is her own son. At the same time, Eline discovers that her lover, Nils Lykke, is her sister's seducer. Lady Inger dies by her son's coffin, and Nils Lykke walks quietly out, his mission accomplished. Evil has triumphed.

Lady Inger of Østraat was the first of Ibsen's plays to be written entirely in prose; it is also the first that would stand up to performance today. In 1857, even after he had had a public success with *The Feast at Solhaug*, Ibsen, writing to Paul Botten Hansen, twice referred to *Lady Inger* as 'my best play'. It is indeed, despite its obvious faults, a remarkably mature and powerful work. Not that it is to be regarded as a harbinger of the new drama; it is rather a brilliant essay in the old tradition. In it, Ibsen has retained, as yet without question, much of the old paraphernalia of plot which was still then supposed to be indigenous to tragedy, as to comedy—mistaken identities, intercepted letters, overheard conversations, lengthy monologues and frequent asides (which last can be deleted from *Lady Inger* without in any way obscuring the action). The language, too, is often stiff, though of considerable quality and precisely phrased. But the characterisation is much more searching than anything he had achieved previously, and the action moves towards its climax with that inevitability which we associate with his later and more famous works. Here, too, for the first time, we hear that tone of controlled yet searching self-analysis which we shall later come to recognise as the authentic Ibsen music. In particular, Lady Inger's conflict of courage and cowardice, her desire to act and her doubts that hold her back, was a theme to which Ibsen was to return again and again in his plays; it is the dilemma of Skule in *The Pretenders*, Mrs Alving in *Ghosts*, Ellida in *The Lady from the Sea*, Rebecca West in *Rosmersholm*, and Hedda Gabler.

It has been suggested that *Lady Inger of Østraat* was technically influenced by Scribe's historical drama *Les Contes de la Reine de Navarre*, which Ibsen had helped to direct that autumn, in October 1854. The rapid succession of short scenes, it is argued, and the various coincidences vital to the plot, are typical of Scribe. Have the critics who make such assertions never read Shakespeare? Mistaken identities, intercepted letters, overheard conversations, monologues and asides are all to be found in both *Hamlet* and *King Lear*, which we know Ibsen had seen in Copenhagen, and which he had almost certainly read; indeed, off-hand, it is difficult to think of a Shakespeare play that does not contain them. And anyone who has ever acted in, or been associated with, a

Shakespeare production knows how, with the free Elizabethan method of staging, Shakespeare was addicted to the frequent use of the short scene. Even if Ibsen had not learned all this from Shakespeare, he would have done so from Holberg. In any event, Blytt tells us that Ibsen offered him the play 'a few weeks' after he had become chairman of the board, which we know to have been on 9 September, and *Les Contes de la Reine de Navarre* was not performed until October. Are we to suppose that Ibsen wrote this long and very complex play in a few days? One repeats that the myth of Ibsen's debt to Scribe, of whom he never recorded a good word, needs to be exploded. Scribe, if shallow in characterisation, was a skilful theatrical craftsman, but there is no evidence that he ever exerted the slightest influence upon Ibsen.

Sixteen years later, in a letter to Peter Hansen (28 October 1870), Ibsen stated that *Lady Inger of Østraat* stemmed 'from a sudden love affair, violently broken off, which you will also find treated in several short poems, such as *Earth Flowers and Potted Plants, A Birdcage*, etc.' This reference to the Rikke Holst interlude has evoked a quantity of obtuse speculation from commentators who have sought to identify Rikke with Eline, and have even suggested that, since there is no relationship in the play which resembles that between Ibsen and Rikke, he must, in a moment of aberration, have been mistakenly referring to some other drama. Surely it is obvious that it is the tragic and nihilistic mood of the play which stemmed from the unhappiness of that summer. Again and again in his later years Ibsen was to remind questioners, unhappily with little effect, that he distilled his experiences into his plays, and did not, except in very rare instances, mirror them directly.

Lady Inger of Østraat might, if its reception had been different, have proved the first major turning-point in Ibsen's career as a dramatist; it was his first step on that road of high tragedy which he was ultimately to extend into previously uncharted country. As fate decreed, however, he was thrown smartly off that road, and it was to be another decade before he ventured to return to it. For *Lady Inger* was as big a failure with the Bergen public as *St John's Night* and *The Warrior's Barrow* had been. They received it so poorly at its first performance on 2 January 1855 that it was repeated only once; and even when, the following year, Ibsen had a success with *The Feast at Solhaug* and tried to persuade them to revive *Lady Inger*, the board refused.[1] It is possible, of course,

---

[1] This may, however, have stemmed not so much from a poor regard for the play as from the inability of the Bergen actors to cope with tragedy. Peter Blytt tells that when, in the winter of 1854–5, they tried to do Victor-Hugo's *Angelo*, Tyran de Padron, the board had to call off the production after the final dress rehearsal because the play was 'obviously far outside the company's range'. (Blytt, *op. cit.*, p. 128.) On 12 July 1855 *Bergens-Posten* printed a late notice of the play: 'If he can only raise pillars of shame, then let them rest, the poor shadows'.

that it may, like so many plays that have failed critically and publicly, have won him the admiration of a discriminating few, but we have no evidence for this.

He does not seem to have found any replacement for Rikke Holst; as we have heard, those who knew him at this period say that he was preternaturally shy and had few friends. As far as we know it was to be almost three years before he again formed any close association with a girl, and then it was to be the one he was to marry. The overall picture we have of Ibsen at this time is very different from that which Christopher Due paints of him at Grimstad only five years earlier, when he had, apparently, become infatuated fairly often. No love poems have survived from the years 1854 and 1855. But this, again, is not so inexplicable a phenomenon as some critics and biographers have tried to make out. Some young men fall in love at the drop of a handkerchief, others rarely and with difficulty, and it is not uncommon for a young man to change in his twenties from one type to the other. Nor should we be surprised that he, who had made several close friends in Christiania, found none in Bergen. Although the two towns were roughly similar in size, Bergen had no university, and, as Lorentz Dietrichson has told us, little culture. Ibsen was not the first man who, on leaving a university city for a small provincial town, has found himself isolated and friendless and sought in vain for someone to love.

Outwardly, too, and especially sartorially, Ibsen was very different from the shabby apprentice, lacking socks and overcoat, whom Due had known at Grimstad. True to the child who, at Venstøp, had admired the sexton's father as he arrayed himself in his fine clothes, Ibsen used what must have been a largish proportion of his salary to dress elegantly. Magdalene Thoresen, seeing Ibsen around 1870 in a velvet coat, 'was reminded of an earlier attempt at the elegant which he once made in Bergen when, very smart, he swung round a corner wearing light yellow kid gloves. In Bergen!' she added uncharitably.[1] Herman Bang, writing in 1889, quotes a description given him by someone who had known Ibsen at Bergen: 'He was so soigné, almost precise and finicky, in his dress. He wore elegant frilled poet's cuffs, with lace edges extending over his hands. And on the street he carried a short little cane. People thought he looked unimpressive, and he suffered from the consciousness of being small—but those who dismissed him as insignificant had never seen his eyes. They could catch fire and throw a glance that pierced you, so that you remembered it long afterwards.'[2] Bang's informant may have been Rikke Holst, for John Paulsen, who interviewed Rikke when the latter was an old woman, records that she described him in almost identical terms: 'Ibsen was at that time

---

[1] From an interview first printed in *Juleroser* (Copenhagen, 1901), subsequently in Karl Larsen's edition of the epic version of *Brand* (Christiania, 1907).
[2] Article in *Af Dagens Krønikhe* (Copenhagen, 1889), p. 341.

very soigné, even pedantic, in his dress. For example, his coat had sleeves which were very broad at the wrist, *engageant* sleeves as they were then called, and these were adorned with curious long lace cuffs, a fashion which the other men did not affect. He always wore frilled shirts...The same precise order ruled in his rooms. There was never a speck of dust on the furniture, and elegant vases of flowers stood in the windows...His physical appearance, with its brown complexion and black hair and full black beard, was interesting rather than handsome.'[1] And Lorentz Dietrichson mainly remembered, from this time, 'his full dark brown beard, covering the whole chin, which was then still quite unusual, his grey cloak, his lively eyes and his quick gait.'[2]

That February, 1855, he wrote a pleasant epithalamium to celebrate the marriage of another of his former landlady's sons, Edvard Sontum: it is the only poem from Ibsen's pen that has survived from this year, apart from those which he was to insert into his new play. The same month, he directed one of the few good plays (apart from Holberg's and his own) which came his way at Bergen: Eugène Labiche's farce, *An Italian Straw Hat*, composed in 1851. Otherwise, the repertory made the usual dismal reading: Scribe, Bayard, Mélesville, Hertz, with German, Danish and (occasionally) Norwegian pieces of equal triviality and, usually, less expertise.

That others besides himself were dissatisfied with such dramatic fare Ibsen would have learned from a drama criticism by Bjørnson which appeared in *Aftenbladet* on 1 February that year. The starting-point of the article was a new French play, *Le Gendre de M. Poirier*, by a thirty-four year old dramatist named Emile Augier, which had been produced in Paris the previous year. Bjørnson wrote admiringly of 'the economy of the dialogue, the careful unfolding of character, so that even in the fourth act the author has new aspects of personality with which to surprise us', and of 'the perspective which is opened...by the dialogue never illuminating the character directly but...as it were merely allowing it to be distantly glimpsed'. This new naturalism is generally agreed to have dated, as far as the French theatre is concerned, from the production of Musset's *Un Caprice* at the Comédie Française in 1847 (though in the novel it can be traced back at least twenty-five years, to Balzac's *Le Peau de Chagrin* (1830) and Stendhal's *Le Rouge et le Noir* (1831), and was to reach its peak in Flaubert's *Madame Bovary* in 1856). Bjørnson, praising the psychological advance which Augier had made on Scribe, expressed the hope

---

[1] *Samliv med Ibsen* (Copenhagen and Christiania, 1906). pp. 120–21.

[2] *Svundne tider*, Vol. I (Christiania, 1894), p. 331. It is interesting that Rikke, unlike other witnesses, remembers his complexion as brown. They were together in the spring and summer only, when he had evidently caught the sun.

that the new movement might help 'to reform the taste of our time for characterless drama'.

Later that year, in *Morgenbladet* on 9 December, Bjørnson developed his demand for realism in the drama at greater length. Again contrasting the work of Musset, Augier and Dumas *fils* with the artificialities of Scribe, he wrote: 'In a time such as ours, one cannot be content with mere hints of character. People are delving more deeply into human nature from every angle, in science as well as in art; we investigate each minutest trait, we dissect and analyse...the smallest flower, the least insect...And in art this current of naturalism reveals itself in a striving for truth rather than beauty, manifesting itself in theatrical terms in a strong demand for individualisation'. In a piece such as Felicien Mallefille's *Le Coeur et la Dot*, Bjørnson continues, 'it is no longer a question of revealing merely that aspect of a person's character for which one happens to have use; no, one puts the whole person into the play, with all his social roots'. The danger is that, in ill-written works, 'he [the character] occupies so much space that he halts the action and destroys the interest'. What playwrights must do is 'to let his [i.e., Scribe's] dramatic machinery and their more detailed characterisation merge to their mutual advantage'; the plot must be the result of 'the characters' own development'. Two years later (in March 1858), Bjørnson was to write in *Bergensposten* that 'Scribean comedy is now finished in France', and that the characters now being created there 'are no longer marionettes moved by invisible strings but human beings, men and women with the pain of life in their faces'.[1]

But Ibsen was unable to read Augier because of his ignorance of French, and some time during the spring or summer of 1855 he made a literary discovery which excited him much more: the Icelandic Sagas. They were the first literature that had excited him for several years, since his discovery in his teens of Voltaire, Oehlenschläger, Holberg and Heiberg, and the Shakespeare he had seen in Copenhagen and Dresden; and they were to be virtually the last. Once Ibsen had thrown off the not very inspiring influence of Oehlenschläger and had absorbed what he could of Shakespeare from seeing him and reading him in bad translations, he was never again to be seriously influenced by any writer, dead or alive. He would sometimes pick up a thought from Kierkegaard or Brandes, or a hint by Bjørnson, and develop it; but he was, as Edmund Gosse observed, one of the very few great writers who worked without a library. For the last half of his life indeed, if not longer, Ibsen read little but newspapers and the Bible (the latter, he would hasten to point out, for the

---

[1] Quoted by Christen Collin in *Bjørnstjerne Bjørnson; hans barndom og ungdom*, II (Christiania, 1907), p. 436.

language only); but he read them, and the newspapers especially, most minutely; his last twelve great prose plays, from which the whole of modern prose drama stems, are like fragments of newspapers written by some all-seeing editor.

The sagas, however, fascinated him. It is remarkable that he had not discovered them before; even such knowledge of the Viking Age as he had required when writing *The Warrior's Barrow* had been gleaned from Oehlenschläger. It was not that no good translations of the sagas were available in Norwegian or Danish, for N. M. Petersen had produced four excellent volumes between 1839 and 1844. But somehow Ibsen had missed them. They excited him as the literature and history of the Middle Ages, which he had studied when preparing *Lady Inger of Østraat*, had failed to do.

At the same time, groping back into the literature of the remote past, he happened upon another form that proved a revelation to him: the mediaeval folk tale. Ibsen had a better excuse for his ignorance of this rich field, for the rediscovery of it in Norway was still barely under way. The pioneer in this had been Jørgen Moe, a farmer's son who was later to become a bishop. He had begun to collect folk tales from his fellow peasants as early as 1834, when a youth of twenty one. A few years later he was joined in his researches by another enthusiast, Peter Christian Asbjørnsen, and in 1841 they published their first collection; their full edition of 1856 was to create among Norwegian writers something like the sensation which Thomas Percy (likewise destined to become a bishop) had aroused in England in 1765 with the publication of his *Reliques of English Poetry*, which were to inspire so much of the literature of the Romantic Movement. Other Norwegians besides Moe and Asbjørnsen were digging up the literary past in the eighteen-fifties; in 1853, M. B. Landstad had published the first of his collections of folk ballads, while from 1853 to 1859 L. M. Lindeman brought out, in instalments, the peasant melodies of Norway. All this fitted well with the nationalistic movement that was afoot in Norway, in literature as in politics; here was a literature that was neither Danish nor Swedish, but truly Norwegian.

Twenty-eight years later, in a foreword which he wrote to *The Feast at Solhaug* in 1883, Ibsen recalled the effect which the discovery of this ancient literature had had upon him at the time:

'The year before [*The Feast at Solhaug*] I had written *Lady Inger of Østraat*. The preparation of this drama had necessitated my delving into the history and literature of the Middle Ages, particularly the later stages of that period. I tried, as well as I could, to live myself back into the habits and customs of those times, the emotional life, the ways of thought and speech. The

period is, however, not especially attractive to dwell in for any length
of time; nor does it provide material particularly suited to dramatic
treatment. I soon, therefore, turned to the saga age. But the sagas of the
kings, and the strict historical traditions of that remote time, did not grip
me; I found myself unable, then, to make any creative dramatic use of the
strifes between kings and chieftains, factions and families. That was to
come later.

'On the other hand, in the Icelandic *family* sagas I found in rich measure
what I required in the way of human clothing for the thoughts, moods and
ideas which at that time were filling, or anyway running around in,
my head. Hitherto I had been ignorant of these Old Norse contributions to
the personal history of our saga age, had indeed scarcely heard of them.
By chance N. M. Petersen's excellent translation (excellent, at least, as
regards the feel of the language) came into my hands. In these family chronicles, with their varied relationships and confrontations between man
and man, woman and woman, above all between human being and
human being, I discovered a rich, vital and personal life; and from my
encounter with all these intensely rounded and individual men and
women there arose in my mind the first rough and misty outline of *The
Vikings in Helgeland*...But then something intervened. This was principally and decisively of a personal nature; but I think it was not without
significance that I had at that time begun to study Landstad's collection
of Norwegian folk ballads which had been published a few years previously. The mood in which I then found myself fitted better with the
literary romanticism of the Middle Ages than with the deeds of the sagas,
better with verse than prose, better with the linguistic music of the folk
ballad than with the characterisation of the sagas. So it happened that
the shapeless, embryonic idea of *The Vikings at Helgeland* gradually
transformed itself into the lyrical drama *The Feast at Solhaug*.'

Ibsen wrote *The Feast at Solhaug* during the summer of 1855. It is partly in
rhymed verse, partly in prose, and is set in the fourteenth century. The plot
must be given briefly. Margit is the bored young wife of a rich and tedious
old landowner named Bengt. She has a younger sister, Signe. The King's
officer, Knut Gaesling, is on a visit to them, with a dual purpose; he intends
to propose to Signe, and is also on the look-out for a former friend of theirs,
Gudmund Alfson, who is suspected of treason. This Gudmund now turns up
at Solhaug, protesting his innocence; and, in an improbably romantic manner,
he declares that he is in love with someone at the house without naming her.
Margit and Signe have both been in love with him, in each case (again some-

what improbably) without the other suspecting, and each now assumes herself to be the one he loves. Margit believes that, if she had not been so foolish as to marry Bengt, Gudmund would long ago have married her; she therefore decides to poison her husband. Meanwhile, Knut has been rejected by Signe and, hearing that she loves Gudmund, sees a double reason for killing him as soon as the day is over (it would offend against the laws of hospitality if he were to murder a fellow-guest during a feast). Bengt now gets drunk, fights Knut to avenge a supposed insult, and is killed by him; whereupon the servants overpower and bind Knut, so that he is now in Gudmund's power. Gudmund chivalrously spares him. News now arrives that the King has discovered that Gudmund is not after all guilty of treason. Knut is freed, Gudmund is now also free, he marries Signe, and all ends happily for everyone except Margit.

The Feast at Solhaug is, except possibly for The Warrior's Barrow, the worst play that Ibsen ever wrote. The plot and characterisation are both extremely banal, and the only merit lies in some of the lyrical writing. The influence of the folk ballad is very apparent; both the style and the atmosphere of the play are full of echoes from Landstad's collection, and so are the characterisation and motivation. Professor Francis Bull has remarked that examples of this are to be found on 'almost every page' of the play; inter alia, Landstad contains songs about characters named Margit, Gudmund and Signelita who have much in common with Ibsen's Margit, Gudmund and Signe. If Ibsen had any illusions about its quality at the time, he soon abandoned them; writing to Peter Hansen in 1870 he dismissed it as 'a trifle that I no longer wish to acknowledge'.

But even the worst of plays may serve a purpose, and The Feast at Solhaug, as Ibsen was to discover when it was staged the following January, was to prove extremely important to him, for two reasons.

Meanwhile, he continued with his work as sceneinstruktør. In June of that year (1855) the board, for some unexplained reason, proposed that Laading and Ibsen should switch jobs. Both protested. 'Three full seasons have now elapsed since Herr Ibsen took over the sceneinstruktion,' wrote Laading to the board, 'so he has all the details at his finger tips far more than I...Whether Ibsen will be able to fill my place as reading supervisor and rest content that the experience which he has gained of stage management should lie unused, he must himself inform you.' The board dropped the idea.

On 30 September 1855, Ibsen, for the first and last time in his career, directed a Shakespeare play—As You Like It, adapted by a Frøken S. Beyer and re-entitled Livet i Skoven, or Life in the Forest. The Bergen public did not appreciate it, and it was dropped after only two performances. T. H. Blanc, the historian of the Bergen theatre, comments: 'The play seems to have proved too difficult for the company's talents.'[1]

That autumn, however, Ibsen had the honour of being elected to a fairly exclusive club, the 22 December Society. The name had no political significance, but arose merely from the fact that on 22 December 1845 twenty-five citizens had met in Bergen to found a literary society which was to meet every fortnight during the winter for lectures and readings; the playing of cards was to be strictly forbidden. Peter Blytt, the chairman of the theatre board, had become president of this society in 1855, and during the autumn he proposed Ibsen as a new member. He was elected unanimously. The records of the society inform us that on 27 November 1855 'Instruktør Ibsen gave a lecture on W. Shackspear [sic] and his influence on Scandinavian Art'. Exasperatingly, the manuscript of this talk has not survived, and we have no record of anything that Ibsen said in it. One would give a lot to know. It seems, at any rate, to have interested the members, for the following month, to celebrate the tenth anniversary of their founding, Johannes Brun was invited to give a dramatic reading of the Falstaff scenes from Henry IV.[2] Ibsen wrote a song for the occasion, and also for the following anniversary in 1856, by which time the society had over eighty members. Neither song is of much poetic value.

On 2 January 1856, The Feast at Solhaug was performed, under Ibsen's direction, at the Bergen Theatre and, thanks to the debased taste of the public, was a success: the first, apart from the very limited praise accorded to The Warrior's Barrow in Christiania, that Ibsen had known. As much as the play itself, people admired the apparently authentic mediaeval peasant costumes and furniture, and the new decor which, like the costumes, Ibsen had designed, or at any rate co-operated on. In his 1883 foreword to the play, Ibsen described the first night reception:

'I was at the time employed as stage instructor at the Bergen theatre, and so personally supervised the rehearsals of my play. The performance was admirable, and of a rare warmth; acted with joy and devotion, it was received in the same spirit…The performance ended with repeated calls for the author and cast. Later that evening the orchestra, accompanied by a large part of the audience, serenaded me outside my windows. I am not sure that I did not permit myself to be so carried away as to deliver a kind of address to the gathering. I know, at any rate, that I felt profoundly happy'.

---

[1] Blanc, op. cit., p. 206.
[2] See the article by Professor Francis Bull in Edda X (1919). He says 'from Henry V', but there are, of course, no Falstaff scenes in that play. The 22 December Society folded in the autumn of 1861.

When, after a subsequent performance, one of the actors made a speech in his honour, Ibsen thanked them for 'the recognition that will strengthen me in my pursuit of the goal towards which I am striving, and which I *shall* achieve'. Later, he said it was the only really happy day he ever spent in Bergen.[1]

The Feast at Solhaug was repeated five times during the next few months, a record previously achieved at the theatre only by C. P. Riis's rustic 'dramatic idyll', *Til sæters* (*At a Mountain Farm*). Ibsen was by now nearly twenty-eight, and he badly needed some kind of success; a poet or a novelist can work unrecognised, but hardly a playwright. The occasion had, though, a side effect which in the long run was to prove vastly more important to his writing.

Among the audience at the Bergen theatre that January evening in 1856 was a thirty-six year old authoress named Magdalene Thoresen. Danish by birth, she had fled from her native country to escape from a love affair with an Icelandic poet, and had married a twice widowed clergyman seventeen years her senior, Hans Conrad Thoresen, the Dean of Bergen. She was a beautiful and remarkable woman, who had already achieved recognition as a novelist and short story writer, and had both written and translated plays for the Bergen theatre, so that she had already met Ibsen several times. Now that he was acclaimed as a successful playwright, she invited him to a literary evening at her house, and he paid his first visit there five days after the premiere of *The Feast at Solhaug*, on 7 January 1856.

Dean Thoresen has been described as 'a greatly gifted man, witty and eloquent, with a voice like the clearest bell, able to do in an hour what another man could not achieve in a week';[2] and as 'a quiet, sedate and lovable man' who 'never went out but was immensely proud of his beautiful wife'.[3] His first wife, Sara, had died in 1841, aged thirty-five, leaving him two daughters, Suzannah and Marie. Suzannah, in 1856, was nineteen, eight years younger than Ibsen. Her closest friend was a girl of the same age named Karoline Reimers; they 'subscribed to the same lending library, and often sat back to back on a sofa reading novels. They promised each other that if the one should have a son and the other a daughter, the two should marry; and so it turned out'.[4] Karoline Reimers was destined to become the wife of Bjørnstjerne Bjørnson; she lived into her ninety-ninth year, and gave her daughter, Bergliot, a vivid description of Suzannah at that time, which Bergliot recorded nearly a century later:

[1] Halvdan Koht, *Henrik Ibsen, Eit Diktarliv* (Oslo, revised edn, 1954) I, p. 117.
[2] Marcus Grønvold, *op. cit.*, p. 144, quoting his father.
[3] Bergliot Ibsen, *De Tre* (Oslo, 1948), p. 13, presumably quoting either her mother or her mother-in-law.
[4] *ibid.*, p. 13.

K

'The Dean's study was lined with books, and Magdalene Thoresen, being an authoress, gave the house an added literary atmosphere. But Suzannah Thoresen was not just generally interested in literature; she was a book-worm, with a voracious appetite...She was especially interested in the drama, being herself of a dramatic temperament. Her descriptive power was on occasion so imaginative that both her sister Marie and her mother would burst into laughter; but then she would laugh herself, for she had a great sense of humour. But what was most deep-rooted in her nature was, and remained, her sense of the epic in life, her feeling for every-thing that was intense and powerful like herself, her understanding of the monumental and the tragic. No wonder that both her sister Marie and her friend Karoline began to whisper that the young dramatist at the city theatre, Henrik Ibsen, was the man for Suzannah.'[1]

Bergliot herself remembered Suzannah only as 'an old woman, crippled by gout, sitting motionless in a chair, sharp of feature and dim of eye'.[2] But a photograph of her in her early thirties, fifteen years after Ibsen met her, shows a lively face, not classically beautiful but attractive and well-proportioned, with unusually fine eyes. She was famous for the beauty of her hair. 'Everyone in Bergen talked about it,' writes Bergliot Ibsen. 'It was even once weighed on a festive occasion in the town; and it was so long that it stretched right down to her feet like a cloak, chestnut brown and splendidly wavy. Her figure had always been somewhat full, but the taste of the time was different from ours. Her sister Marie was the prettier, but Suzannah's face acquired a beauty from the strength and vitality that coursed through her.'[3]

Suzannah's views on most matters were, partly no doubt thanks to the influence of her stepmother, advanced to the point of radicalism, and she was probably the first 'new woman', apart from Magdalene herself, whom Ibsen had ever met. It is easy to imagine the effect she must have made on the lonely and restless young poet; less easy to guess whether Magdalene, never averse to the admiration of young men (she was later to have a celebrated affair with Georg Brandes, twenty-two years her junior), was pleased to note this, or a little jealous. Ibsen, at any rate, was immediately attracted by Suzannah, and she by him. Their second and decisive meeting took place later that month at a ball in Bergen given by the local Philharmonic Society. Here, Bergliot tells us (and her mother and both parents-in-law were present on the occasion) 'he did not

---

[1] ibid., pp. 13–14.
[2] ibid., p. 17.
[3] ibid., p. 17.

dance, and neither did she. They talked together deep into the night; and that same night he wrote to her that if she would join her destiny to his, he could become something great in the world'. Later he was to recreate the atmosphere of that evening in an exquisite love poem, entitled *To the Only One*.[1]

Ibsen now became a constant visitor to the Thoresen household; which, as Bergliot Ibsen observed, presumably on her mother's information, 'must surely have both astonished and vexed the admired Magdalene Thoresen, to see the young Ibsen paying court to her stepdaughter and not to herself'.[2] Before the end of the month he sought formal permission to ask for Suzannah's hand. Halvdan Koht, who knew both Ibsen and Suzannah and presumably had the story from one or other of them, or perhaps from Karoline Reimers-Bjørnson, tells what followed:

'He went in his best clothes to receive an answer, and was shown into an empty room to wait for her. Time passed, and she did not come. He paced to and fro, sat down, got up, became more and more restless. Finally, in despair, he moved towards the door. Then he heard a laugh from beneath the sofa, and a head peeped out; she had been hiding there all the time. She gave him her answer, and they became engaged'.[3]

His position and prospects were, however, not yet adequate to support a wife, and it was to be two and a half years before they could marry.

Magdalene Thoresen commented briefly: 'The engagement went off very quietly, and gave not the slightest occasion for strong outbursts of emotion'.[4] Her attitude towards her future stepson-in-law remained, throughout her long life, curiously ambivalent. 'Henrik Ibsen,' she continues in the same memoir, recorded in 1871, 'was a silent, withdrawn person whom no one got closer to than he, Ibsen, wished. This strong reserve became the weapon with which he kept clear the ground about him...Even in one of his more

---

[1] It has sometimes been stated that he sent her this poem that same night as a form of proposal, but this seems rather doubtful. He wrote several other poems to Suzannah during their courtship, but only one other has survived; she destroyed the rest, and also, it seems, all his early letters to her, shortly before her death. 'Our relationship,' she said, 'concerns no one but ourselves.' She was, to the last, the most formidably inflexible of women.

[2] Bergliot Ibsen, *op. cit.*, p. 18.

[3] Koht, *op. cit.*, I, p. 125.

[4] Interview with G. Knudtzon on 28 April 1871, checked and added to by Magdalene, first printed in *Juleroser* (Copenhagen, 1901), and reprinted with comments in Karl Larsen's introduction to his edition of *Henrik Ibsens episke Brand* (Copenhagen and Christiania, 1907).

inspired moods, when he would be caught up in a swift exchange of conversation and ideas, his personality was on guard, and the famous "three steps from life" were never crossed...Even with the woman who approached him willingly and admiringly he seemed to lack the abandon to yield to her power of enchantment. As a young man he had a certain awkwardness about him, as though groping for a foothold, which in most people would have suggested a mental confusion. But his clear glance was so firm and sure that no one could doubt that this man knew where he was going. Yet one couldn't help smiling at him.'

'Even with the woman who approached him willingly and admiringly...' It is difficult not to believe that Magdalene was speaking here from personal experience. Ibsen, after all, was eight years her junior; and Bjørnson, who was to succeed Ibsen at Bergen the following year, was four years younger than Ibsen. 'I know immediately,' she recorded later, 'if I make an impression on people and gain power over them. It happened with Bjørnson. We two understood each other at once, we shared the same instincts...I was born anew, I understood myself, it was then that I first really became a writer. No one has been as spiritually akin to me as he was, he is in truth my spiritual father. I had to love him.'[1] The pattern was to be repeated with the yet younger Georg Brandes.

Magdalene, in the same memoir, goes on to make an interesting comparison between Ibsen and another writer of genius whom she had met in her own country of Denmark. 'One couldn't restrain an involuntary smile—and that awoke a memory. As a young girl I had once met Søren Kierkegaard. It now occurs to me that there was a striking similarity between these two great spirits. Outwardly the resemblance was small; Søren Kierkegaard was longstriding and gangling, while Ibsen took short paces and had the squat build of a miner. What similarity there was must, therefore, have lain deeper; and so it was. I have never seen in any other two persons, male or female, so marked a compulsion to be alone with themselves.'

That spring of 1856 was a good one for Ibsen. On 13 March *The Feast at Solhaug* was produced in Christiania, and received a considerable ovation. Six days later it was published there by Christian Tønsberg—the first book by Ibsen to appear since *Catiline*, and the first to carry his name on the title page.[2] Critical opinion, admittedly, was less favourable than the reception by the first night audience had been; he was accused of having plagiarised both Henrik Hertz's *Svend Dyring's House*, an inferior melodrama written ten years earlier

[1] *Breve fra Magdalene Thoresen* (Copenhagen, 1919), p. 43.
[2] It sold poorly, however; it took fifteen years to exhaust the small edition.

(and which Ibsen had directed on 24 February 1856 in Bergen), and Heinrich von Kleist's *Kätchen von Heilbronn*—a charge which the Danish press later repeated, and which Ibsen was angrily to rebut in his 1883 foreword to *The Feast at Solhaug*, concluding his assault on the critics by expressing the hope that 'people may in the future allow to each of us three Henriks undisputed possession of what rightly belongs to him'. One of the few critics to praise the play in print was Bjørnson who, we must remember, had at this time scarcely met Ibsen, and who wrote a dynamic notice of the work in *Morgenbladet*. 'It was,' commented Ibsen in the same foreword, 'not in the real sense a review or a criticism, but rather a brilliant free fantasy, a poetic improvisation on the subject of the play and its performance.' *The Feast at Solhaug* was repeated five times in Christiania that season, a sign of fair success for a comparatively serious work.

While all this was happening in Christiania, Ibsen was far to the north in Trondhjem where, under his supervision, the Bergen company had just arrived to play a short season. He wrote four business-like reports to his board that March; practical matters kept him very busy. 'I am pleased to inform you,' he told them on 3 March, 'that we all arrived here in good order on Sunday afternoon. During Monday and Tuesday we obtained the permission of the local authorities to hold performances, engaged orchestral players, singers, walk-ons, a property master, etc. Subscription lists were issued and circulated in the town. I have succeeded in agreeing inexpensive terms for the hire and improvement of the more essential items of decor...Yesterday (Wednesday) we presented *Bureaucracy*[1] and *The Monkey*.[2] Fru Isaachsen has still lost her voice, so I gave her role (in the first-named play) to Frøken Jensen, who acquitted herself well...The takings at yesterday's performance amounted to 122 specie-dollars (£30), which must be reckoned good, especially considering the dreadful weather and the choice of plays; *Bureaucracy* has a poor reputation here, having been twice very ill played by Danish actors (and whistled), while *The Monkey* has been acted here innumerable times. But...both plays were greeted with loud and sustained applause. Interest in our theatre is great...The gas lighting is calculated to cost roughly 3 specie-dollars (15s.) per performance, rehearsals included.'

Having got the Trondhjem season safely launched, he sought permission to come home before the rest of the company. 'Although actual theatrical matters occupy only a small part of my time during our stay here in Trondhjem,' he wrote to the board on 31 March, 'daily trivialities prevent me from

---

[1] A comedy by F. L. Høedt based on Jean François Bayard's *Un Château des Cartes*.
[2] A vaudeville by Johanne Luise Heiberg.

concentrating in peace on a task which it is essential that I complete as soon as possible; I therefore beg your permission to return to Bergen by the next steamer.' He was not, as far as we know, working on any new play at the time, but the company was due to stay in Trondhjem for a further two months, and three months, especially in the Scandinavian spring, is a dangerously long time to leave a self-willed young lady without an escort. The board, whether or not they knew the real reason for his restlessness (and in a town as small as Bergen, one suspects that they did) agreed to his request and sent Laading up to replace him. A month later *The Feast at Solhaug* was added to the repertory there, and on 26 May Laading reported that it was a success. 'After the performance,' he added, 'we gathered on the stage and drank Ibsen's health on the house. After the dessert the bride and bridegroom [*sic*] were toasted, and H. Nielsen was authorised to convey to Ibsen and his chosen one the good wishes of the entire company.'

That summer the theatre at Bergen was honoured, and nearly bankrupted, by two royal visits. In July Crown Prince Carl, soon to become King Carl XV, announced his intention of descending on the town, together with the young Prince of Orange. The theatre was redecorated for the occasion, an expense which could ill be afforded; and a grand banquet was laid on, including, so Peter Blytt (who, as chairman of the board, was principally responsible) tells us, 'every wine of the choicest vintage'. The two princes were expected in the early afternoon, and the reception committee, together with the garrison, a band and most of the populace, assembled at three o'clock to welcome him. They waited; hour after hour passed; but no prince appeared. Evening came, and still there was no sign. Eventually, at midnight, the royal vessel was sighted, and anchored a mile offshore. The Crown Prince had enjoyed the ale and, no doubt, the other attractions provided for him at Hardanger so much that he had refused to leave, 'despite repeated reminders from his distinguished entourage'. Now, however, he was here, and would soon surely be rowed ashore in the royal barge by the pick of Bergen's oarsmen, who had joined the ship at Hardanger for this purpose. But no barge was to be seen, and it was not until nearly one o'clock in the morning that the princes finally landed, ten hours late, from a small dinghy. The Bergen oarsmen had, shameful to relate, regaled themselves over-merrily like their master, and had smashed the barge against the buoy.

The royal visitors stepped ashore amid huzzas, but there were further worries in store. The Crown Prince's equerry asked what play was to be performed on the morrow and, when informed that it was to be a new musical comedy 'with witty songs' by Jens Christian Hostrup entitled *Fun in the Army*, declared that under no circumstances could this be shown, since the Crown Prince regarded one of the characters as an insult to Sweden. At a few hours notice, therefore, the theatre had to substitute J. L. Heiberg's vaudeville *No*, which passed without offence. Even then, their troubles were not over. When, at the banquet, the Crown Prince was asked what he would like to drink, he graciously enquired what they had. 'I think', said Blytt proudly, 'we can say we have anything that your Royal Highness could demand.' The Crown Prince replied that if this was so, he would like nothing better than a glass of Hardanger ale, which he had sampled the previous day for the first time and thought the best beer he had ever tasted. This was, of course, the one thing that the organisers had not thought of, and Blytt had to keep the Crown Prince engaged in what must have been a thirsty conversation while emissaries hastened into the town to knock up the more discriminating beer-drinkers and ask if they could supply the need. But none of the ale could be found, and 'their Royal Highnesses had to slake their thirst with other beverages, which Orange, who was scarcely more than 17 or 18, did so thoroughly that H.R.H. became quite unsteady'.[1]

That was awkward enough for everyone concerned with the theatre, but it was nothing to what followed. On the afternoon of Saturday 23 August Prince Napoleon, the son of King Jerome Napoleon and nephew to Napoleon I, landed completely unannounced in the city, asked if it contained a theatre and, on learning that it did, 'thrice expressed the wish to see a performance' on the following day, before departing on the Monday. The theatre was by now closed for the summer recess, the actors were all holidaying out of town, and the Prince's request did not reach Peter Blytt until ten o'clock that Saturday night, when he was in bed with a painful attack of gout, and had to go to be presented to the Prince wearing one shoe and one galosh, the afflicted foot being too swollen to take any more elaborate form of footwear. Blytt did not quite see how the company could be reassembled and re-rehearsed in what was, after all, less than twenty-four hours; however, he said he would see what could be done, and sent a message to Ibsen telling him to come and see him at once.

Ibsen, who had also gone to bed, in due course appeared, 'evidently in no good humour', and told the board that what they were asking was quite impossible. Blytt asked whether, since most of the company, including the leading players, were known to be together at Kolstien just outside town, a messenger could not be sent to summon them back. Reluctantly Ibsen wrote a letter, asking them to return first thing in the morning; then, after it had been despatched, 'became more abrupt and unforthcoming than usual. He spoke

---

[1] This anecdote and the one which follows are related in detail by Blytt (*op. cit.*, pp. 88 *ff.*).

only when directly addressed, and made no suggestions as to how the various difficulties might be overcome. Suddenly he jumped up and said with vehement irritability: "No, it's no good—I've just remembered. We have no orchestra. All the wind instruments have been commandeered for tomorrow by the steamer *Patriot* for its cruise to Hardanger. I'd forgotten."'

Blytt said that this could surely be countermanded. Ibsen still shook his head. Then Blytt had a brilliant idea. 'It would be a pity if we had to cancel the performance,' he said, 'for the play we had in mind to show his Royal Highness was *The Feast at Solhaug*. It is as Norwegian as anything in our repertory—Norwegian author, Norwegian subject, Norwegian costumes—all of which unfamiliar material cannot but enrapture Prince Napoleon.' At this, Blytt tells, 'a marked change became noticeable in Ibsen. He suddenly became transformed into a bundle of energy and vitality, and looked interested, happy and hopeful. The difficulties began to vanish'. Ibsen promised to conduct a rehearsal at eight the next morning. The wives of the board, plus Magdalene Thoresen, were bidden to prepare a supper of, indigestible as it sounds, 'ice cream, cakes, fruit, confectionery and champagne', and to lend their best china and silver, 'there being no hotel in the town then'. Real gold and silver cups for use on stage in the performance were to be borrowed from local goldsmiths, and posters were to be run off by a relative of one member of the board who fortunately happened to be a printer, so that the citizens might be informed and a full audience assembled.

Early the next morning Blytt received a note from Ibsen telling him that 'the company had arrived early and in the best of spirits, delighted at the honour of being asked to play before Prince Napoleon'. And at seven o'clock that Sunday evening the performance took place. Prince Napoleon, who knew no Norwegian, had asked for a written synopsis of the play in French; but the few French and French-speaking people in the city were all engaged in the preparations for the banquet, except for the local barber who was regarded as unsuitable. Blytt, however, knew German and, on enquiring whether the Prince understood that language, and finding that he did, having, surprisingly, taught it once in Alsace ('the reader of these lines may shake his head in doubt, but I can swear on my honour and conscience that Prince Napoleon actually told me this'), stood behind him throughout the performance, despite his gout (and still clad in a galosh?), giving the Prince and his suite, which included Ernest Renan, a brief resumé before each act of what was to come.

During the second interval the author and his company were presented, whereupon 'Ibsen offered the Prince a handwritten copy of the play bound in red Morocco. He received it graciously, took wine with Ibsen, and promised that he would see that the play was translated into French and performed at the

Imperial private theatre at St Cloud.[1] He also ordered a copy, exactly similar in colour and cut, to be made of the costume that Louise Brun had worn [as Margit], which, executed in silk and velvet, he proposed to present to the Empress Eugénie. This, before being despatched, was exhibited in Bergen, and aroused much admiration'. The Prince enjoyed his visit so much that he postponed his departure by a day, and attended a special ball hastily arranged by some local bigwigs, to which Ibsen and several of the company but, to Blytt's rage, on account of some private quarrel, none of the board were invited.

Some time during that summer or autumn Ibsen settled down, no doubt with greatly increased confidence, to write another play for the next January anniversary. After the success of The Feast at Solhaug it seemed obvious to attempt another comedy in the balladic manner; and he bethought himself of the theme on which he had begun to work during his first year at Christiania in 1850, and raked out the unfinished manuscript of The Ptarmigan of Justedal.

To complete this in its original metre would have meant abandoning the style which had served him so well in The Feast at Solhaug, for The Ptarmigan at Justedal was, so far as it went, written in unrhymed blank verse, and Ibsen wished to use again a mixture of prose and rhymed verse of varying rhythms as found in the ballads. He therefore rewrote it completely, retaining only the original idea of a girl (still named Alfhild) who was the sole survivor in a valley devastated by the Black Death, and thus lived a wild, bird-like existence uncontaminated by the materialism of civilisation; and also the character of the wandering singer. Apart from this he kept nothing. Not a single line of The Ptarmigan in Justedal is carried over.

He found the theme for his new play in a ballad in Landstad's collection about a character named Olaf Liljekrans, who, whilst out riding the evening before his wedding, is killed by fairies because he will not let them seduce him into joining them. Ibsen set his drama in the Middle Ages, in a village in the Norwegian mountains. Two families have waged a vendetta for generations; now their two present heads, Arne of Guldvik and Dame Kirsten Liljekrans, have decided to end the quarrel and merge their fortunes by marrying Dame Kirsten's son Olaf to Arne's daughter Ingeborg. In a spirited opening scene, Arne and his followers, on their way to the wedding, are met by Dame Kirsten in a state of great confusion; Olaf has disappeared. Wandering in the mountains, he has met the strange, half-elfin girl Alfhild, and has been bewitched by her innocence (as Johannes, in St John's Night, was bewitched by the innocence of the unworldly Anne). Arne suspects trickery, and his daughter, Ingeborg, is furious; she is in any case half-infatuated with her father's servant,

[1] Neither of which things happened.

Hemming. However, Olaf and Alfhild are now discovered, and are persuaded to come down to the village; Dame Kirsten thinks she can settle things by marrying off Alfhild to one of her servants.

Alfhild is told that a wedding will be arranged for her, and assumes in her innocence that her husband is to be Olaf. He, meanwhile, back among civilised people, weakly agrees to marry Ingeborg. When Alfhild discovers the truth, she bars the doors and windows of the house, sets fire to it and flees back into the mountains. The guests manage to get out, and Ingeborg runs away with Hemming, also into the mountains; she no longer wishes to marry a man who does not love her. Dame Kirsten, Arne and their followers pursue Alfhild and capture her; then, on the mountain-side, Dame Kirsten, as is her right under feudal law, sentences Alfhild to be thrown to her death unless any man can be found willing to marry her. She proclaims this twice, and no one answers; at the third and final proclamation, however, Olaf claims her as his. Dame Kirsten has no alternative but to accept the situation, and Arne reluctantly has to agree to his daughter, Ingeborg, marrying his servant Hemming (being much more worried at the prospect of losing his best servant than at his daughter marrying beneath her).

Olaf Liljekrans was immediately accepted by the theatre for production the following January. During the last three months of 1856, before he got down to directing it, Ibsen found himself staging several worthwhile plays of a much better class than had usually fallen to his lot—none of them, needless to say, new. In October he produced two of Holberg's best comedies, *The Scatterbrain* and *Erasmus Montanus;* in November, Oehlenschläger's *The Vikings in Byzantium;* and in December, Scribe's best comedy, and perhaps the only play by him that stands revival today, *A Glass of Water,* which is set at the court of Queen Anne and has as its main characters the Queen, Bolingbroke and the Duchess of Marlborough. (What with this play, Dumas's *Katharine Howard,* and two comedies by Alexandre Duval called *La Jeunnesse d'Henri V* and *Edouard en Ecosse, ou La Nuit d'un Proscrit,* which he had directed earlier, Ibsen was learning a lot of bad English history). He also busied himself with preparing a lecture on *The Heroic Ballad and its Significance to Modern Poetry* which he was due to deliver to the 22 December Society the following February, and which he later expanded into a lengthy essay.

After the success of *The Feast at Solhaug,* there was a great rush for seats for *Olaf Liljekrans* when it was announced for 2 January 1857. According to *Bergens Tidende,* 'the demand was so great that only the stronger succeeded in forcing their way to the box office, under the present somewhat unfortunate arrangements for the sale of tickets'. It was quite cordially received at its first performance, and the board rewarded Ibsen with an honorarium of 100 specie-dollars (£25), a large sum when one considers his salary; but after his previous play expectations had been high, and among the public, and even more so among the critics, there was a feeling of disappointment. Peter Blytt noted that it was 'little understood, and was not a success; the audience which had filled the theatre, hugely expectant, left in a cool mood'.[1] Ibsen took a curtain call, and Marcus Grønvold, who was present, remembered him many years later 'pale, thin and with a full black beard'.[2] *Bergens Tidende* admired the 'pretty versification, and often beautiful and poetic images', but plainly thought little of the plot, which it summarised disparagingly; and the correspondent of the Christiania *Aftenbladet* expressed himself bewildered by 'all the confusion' of the action. (Ibsen reacted to the latter criticism with a sharp letter demanding that the reviewer justify his 'mischievous and irresponsible' remarks, but received no reply). The play was repeated only once, on 4 January, and was never performed again in Ibsen's lifetime; nor was it published until shortly before his death, over forty years later. Ibsen himself rejected it as completely as *St John's Night*. When writing to Julius Elias in 1897 about his various early works, he deliberately omitted all mention of it, and subsequent commentators have rather slavishly accepted his judgment.

In fact, *Olaf Liljekrans* is by modern standards a much better play than *The Feast at Solhaug*, or indeed than any other play that Ibsen had yet written except *Lady Inger of Østraat*. The principal characters are all sharply drawn: Olaf and Alfhild, confused and unhappy poetic creatures in a materialistic world; the crusty and avaricious Arne, the domineering Dame Kirsten, the spoiled, self-willed Ingeborg and the proud, lonely minstrel Thorgejr, who acts as a kind of chorus to the action. The plot, which so confused the critic of *Aftenbladet*, is more complex than that of *The Feast at Solhaug*, which one would have thought a trifle uncomplicated even for the Bergen public, but it is less unravellable than that of *Lady Inger;* to a modern eye its complexity, yet lack of obscurity, is one of its virtues. The rhymed verse anticipates *Peer Gynt* in the freedom with which it changes from one rhythm to another; and here and there one perceives motifs which were to be echoed more strongly in his later, maturer work. The contrast between the purity of life on the mountain and the corruption in the valley was one on which Ibsen was to dwell in his long poem *On the Heights*, in *Brand* and, forty years later, in *When We Dead Awaken*. The reference to Alfhild's mother Ingrid, who was stolen by the minstrel Thorgejr on her wedding night and carried by him up into the mountain, is a clear anticipation of what was to happen to that other Ingrid in *Peer Gynt*. Moreoever, Ingeborg's

---

[1] Blytt, *op. cit.*, p. 12.
[2] Grønvold, *op. cit.*, p. 140.

and Hemming's discovery in the last act that life on the mountain is not as idyllic as they had supposed, and that to feed and clothe oneself are practical problems that even the most romantic among us must face, shows that Ibsen, unlike some of his contemporaries who were attempting the same kind of play, had no illusions about the supposedly idyllic life of the countryside.

The main difficulty to a modern reader, and one which would probably prove insuperable upon the stage, lies in Alfhild herself. Two types of character are notoriously difficult to make convincing in the theatre, mad people and peasants, and a mad peasant-girl offers a formidable challenge to any actress and audience. Gerd, in *Brand*, can be made acceptable because she appears only in three brief scenes; but Alfhild is the leading character in *Olaf Liljekrans*, and Ibsen has, it must be admitted, put a deal of rather mawkish dialogue into her mouth. The play, depending as it does so much upon the lyrical quality and subtle rhyming of the dialogue, would be monstrously difficult to translate, and will probably never be adequately translated; but it is not to be dismissed as negligible.[1]

One curious relic of *Olaf Liljekrans* has survived in the form of six coloured drawings from Ibsen's hand. They have the appearance of costume designs; all are of characters in mediaeval rustic dress. Two, which are similar, show a young man in national costume, confused and distraught, his fists clenched; the others, respectively, are of an oldish man with a staff, a stern middle-aged woman with arms akimbo and a threatening expression, and two young girls, both wearing bridal crowns, the one shy and innocent, the other sharp-eyed and purposeful. We have no direct evidence that these represent the characters in *Olaf Liljekrans*, but they correspond precisely to Olaf, Arne of Kildal (or possibly Thorgejr), Dame Kirsten, Alfhild and Ingeborg.

On 2 February 1857 Ibsen delivered a lecture on *The Heroic Ballad and its Significance to Modern Poetry* to the 22 December Society. On 17 April he sent an expanded version of this to Paul Botten Hansen in Christiania, hoping that the latter might accept it for publication in *Illustreret Nyhedsblad*, a literary periodical which he was now editing. The letter which accompanied this essay is, apart from business reports and requests to the board of the Bergen theatre, a note to the publisher of *The Feast at Solhaug*, the brief letter to Botten Hansen in 1853 which has already been referred to, and a line of thanks to a lady in

---

[1] The prose, too, bears the marked and not altogether fortunate influence of the Icelandic sagas (or Petersen's translation of them), in the frequent inversion of the natural word order—'Little shall it boot you....', etc. The unnaturalness of verse works in the theatre; unnatural prose seldom does, except in comedy. But the discovery of this fact, and its corollary, that high tragedy could be written in ordinary colloquial prose, still lay many years ahead.

Bergen for praising *The Feast at Solhaug,* the first letter that we have from Ibsen's hand since that which he wrote to Ole Schulerud from Grimstad seven years previously, enclosing his elegy on the death of Oehlenschläger:

Bergen, 17 April 1857

My dear old friend!

I send you herewith, first and foremost, my warmest greetings, and secondly, some observations on the Heroic Ballad, in the hope that they may be found worthy of acceptance in your paper. Should you be willing to make use of the article, I beg that you print it in as large instalments as possible, and above all that you break it where most appropriate, and finally, that you pay particular care to correcting any errors oj spelling or punctuation that you may find; for as I have, as you will see, had the manuscript fair-copied by someone else, and have only managed to glance through it.

I have often meant to write to you, but have always put it off, I once thought of sending you some travel articles, but nothing came of that either—however, this summer I intend to go on a long tour, and then perhaps I shall be able to send something which you can use.

Of my life here I can think of nothing of interest to tell you, except that last year I became—engaged to a daughter of Dean Thoresen here in Bergen (her stepmother is the authoress of A Witness *and one or two other things which you have at various times reviewed in* Nyhedsbladet).

I must thank you most warmly for your notice of The Feast at Solhaug; *I sent my new play,* Olaf Liljekrans, *to the Christiania Theatre a couple of months ago, but Borgaard is not one of those who hurry about anything. My best play,* Lady Inger of Østraat, *he has refused to include in his repertory unless I make several changes, which I wasn't prepared to agree to; around the New Year I sent it to Chr. Tønsberg in the hope that he might publish it, which he couldn't for the time being, and since it is extremely important for me to get this, my best play, published, I beg you to take the matter in hand and do what you can for me. The play is with Tønsberg, read it through and—find me a publisher! I don't mind on what terms—I'll gladly forego payment if you can only get it printed—I'm sure that if you could be so kind as to try to do this for me, we'd succeed. It has occurred to me that it might possibly be published in aid of the Students' Union Building Fund—I would gladly preface the play with a short prologue dedicated to the youth of our three countries and the future of Scandinavianism. Dear friend! please help me—I give you a free hand with* Lady Inger, *bully a publisher till he gives in!!*

Please send me a line as quickly as possible! Let me know how everything is with you and with our mutual friends in Christiania.

Best wishes,

Your affectionate

Henr: Ibsen

Eleven days later he writes again to Botten Hansen:

Bergen, 28 April 1857

Dear friend!

A brief line only, since the post is about to leave. Call my article, if you agree: On the Heroic Ballad and its Significance to Modern Poetry. *I cannot immediately think of any title which more accurately describes its content—*A Note on...etc. *might not be bad—I could have written at ten times the length on this subject—but since the expression is '*Ole-Vigsk*'—forget it!*

Your suggestion of printing Lady Inger *in Nyhedsbladet, and then doing an offprint, I think absolutely splendid. But the play won't possibly fit into two numbers; the best thing would be if each issue could contain* one *act. I trust that the offprint will be tastefully and attractively done, and give you full authority to handle the play as though it were your own property, and in particular to recover the manuscript which I previously offered to Hr Tønsberg, for which purpose I enclose the necessary authorisation.*

I should dearly like to see Olaf Liljekrans *published in a similar manner as soon as it has been acted at the Christiania Theatre; but I still haven't heard a word from Borgaard about this. I feel strongly inclined to start a campaign against him about his refusal to stage* Lady Inger *in its present form. According to his letters he finds the play 'poetic, full of good characterisations and powerful dramatic moments'—and yet— well, you'll be able to understand his motives when you read the play.*

As regards payment etc., I beg you to arrange everything as you think best, I shall be happy with whatever you decide. One thing more: in Lady Inger *I have once or twice referred to the Lady's dead husband as Lord High Steward Henrik Gyldenløve, but I have since found that he was called 'Niels Henrikson Gyldenløve'—but since there are already two Nielses among the characters apart from him, will you please just call him 'Lord High Steward Gyldenløve' (with no Christian name). If you could drop me a line and tell me what you think of the play as soon as you have read it, I should be particularly grateful.*

If you meet O. Schulerud, give him my regards. Abildgaard—yes, how are things with him? Why don't you make a trip to these parts? You'd find it rewarding; the landscape is magnificent; quite something apart.

Best wishes for now—I know you will do whatever is best for me.

Yours affectionately,
Henr. Ibsen.

I am already working on a new play; it will be rather different from my previous works, in both tone and content.

H.I.

This 'new play' was *The Vikings at Helgeland*, which he had begun to write in verse, but was to complete in prose in Christiania during the autumn.[1] His contract at Bergen had expired on 1 April, and on 11 April he had signed for one more year; but in the event he was to stay in Bergen only for another five months.

Ibsen's article on *The Heroic Ballad* appeared in *Illustreret Nyhedsblad* on 10 and 17 May 1857, in two instalments each of about 3,500 words. It is a skilfully reasoned defence of his use of the ballad style in *The Feast at Solhaug* and *Olaf Liljekrans*. 'The time will come,' he wrote, 'when our national poetry will return to the ballad as to an inexhaustible gold-mine; cleansed, renewed to its original purity, and elevated through art, it will then once again strike root in the people.' He also made the interesting point that 'it must some day surely be admitted that the iambic pentameter is far from being the most suitable metre for the treatment of ancient Scandinavian themes. This verse form is completely foreign to our national prosody, and only through a national *form* can full justice be done to national subjects...The flexible metre of the ballad allows many liberties that are of great importance to dramatic dialogue, and there can be little doubt that this poetic source will sooner or later be used by poets who will exploit it to build upon the foundation laid by Oehlenschläger; for it is surely clear that his work can only be regarded as a foundation, and by this I imply no denigration of his talent, since it is a characteristic of whatever is good and beautiful that it is not a complete end in itself but contains within it the germs of a more absolute fulfilment.'

Ibsen then goes on to make the point that the ancient ballad succeeds as no modern form does in reconciling the two worlds of the natural and the supernatural. 'The Asa-worshipper, who was ignorant of the power of faith, created for himself a world in which the laws of reason were completely suspended; in this, the supernatural became *All*, and consequently *Nothing*, and thus he found a *modus vivendi*, this he succeeded in reconciling faith with reason. The romantic view of life, on the other hand, follows another course, it pays homage to Shakespeare's thesis that "there are more things in heaven and earth than are dreamed of in our philosophy"; it concedes the power and validity of reason, but together with, surrounding and permeating this is the Mystery, the riddling, the inexplicable, the Christian if one wishes so to call it, since Christianity is itself a mystery; it preaches faith in those things "which are beyond comprehension". This is where the mythical saga differs essentially from the ballad; the one is to the other as an ordinary story is to a fairy tale; the ordinary

---

[1] According to Henrik Jæger's notes of his conversations with Ibsen on 2 September 1887 (Midbøe, *op. cit.*, p. 143), Ibsen said that he finished the first two acts of *The Vikings at Helgeland* before leaving Bergen.

story does not embrace the miraculous, the fairy tale is rooted therein. It is this world, where the natural and supernatural co-exist, that the ballad reveals to us.'

Hettner's teaching is apparent here; and the problem of reconciling the best of heathenism with the best of Christianity was one that he was to consider in *The Vikings at Helgeland* and to explore more deeply in *Emperor and Galilean*.

We know, disappointingly, virtually nothing of Ibsen's activities during this, his last summer in Bergen. He must have felt that the little town had nothing more to offer him, artistically or materially. He could not marry Suzannah on any salary that the Bergen theatre seemed likely to pay him in the foreseeable future; he badly needed the security of married life, they had already been engaged for a year and a half, and he must have felt that if this delay were to continue indefinitely, he might well lose her. Nor can the apparently unending prospect of directing Scribe and his followers have offered any incentive to remain.

Suddenly an avenue of escape appeared. He got leave from 9 July until the end of August, and on 17 July he wrote to Botten Hansen in the capital:

My dear friend,
Tomorrow I leave on a three weeks visit to Christiania. Should you by any chance know how one acquires a decent room for such a period, you would be doing me a great service. I hope this letter will find you in town—I am trusting to Nyhedsbladet to keep you there—even now when everyone is moving out into the country—for the chief purpose of my trip is to enjoy myself and see old friends again. In great haste—
Your affectionate
Henr. Ibsen.

He arrived in Christiania on 21 July. Two days later he wrote the following letter:

Christiania, 23 July 1857
To the Directors of the Norwegian Theatre at Bergen:
On my arrival in Christiania I saw in the newspapers a report which has probably by now also reached Bergen, and which I should accordingly like to correct. It asserts that the directors of the Norwegian Theatre in Christiania have entered into negotiations with me with a view to my taking over the post of artistic director at the Norwegian Theatre, recently vacated by Cronborg.
The facts are as follows. Some time before my departure from Bergen G. Krohn[1] received a letter from Engineer-Lieutenant Lund in which the head of the Norwegian

---

[1] An actor at the Bergen Theatre. He later joined Ibsen at the Christiania Norwegian Theatre.

Theatre enquired whether he knew of anyone in Bergen who might be willing to accept the aforesaid post. Krohn disclosed to me the contents of this letter (which was confidential), and I told him that if I could obtain release from my contract with the Bergen Theatre, and if the terms proposed by Christiania should prove acceptable, I might not be unwilling to accept such an offer. Krohn replied to them on these lines, and on the day I left Bergen I received from Lieut. Lund, on behalf of his directors, an offer to take over the aforesaid post at an annual salary of 600 specie-dollars, with the promise of a gratuity and an increase in salary as soon as the theatre could afford it.

The reason, gentlemen, that I did not inform you of this situation lay simply in the uncertainty which I felt about the whole matter; I felt I had to come and assure myself at first-hand of the theatre's circumstances and prospects, etc. This I have now done, and I am now satisfied that the Christiania Theatre is as securely established as that of Bergen, and that here, as there, there is a chance that something may be achieved. I need not stress the advantages there would be to me in living in the capital, they are overwhelming, and painful as it would be to me to leave Bergen and the Bergen Theatre, I cannot but question whether it would not be indefensible of me to reject the opportunity which now presents itself of taking up a not unrewarding post. I speak in terms of salary and material advantages, but I am, please believe me, not merely being mercenary, or ungrateful, I shall never forget the debt I owe to the Bergen Theatre, but I also have duties towards myself, and I have long found working conditions at the Bergen Theatre oppressive, every way in which I might achieve anything has been barred to me, my hands have never been free, and I have as a result felt daily frustrated by the consciousness of having to work without being able to accomplish what I desired. In now addressing myself to you and asking whether, in the event of my agreeing terms with the Christiania Theatre, I may be released from my duties at Bergen, and how soon—I regard myself as appealing not merely to my superiors, but also to benevolent counsellors who will not refuse to look at the situation from what is, to me, its most important aspect. Should I be released from the remainder of my contract, I should naturally feel bound to refund my last month's salary, which has been paid in full. I need scarcely add that, offered equal conditions, I should prefer to remain at the Bergen Theatre, where I regard myself as having grown up, but I know that the theatre cannot stretch its resources further than has already been done, and I feel sure you will not be surprised that I feel compelled to seize this opportunity of a securer future. I await your reply eagerly.

Your obedient servant,

Henr. Ibsen

During the days of waiting to know their decision, he renewed his acquaintance with Bjørnstjerne Bjørnson, whom he had met occasionally during his student period in Christiania and who was just completing *Synnøve Solbakken*, the

peasant novel that was to make him famous. 'Ibsen has come from Bergen—
Read his *Feast at Solhaug*'! wrote Bjørnson to the Danish critic Clemens Petersen
on 2 August; adding: 'I love him!!' On 4 August Herman Laading replied to
Ibsen on behalf of the Bergen directors 'regretting that your application should
come at a time when, as you must know, any reduction in the number of our
instructors will be especially felt, since with the departure of Brun [in April]
practically the whole of our repertory has been dislocated; but the board feel
that the obvious advantages which must ensue to you from your new appointment and from living in the capital must override other considerations. We
therefore release you from your contract with the Bergen Theatre, and
wish you every luck in your work for your new theatre, whose goal is our
own.'

On 11 August 1857 Ibsen signed a contract with the Norwegian Theatre of
Christiania. On 21 August *Morgenbladet* announced: 'Hr Ibsen's appointment as
stage instructor and artistic director at the Christiania Norwegian Theatre has
now been confirmed. His salary is to comprise $7\frac{1}{2}\%$ of the theatre's gross
takings against a guaranteed minimum salary of 600 specie-dollars (£150) per
year. He has, as is well known, worked for five years at the Bergen Theatre,
whither he has now returned to make preparations for his final removal. He
is expected here at the end of the month.'

Ibsen left Bergen as unheralded as he had arrived—indeed, more so, for no
newspaper thought it worth while to inform its readers of his departure, the
date of which remains unknown. He said farewell to his fiancée and on 3
September took up his new post in Christiania.

He had, including his study trip to Copenhagen and Dresden, spent five years
and ten months in Bergen. They had, after the first excitement, been extremely
frustrating. As a director, his hands had been tied; as an author, he had repeatedly seen every attempt he had made to experiment and diverge from either
the antiquated conventions of static verse tragedy, or the banalities of nationalistic rustic comedy, derided. His voyage abroad had opened his eyes to the potentialities of theatrical art; he had seen *Hamlet* and *King Lear*, met Heiberg and
Hans Andersen, seen Michael Wiehe and N. P. Nielsen, Johanne Luise Heiberg
and Frederik Høedt, Emil Devrient and Boguwil Dawison act. Bergen must
have seemed more than usually provincial to him after that, and he must have
been hideously aware of the inadequacy of the performances which he directed,
whether of his own plays or of others.

Nevertheless, it is easy to overstress his depression. He may well have felt
that, in spite of everything, he had developed his powers not unprofitably
during those five years. He had written four full-length plays in that time, and
re-written a fifth; admittedly, all but one had failed, but there is some evidence

that even the 'failures' were admired by a discerning minority. Some writers and artists, particularly if they are restless experimentalists, as Ibsen was to be all his life, are content with such recognition; conscious of the power and quality of their work, they know with the certainty of religionists that they are right and other people wrong. What they normally need is one other person who shares their faith in themselves; and this he had now found. As he packed his bags that August day in Bergen, Ibsen may well have felt that his time of fulfilment and recognition was at hand. If so, he was to be unpleasantly disillusioned. The six and a half years he was to spend in Christiania were to be far more chilling to his spirit than anything he had experienced in Bergen, or Grimstad, or Skien.

SIX

✵ The Chicken Ladder

(1857-1859)

THE NORWEGIAN THEATRE OF CHRISTIANIA, of which Ibsen now, in the autumn of 1857, found himself artistic director, was a more recent enterprise than its counterpart in Bergen, and we must briefly examine its origins. At first a drama school, it had been founded in 1852 as an angry reaction by a few extreme patriots against what they regarded as the failure of the Bergen Theatre to live up to its expressed ideals.

The previous year, 1851, some working-class amateurs had given a few performances in the vernacular at a Christiania theatre owned by Benedict Klingenberg to raise money for such of their fellows as had been arrested for supporting Marcus Thrane's socialist agitations. These performances had increased the demand, already strong in the capital, for a theatre to express the growing tide of nationalistic enthusiasm. Klingenberg had accordingly visited Bergen, and had been badly disillusioned by what he saw. Not only were very few of the plays in the repertory Norwegian, and the near-Danish *riksmaal* as much in evidence as the vernacular; worst of all, Klingenberg was appalled to note that many of the actors spoke with a deliberately Danish intonation. On his return to Christiania he formed a committee of three (the other two members, oddly enough, both being Danes) to establish, as they proclaimed in turgid language, 'a training school for Norwegians who might have a talent for, and wish to pursue, a dramatic career, but who lack the opportunity to acquire sufficient education to enter the [Danish-controlled] Christiania Theatre, where, in any event, the essentially foreign character of the organisation proffers many obstacles to the advancement of those of native birth'.

This training school had opened in Møllergaden on 11 October 1852 with eleven pupils, mostly working-class and ill-educated. Cronborg, one of the two Danish committee members and a former instructor at the Christiania Theatre, was appointed general instructor and, since one of the declared aims of the school was to preserve and encourage the Norwegian language, a celebrated champion of the vernacular, a pernickety linguist named Knud Knudsen, was engaged as 'language teacher'. Public performances were given; and the committee were so encouraged by the results that two years later, in the autumn of 1854, they dropped the description of 'school' and proudly re-titled their foundation the Norwegian Christiania Theatre.

The idea of a Norwegian theatre had by no means been received with unqualified enthusiasm in the capital. Knud Knudsen tells in his memoirs how indignant the higher stratum of Christiania society, 'more Danish than the Danes themselves', was to find actors in the theatre at Møllergaden speaking in the accent and idiom which Norwegians used, indeed, in private conversation, but regarded as unsuitable for public occasions; just as, a century earlier in Copenhagen, before Holberg had begun to write, we learn that the Danish language was never heard in a gentleman's house, and that polite Danes were wont to say that a man wrote Latin to his friends, talked French to the ladies, called his dogs in German and used Danish only for swearing at his servants. Particular offence was caused by the fact that many of the actors at Møllergaden were from the eastern country districts of Norway and spoke in the despised 'eastland' dialect. Bergenese was just acceptable, but eastland dialect, no. This contempt of the educated public had a damaging effect on the Norwegian company, who soon realised that if they were to progress in their career they would have, sooner or later, to perform elsewhere in Danish, however fervent their patriotism might be. Nor did the unfashionable situation of the new theatre help. Møllergaden was an ugly and dirty street, full of doubtful inns where drunken individuals engaged in horse-coping and similar ungenteel transactions. When the young Laura Svendsen (later Laura Gundersen) was asked by a relative why she did not perform at the Norwegian Theatre, she replied that she would sooner beg in the gutter.

The Christiania Theatre (such being the official title of the 'Danish' Theatre at Bankpladsen), not surprisingly gave little encouragement to its new rival. An application from Knudsen and his committee for free tickets for their actors to the performances at Bankpladsen was refused; and whenever a promising player appeared at Møllergaden, the Christiania Theatre immediately tried to seduce him or her away with the carrot of higher pay. From the state, as might have been expected, the new theatre received no more help than Bull had. Requests for financial support were repeatedly refused, the most recent appeal, only three months before Ibsen took up his post, having been rather unluckily rejected in the Storthing by 57 votes to 49, a majority of eight.

The Christiania Norwegian Theatre soon found, as the Bergen Theatre had done, that to fulfil the ideals of experimentalism is easier in theory than in practice. Such new Norwegian plays as came their way were naïve and either undramatic or melodramatic. Nor could they follow the common practice of experimental theatres today when new plays fail, by taking refuge in the classics, firstly because the classics could not be translated into *landsmaal* any more than they might today be rendered into, say Dorset dialect, and secondly because the inexperienced actors were totally incapable of the heights demanded by classical tragedy or of the technique required for classical comedy. The translations, too, were mainly of poor quality, conveying little poetry or wit. Soon the directors found themselves compelled, like their fellows at Bergen, to fall back upon the staple diet of Danish vaudeville and French farce and musical comedy, so that it came to be said that a good singing voice was more likely to get an actor a leading part than acting ability. The usual evening bill consisted of two or three short pieces varied with songs, declamations and *tableaux vivants*. After five years of activity no new authors had been discovered and neither the repertory nor the talents of the company had noticeably been broadened. By the spring of 1857 things were so bad that the committee considered winding up the whole project; but they decided to continue, and it was to remedy matters that they imported Ibsen to replace Cronborg as artistic instructor. Cronborg, apart from being a Dane, had been an actor very much in the traditional manner. They had appointed him because no qualified Norwegian existed; now that, in Ibsen, one had arisen, they gave him the job.

The reputation of the Norwegian Christiania Theatre when Ibsen arrived to take over on 3 September 1857 was, then, very low. Even those who sympathised with its aims found it difficult to give their whole-hearted approval. Lorentz Dietrichson, by now a student at Christiania University, recalled: 'It did not stand very high in our favour when Henrik Ibsen became director, however nationalistically fervid we might be. The lesson that mediocre Norwegian art was better for us than good Danish art did not altogether strike home...The pronounced eastland accent of the Møllergaden players, the amateurish new plays that were presented there, and above all the desperate attempts at neology with which the theatre diverted itself...failed to win our unqualified assent. This language movement made in all a dry and desiccating impression, frequently seeming to sacrifice drama to grammar. The public decided that it did not visit the theatre in order to learn grammar.'[1] The newspapers, however, showed good will. During the summer of 1857, when the theatre was at its lowest ebb, both *Morgenbladet* and *Christiania-Posten* exhorted their readers to support it; and *Aftenbladet*, encouraging its subscribers to attend Cronborg's benefit performance on 10 August and a farewell evening for him on 13 August, concluded: 'Nor should it be forgotten that the theatre must now be regarded as having taken a step closer to its ultimate goal by ap-

---

[1] Dietrichson, *op. cit.*, I, pp. 269–72.

pointing a native Norwegian as artistic director.' One can understand how, to Ibsen, it must have seemed a promising field for activity.

Ibsen took lodgings in a house at the corner of Akersgaden and Carl Johansgade, and got down to work at once. Only a fortnight after his arrival, on 18 September, a double bill of two Norwegian plays was performed under his direction. Both were familiar works, by writers who had died ten to fifteen years previously: Henrik Bjerregaard's musical, *A Tale of the Mountains*, and Henrik Wergeland's sequel to that play. Ibsen contributed a rhymed prologue in praise of the two dead dramatists, and *Morgenbladet* remarked that 'the stage management showed evidence of considerable care, and augurs well for Herr Ibsen's direction of the theatre'. *A Tale of the Mountains* proved a public success, and was performed twenty-two times that season.

Most of the repertory that autumn consisted of revivals of plays produced in previous seasons—a fact that has surprised some commentators, but which is simply explained in Ibsen's report to his board two years later, on 2 July 1859. 'Nothing had been prepared...and there was nothing new to begin with.' The titles read dismally. *Cousin Lotta*, a vaudeville by C. M. Wengel; *The Cobbler and the Countess*, a musical by Ibsen's mentor in Copenhagen, Thomas Overskou, based on a French piece named *Riquiqui; A Foolish Girl*, a vaudeville by Erik Bøgh, adapted from a French comedy which had in turn been adapted from a play by Calderon (*Casa con dos puertos mala es de guardar*); and J. H. Wessel's old musical parody, *Love without Stockings*. The only three new additions to the repertory before Christmas were on the same level: R. Benedix's comedy *Die Lügnerin*, which had to be withdrawn after one performance; *Lazarilla*, an operette based on Scribe's comic opera *La Chanteuse Voilée*, which was a success and achieved sixteen performances before the summer closure; and Alexandre Duval's comedy, *La Jeunesse d'Henri V*, which Ibsen had already directed in Bergen, and which managed nine performances. A revival of Holberg's *Jeppe of the Hill*, an old favourite about a peasant who finds himself rich for an afternoon, was the only play of genuine distinction to be produced that season.

Not that the quality of the repertory at the Danish-controlled Christiania Theatre was any different, or any better. This was clearly what the public wanted. Ibsen, in addition to his work at the Møllergaden theatre, wrote occasional reviews for Botten Hansen's *Illustreret Nyhedsblad* of the productions at Bankpladsen, an arrangement which strikes a modern reader as somewhat unprofessional but which does not appear to have caused any surprise or offence then. On 11 October 1857, less than six weeks after his arrival in Christiania, we find him castigating the theatregoers of the capital for their lack of taste. The play under review was Hans Andersen's *A Country Tale*, adapted from Salomon Mosenthal's *Der Sonnenwendhof;* and Ibsen warned his readers that it could hardly expect a long run, since 'its quality is essentially poetic. This is the age,' he continued, 'of transparencies, of clever technical effects. Technique, in the most superficial meaning of the word, is the only thing the public is capable of appreciating, and the theatre is perfectly justified, from a financial standpoint, in continuing as hitherto to present the more recent French works which have for so long constituted the basic diet of our repertory. These plays commonly display a skilled technique, which the public likes, and, which is probably even more to their taste, they have nothing whatever to do with poetry.' Ibsen goes on to express sentiments which may surprise those, still, sadly, a majority, who think of him principally as a social realist on the strength of a few plays which he wrote in the middle of his career. Many people, he writes, 'will regard this play as both untrue and unwholesome, because it does not bear a photographic resemblance to reality...People demand reality, no more and no less. That art should elevate is not a popular conception.' The only limitation of photography, he concludes ironically, is that it cannot, except in an abstract kind of way, reproduce colour; but this, doubtless, will soon be remedied, and an even greater realism will result, a tendency which art and poetry will doubtless follow in their quest for further popularity.

Two months later, in a tribute to the actor Anton Wilhelm Wiehe published in *Illustreret Nyhedsblad* on 13 December, Ibsen returned to the attack on modern French drama and photographic realism. Denouncing the former as 'lacy weavings', which 'so sadly flaunt virtuosity at the expense of art', and 'can only degrade art into the vulgar emptiness of "effect",' he praises Wiehe for his 'spirited pursuit, not of banal realism, but of truth, that loftier, symbolic representation of life which is the only thing artistically worth fighting for, yet the existence of which is acknowledged by so few'—a bitter comment from one who, during his six years at Bergen, had seen ridiculed every attempt he had made to rise above the contemporary level of taste, and only his one exercise in banality, *The Feast at Solhaug,* applauded. He was, over the next six years, to find the taste of the Christiania public as inflexibly wedded as that of Bergen to the mediocre and the trivial. The former, however proudly it might boast itself to be the country's capital, remained as determinedly provincial as the latter.

A further insight into Ibsen's feelings at this time concerning the proper purpose of drama is given in a long review by him, amounting to over seven thousand words, which appeared in the next two issues of *Illustreret Nyhedsblad* on 20 and 27 December 1857. The subject in question was a historical drama, *Lord William Russell,* by Andreas Munch, (1811–1884), a reputable Norwegian writer who had sat with Ibsen and Bjørnson in the author's box at the première

of the latter's *Between the Battles* the previous month. Lord William Russell was
an English Catholic who was executed in 1683 for supposed complicity in the
Rye House Plot to assassinate King Charles II, and it is apparent from Ibsen's
very favourable review that both the theme and Munch's treatment of it, had
considerably excited him. Attacking 'the traditional demands which are made
of tragedy in general,' he writes: 'It has become customary to expect from
tragic characters a loftiness, a purification, a greatness of thought and expression, will and action, that will fulfil the function of the Greek cothurn—
namely, to give us the feeling that we are outside the realm of everyday life.
But this achieves the exact opposite of its purpose; the world portrayed by the
dramatist is rendered completely foreign to the spectator, no bond exists between us and the protagonist as he struggles and is defeated, and so he cannot
fully engage our sympathy.' One of the great virtues of Munch's play, Ibsen
says, is that whereas 'traditional tragedy presents minor Gods, A. Munch's
work presents great mortal men'. Sixteen years later he was to explain his
final abandonment of poetry as a dramatic medium in similar words.[1]

Ibsen then expatiates briefly on the proper treatment of symbolism, in a
paragraph which should be compulsory reading for the many commentators
who have written ignorantly about this aspect of Ibsen's work. 'Every notable
human being,' he writes, 'is symbolic, both in his career and in his relationship
to history. But bad writers, misconstruing the theory that the significant
phenomena of life should be intensified in art, make this symbolism conscious...
Instead of it existing hidden in the work, like a vein of silver ore in a mountain,
it is continually being dragged into the light of day.' One of the virtues of
Munch's play, says Ibsen, is that 'he has allowed the symbolism to stand there
without commentary like a runic inscription, leaving it to each member of the
audience to interpret it according to his or her individual needs...It is no
conscious battle of ideas that enacts itself before us, any more than that ever
happens in reality; what we see is human conflicts, behind which, yet inter-
woven with them, ideas conflict and conquer or are vanquished. And the play
does not end at the fall of the curtain on the fifth act. The true end lies beyond;
the poet indicates the direction in which we may seek; it is now up to each one
of us to find his or her own way there.'

These two ideas, that tragedy should present recognisable human beings
rather than superhuman creatures, and that symbolism should be integral
rather than overt, were, in time, to become two of his principal dogmas as a
dramatist. At this early stage of his dramatic career, however, cut off by his

---

[1] 'What I sought to depict was human beings, and therefore I would not let them talk
"the language of the gods",' (Letter to Edmund Gosse, 15 January 1874).

ignorance of all foreign languages except German from practically all great specimens of drama, save in clumsy translations and adaptations, and blinded by the claims of the nationalistic movement and his excitement at the discovery of ancient Scandinavian literature, he was still groping inexpertly towards a satisfactory form. This isolation from the main tradition of classical tragedy was, eventually, to prove his strength, compelling him to strike out hugely on his own. But the confusion and uncertainty in which he now, at the age of twenty-nine, found himself, are clearly shown in the play which he had completed a few weeks before writing the *Lord William Russell* review, *The Vikings at Helgeland*.

As explained, Ibsen had conceived this tragedy two years earlier in Bergen, as a result of reading N. M. Petersen's translation of the Icelandic sagas, but had turned aside, under the influence of the folk ballad, to write *The Feast at Solhaug*. When he returned to it, during the spring of 1857 ('a new play... rather different from my previous works, in both tone and content', as he had explained to Botten Hansen on 28 April of that year), he began to write it in verse, but abandoned that medium in favour of a prose based on the Homerically simple yet formalised language of the sagas. That Ibsen was aware of the difficulties of dramatising saga material is evident from certain passages in the essay on the Heroic Ballad which he had sent to *Illustreret Nyhedsblad* on 17 April 1857, when he was already working on the play. 'The saga,' he had written, 'is huge, cold, remote, self-sufficient, epic, quintessentially objective... We cannot see the saga age except in this cold, epic light...If a writer is to create a dramatic work out of this epic material, he must inevitably introduce a foreign element...The age and the milieu which had originally been offered us in an abstract and plastic form he now presents as a painting, with colours, light and shadows...This dramatic treatment brings the saga age closer to reality, but that is exactly what should not happen. The statue does not gain by acquiring natural skin tints and real hair and eyes.'

This incompatibility between saga material and dramatic form was a problem which Ibsen found himself unable to solve. The ancient Greek dramatists had solved it, but Ibsen knew no Greek and had very possibly never read a Greek play, even in bad translation; nor was the Norwegian theatre of the nineteenth century a medium remotely suited to epic presentation. *The Vikings at Helgeland* is a remarkable literary pastiche, and contains, buried in the impossible form of this pastiche, the kernel of what, over thirty years later, in a very different setting, was to become one of his greatest plays. It was the closest he had yet come to writing a great play; the construction, the consistency and development of the characterisation, and the sense of an inevitable working out of destiny evolving directly from given characters in given situations are, for the first time in his work, under mature and successful control. Only the remoteness of these ancient, heroic figures, and, more especially, of the conventions which governed their lives, defeated him.

The Vikings at Helgeland is set in northern Norway during the tenth century. As in The Feast at Solhaug (and, earlier, Catiline), the two principal women are diametrically contrasted characters: Hjørdis is a ruthless and formidable visionary, Dagny gentle, uxorious and practical. Each is married to a man who is her own opposite: Hjørdis to the peaceful Gunnar, Dagny to a great warrior, Sigurd, Gunnar's foster-brother. Hjørdis despises her husband for his gentleness; only one thing binds her to him. As a girl in Iceland she had, in a splendid symbol, been guarded in her room by a huge white bear 'of the strength of twenty men'; no man might win her until he had killed this monster. One night, Gunnar had done this, and so she had become his wife; but their marriage has not been happy. She admires Sigurd, and he her; but he remains faithful to Dagny. During a feast, Hjørdis tries to start a quarrel between her husband and Sigurd; this so enrages Dagny that she reveals what Sigurd has told her, that it was he, and not Gunnar, who killed the white bear, in order that his foster-brother might win the woman he loved. Then, in the most effective, because it is psychologically the most modern scene in the play, Hjørdis and Sigurd, left alone, reveal their love for each other; neither has been happy in marriage; their good and gentle partners have not been what they wanted, and needed. Hjørdis tries to tempt Sigurd to kill Gunnar; but instead, he challenges Gunnar to single combat, knowing that, if he wins, the ancient laws of vendetta will compel Hjørdis to kill him. In the final act Hjørdis, believing that she and Sigurd can only be united in death, shoots him with her bow; but before he dies, he reveals to her that now they can never be together, since he, unknown to her, has embraced the Christian faith, and Christians and heathens can never meet after death. Hjørdis then kills herself in despair.

Thus bleakly outlined, The Vikings at Helgeland may seem little, if at all, superior to the static Viking dramas of Oehlenschläger; and the remoteness of the setting, the deliberate pastiche of the prose and the Homeric simplicity of the characters make it unlikely that it could ever successfully be staged before a modern and sophisticated audience. In its own century it was to prove the most successful of Ibsen's early plays; the audiences who admired the Devrients and Frédéric Lemaître, Sarah Bernhardt and Henry Irving, liked their heroes and heroines to be huger than life, and The Vikings of Helgeland was to be performed more often in Christiania before 1900 than any of even his mature works. But for a play to work today one must be able to some extent at least to identify oneself with the characters; and the ethics and motivations of these mighty archetypal figures are wholly foreign to our own.

Nevertheless, *The Vikings at Helgeland* is of extraordinary interest to anyone who reads it with a knowledge of what Ibsen was later to write. Beneath the formalised characters of this ancient world with their strange conceptions of honour lies the story of Hedda Gabler. Hedda, like Hjørdis, dreamed romantically of heroes, was guarded against them by a 'white bear' (in Hedda's case, a horror of things physical), married a gentle and unheroic man, was jealous of the tender and uxorious girl to whom her hero attached himself and, in her frustration, sent him to his death and took her own life. There is even a scene in the second act of *The Vikings at Helgeland* in which Hjørdis passionately seizes her rival, Dagny, and clasps her tightly, at which Dagny cries: 'Let me go! I don't want to listen to you!' just as Thea Elvsted, when passionately clasped by Hedda in the second act of that play, cries: 'Let me go! I'm frightened of you!' And the great scene in the third act when Hjørdis and Sigurd sit down quietly together and reveal to each other for the first time their mutual love that can never find fulfilment, carries strong anticipatory echoes of that famous scene between Hedda and Eilert Løvborg on the sofa with the photograph album. The sense, too, of fate spinning her inflexible web around men, and of evil spirits ruling their world—'but their power is small unless they find willing helpers within our hearts, and happiness is granted to him who has the strength to fight against fate' (as Hjørdis tells Sigurd)—is something with which we shall become familiar in every mature play of Ibsen's from *The Pretenders* to *When We Dead Awaken*. Structurally, too, *The Vikings at Helgeland* shows an important advance on his previous plays in two important respects. It is blessedly free from the coincidences and improbabilities of *Lady Inger* and *The Feast at Solhaug*; and it does not contain a single monologue (though Ibsen was to revert to the monologue, with calculated effect, for a period later.)

Ibsen's first months in Christiania during that autumn of 1857 must have seemed full of encouragement. Apart from the relief of directing a theatre without having to share the work with a *dramaturg* of superior upbringing and education, other irons were beginning to glow in the fire. On 4 November *The Feast at Solhaug* was performed at the Royal Dramatic Theatre in Stockholm, the first time any of his plays had been staged outside Norway, and it was well received. The same month, *The Vikings at Helgeland* was accepted by the directors of the Danish-controlled Christiania Theatre for production the following spring. He had offered the play to them rather than to his own theatre on the assumption, rightly as it turned out, that his own actors at the Norwegian Theatre were as incapable of high tragedy as the actors at Bergen had been. And as though his work at the theatre were not sufficient to occupy him fully, he applied on 13 November for a University bursary in Scandinavian literature of 260 specie-dollars a year (largely, one imagines, on the strength of his essay on the heroic ballad). In his letter to the authorities he admitted that he 'has indeed not much to plead in support of his application, but ventures to nominate himself since he has good grounds for supposing that other applicants find themselves similarly placed'. Two months later, however, on 13 January 1858, he withdrew his application, having presumably decided that the reorganisation and direction of the Norwegian Theatre was not, after all, a part-time job.

The newspapers, meanwhile, were taking notice of the improved standard of production at the Norwegian Theatre. That February a correspondent in *Aftenbladet*, after complaining at the way in which the gallery is allowed to dominate the style of performance, so that 'inconceivable exaggerations, vulgarities and untruthfulnesses' evoke 'hysterical applause', praised the 'more faithful, if less technically skilled, interpretation of the author's ideas...than is often the case at the other, the Danish Theatre, despite the larger size and superior experience of the company at the latter.' If only, the writer continued, critics would give a lead, the unfortunate public interruptions during performance, which are at present in danger of destroying the good work of the new artistic director, might cease. 'However, Herr Ibsen will surely, being a man of creative power and sensibility, be able to guard against the effect of this repeated caterwauling on his sense of theatrical vocation; yet it needs to be remarked that at present he stands virtually alone, and alone in his vision; and it should not be so.' It was to remain so for longer than the anonymous author of these lines could have guessed.

Another article at about the same time in *Christiania-Posten* gives an interesting picture of the difference between the new Norwegian Theatre and the Danish-controlled one at Bankpladsen. The audience of the one, we learn, comes in 'working clothes', the other in 'going-out dress'. In the Danish Theatre the main purpose is to see and be seen, especially since it has acquired a new chandelier. 'In the Norwegian Theatre the lighting is not quite so bright; there are no boxes to underline differences of class and wealth, and the short jacket of the hill peasant may be seen side by side with a coat of the most elegant cut. Yet if one of the regular Thursday patrons of the Christiania Theatre were to visit Møllergaden *incognito* he might find to his surprise that the acting was not so bad nor the audience so obtuse as he had confidently imagined.' By and large the repertories of the two companies were very similar,[1]

---

[1] During Ibsen's five years at the Norwegian Theatre, the Christiania Theatre at Bankpladsen presented the following classics, mostly in clumsy and unfaithful adaptations: Sheridan's *The Rivals* (September 1857); Shakespeare's *All's Well that Ends Well* (December 1857) and *The Taming of the Shrew* (March 1858); Colman's and Garrick's *The Jealous Wife* (October 1858); Goldsmith's *She Stoops to Conquer* (November 1858); Molière's

since both depended mostly on Danish adaptations of contemporary French and, occasionally, German comedies, musical or not. In anything requiring singing the Norwegian Theatre seems to have had a slight edge over its rival; moreover, the playing there was in general brisker, and so, we are told, was the scene-changing.

An interesting portrait of Ibsen at this juncture in his career is provided for us by Bjørnstjerne Bjørnson, who had recently returned from a year in Denmark and of whom, for the first time, Ibsen had begun to see a good deal. At the premiere on 27 October of Bjørnson's first play, *Between the Battles* (a fine one-acter, set in a moment of peace during a bloody civil war, and vitiated only by a certain glibness of climax which was to be one of Bjørnson's besetting faults as a dramatist), Ibsen had sat beside him in the author's box; and in a letter that November (which Bjørnson, as so often, forgot or did not bother to date) to the young but influential Danish critic Clemens Petersen, Bjørnson, who had evidently read *The Vikings at Helgeland* in manuscript, gives his impressions of his fellow-playwright. He found Ibsen, for his tastes, too derivative. 'I'm afraid,' he wrote to Petersen, 'he must find a new and a different road before I can have any faith in him. In *The Feast at Solhaug* he has so buried himself in the heroic ballad that he ended up by becoming a ballad incarnate. To the point where he made the language his own. Then he moved on to the saga, and now he's emerging from that with all its expressions, its language, word for word, its least nuance and its dead poetry. He is a greater virtuoso than Ole Bull, let alone Henrik Hertz. He has a curiously dreamy personality which can't immerse itself in life but only in dead poetry...In *The Vikings at Helgeland* he has recreated Sigurd Dragon's-Bane and the whole of that vast song-cycle and the legends which belong to it. He has pastiched it and dramatised it absolutely. That I must grant, and praise him for it, and yet I find myself fuming with indignation, just because he's so good and trusting that I can't bring myself to speak out. If it weren't that he's not big

---

L'Ecole des Femmes (September 1859); Sheridan's *The School for Scandal* (October 1859); Shakespeare's *Much Ado about Nothing* (January 1860); Molière's *Le Médecin Malgré Lui* (April 1860); Shakespeare's *Twelfth Night* (November 1860), *The Merchant of Venice* (September 1861), and *As You Like It* (January 1863). In other words, the Danish Theatre presented on an average only two classics a year; otherwise the repertories were similar. (*Hamlet*, astonishingly, was not staged in Christiania until as late as 1870, apart from a single performance of Act 3 only in 1830). During Ibsen's five and a half years of directorship, from 1857–63, the Norwegian Theatre, while not attempting Shakespeare, presented 2 Molières, 1 Musset, 1 Goldoni, 1 Calderon, and 9 Holbergs. For the record, they also, during this period, presented 9 Scribes, 14 plays by Erik Bøgh, 10 by Mélesville, 8 by J. F. Bayard, 4 Heibergs, 4 Hans Andersens, 3 Labiches, 1 Sardou, 1 Kotzebue and 1 Dumas père.

enough to believe me free from envy I'd have told him the truth all the same, in a quiet moment, if possible while I was pressing his hand...Ibsen is making every ordinary human being who lived in Erik Bloodaxe's time just like Sigurd Dragon's-Bane. I can't believe that people who lived then were superhuman and godlike. No, damn it, they were human!'

It is scarcely possible to imagine two more contrasted characters than Ibsen and Bjørnson. Even Dickens and Thackeray were less dissimilar. Ibsen was small, gauche, self-distrustful, shy of women, physically unattractive and, artistically, a slow developer. Bjørnson was tall, powerfully built, self-confident, gregarious, an intensive and successful womaniser and a brilliant public speaker, who achieved literary fame in his middle twenties. For half a century a violent and extraordinary love-hatred relationship was to exist between them, harsh words and condemnations alternating bewilderingly with protestations of admiration and devotion. The wonder is, not that their friendship was so perpetually troubled, but that somehow, in defiance of all probability, it eventually managed to survive.

We have disappointingly few letters from Ibsen's hand during the six and a half years that he was now to spend in Christiania. He must, lamentable correspondent though he was, have written at least occasionally to Suzannah in Bergen during the nine months they were separated (from September 1857 to June 1858), but she apparently destroyed his early letters as she did his early poems. 'Our relationship concerns no one but ourselves.' The only letter of interest which we have from Ibsen's hand during this period is one dated 30 January 1858 to a friend seven years younger than himself, one Carl Johan Anker, who was now serving in the Norwegian Guard in Stockholm and with whom he had gone on a walking tour from Bergen to Hardanger and back in the summer of 1856. After the usual apology for silence, with which so many of his letters were to begin, he recalled their excursion affectionately, and continued: 'I have often wondered what you must have thought of me then, whether you didn't find me walled about with a kind of off-putting coldness which makes any close relationship with me difficult. And yet I found it incomparably easier to make contact with you than with anyone else, for I found in you a spiritual youthfulness, a joy in life, a chivalry of outlook which warmed my heart. Keep all this! Believe me, it is not pleasant to see the world from an October standpoint; though, strangely, there was once a time when I wanted nothing more. I have passionately longed for, yes, almost *prayed* for, a great grief which might fill my existence, give content to my life. It was foolish, and I have fought my way out of that state of mind—but the memory of it will always remain.' This is a very different Ibsen from the 'merry and vital' young man whom Christopher Due remembered from Grimstad. Yet we should not, as some commentators have done, be unduly surprised at this. The shyest people usually have one or two friends from youth, usually (as Due seems to have been) simple and warm-hearted extroverts, who remember them as open almost to the point of ebullience.

The first months in Christiania had been full of promise; the New Year (1858) was to bring two sharp disappointments. In February J. L. Heiberg refused *The Vikings at Helgeland* for the Royal Theatre at Copenhagen. 'The Icelandic Sagas,' he wrote, 'have so markedly epic a character that they can only be mutilated by dramatisation. The wildness and crudity that they depict' are palliated in the original by the epic method of presentation. But the moment one dramatises them one is merely left with the subject-matter in all its rawness.' This judgment of Heiberg's has been condemned as dogmatic; but it is one with which most modern critics would surely agree (though one might think that a theatre director who regarded the trivia of Hertz as worth staging could have taken a chance with so patently more talented a play). A worse blow was, however, to follow. On 9 March Ibsen learned that Carl Borgaard, the head of the Danish-controlled Christiania Theatre, who had accepted *The Vikings at Helgeland* for production that spring, was proposing to postpone production for a year 'since the economic position of the theatre and its immediate prospects do not permit of the payment of honoraria for original works during the current season'.

Ibsen reacted promptly and furiously. The day after he heard the news, on 10 March, he published a violent attack on the Christiania Theatre in *Aftenbladet*. Ever since its inception, he declared, the theatre had jealously clung to everything Danish. The establishment of a Norwegian theatre in the capital had now resulted in their deciding to leave the production of all Norwegian plays to their rival, although they well knew that certain works, especially those written in the mould of classical tragedy, could be adequately performed only by trained actors such as the Danish, but not the Norwegian Theatre possessed. The unofficial truce which had existed between the two Christiania theatres must, he said, now be ended. 'The time has come,' he wrote, 'when the peace of our theatrical world must and shall be broken. Either we must have a Norwegian Theatre which understands, and has the power to work for, our national artistic interests, or we must all pledge our allegiance to our so-called principal theatre, we must all stream towards its doors even when it regales us thrice weekly with translations scrabbled together from the four corners of the earth...And yet,' he concluded sadly, 'the time has now come when a worthwhile national theatre could be established. If the Danish Theatre with its foreign tendencies and anti-nationalism did not block the path, one could from the best Norwegian talent at the three theatres [i.e., including that at

Bergen] create a company which would realise the dream of a national theatre, a theatre which would work hand in hand with our blossoming literature.' On 14 March, Botten Hansen wrote in *Illustreret Nyhedsblad* supporting Ibsen, pointing out that the Danish Theatre's main success of the past few months had in fact been a Norwegian play, Munch's *Lord William Russell*, and that their excuse of not being able to pay for original works rang thin in view of the fact that they had only recently raised the salaries of several of their company.

A reply to Ibsen's accusation appeared in *Christiania-Posten* from the pen of one Richard Petersen, a civil servant who later, not inappropriately, became a prison governor. In a bitter personal attack on Ibsen, Petersen dismissed him as 'a small-time poet', with no right to set himself up as spokesman for the nationalistic cause in literature. Ridiculing him for 'identifying himself with all native dramatic literature', he concluded: 'Herr Ibsen is a playwright of gigantic insignificance, about whom our nation cannot with any enthusiasm plant a protective palisade. *The Feast at Solhaug* is altogether too lacking in originality to encourage any hopes for his future, and his next [*sic*] stage work, *Lady Inger of Østraat*, is devoid of idealism and poetry to a degree which can only be described as astounding. Every character in this play bears the stamp of baseness...Under the circumstances Herr Ibsen should surely appreciate that the public no longer awaits his *Vikings* with any excitement, and that the present is not the most appropriate time to present a play of probably mediocre quality.'

Ibsen plunged back into the fray with two further articles in *Aftenposten*, but a more effective, because independent, championship of his cause came from Bjørnson, who had in November succeeded Ibsen as *sceneinstruktør* at the Bergen theatre. *The Vikings at Helgeland*, wrote Bjørnson in *Bergens-Posten*, was 'the best play that has yet been written in Norway. When it is staged, it will reveal itself as endowed with a scenic power unmatched by anything previous in Norwegian drama'. Bjørnson also wrote to *Aftenbladet* asserting that the Danish Christiania Theatre had now served its purpose, praising Ibsen and *The Vikings* in particular, and concluding: 'If any feeling of decency exists in this country, we must put a stop to this scandalous maltreatment of Norwegian authors, and especially to the tendency to tread them into the mud merely to sustain the crumbling foundations of a Danish theatre.'

On 25 April 1857, *The Vikings at Helgeland* was published as a special supplement to *Illustreret Nyhedsblad*. 2,200 copies were printed; which, since the magazine had, at that time, some thirteen to fourteen hundred subscribers,

---

¹ This is hardly the opinion of the play which he had expressed to Clement Petersen; but Bjørnson, like Walt Whitman, regarded self-contradiction as a sign of mental flexibility. ('I contradict myself?' wrote Whitman. 'Very well then. I contradict myself').

M

meant that about eight hundred copies were available for sale in the shops. The reviews were mixed, but in general the reception was favourable rather than otherwise—*Morgenbladet* hailed it as 'a true national drama'—and the good notices were the first praise that Ibsen had received for any new work since the staging of *The Feast at Solhaug* in Bergen over two years before.

During all this controversy, Ibsen had been directing the usual succession of appalling plays at the Norwegian Theatre: Thomas Overskou's *A Chapter of Misunderstandings*; *Uncle*, a musical comedy by R. Benedix; *Clifford le Voleur*, a drama by Mélesville and Dubetrier; and a French musical entitled *The Day before the Battle of Marengo*. Scribe had, naturally, been represented, by three works, *Les Premières Amours*, *La Marraine* and *La Chanteuse Voilée*, the last-named, with its sixteen performances, proving the principal success of the season. Nothing of any quality had been performed since Christmas except Holberg's comedy, *Henrik and Pernilla*, and that had been a revival of an earlier production. The only plays by living Norwegian authors had been Rolf Olsen's *Anna Kolbjørnsdatter*, and revivals of two old vaudeville successes, C. P. Riis's *To The Mountains* and H. Ø. Blom's *Tordenskiold*.

This lack of new plays, and in particular of new Norwegian plays, was noted by the board of the Norwegian Theatre at its annual general meeting that summer, and they instructed Ibsen to try to introduce more fresh material into the repertory for the coming season. A prize of 100 specie-dollars (£25) had in fact been offered on 22 November 1857 for 'a full-length drama (at least three acts), preferably a musical, the subject-matter to be taken from our own history and the piece suited to the talents of the company'; but only three entries had been submitted, and none had been adjudged worthy of production. Nevertheless, the season had, on the whole, proved not unsuccessful. The takings, which totalled some 9,000 specie-dollars (£2,250), had been higher than in the preceding year, and the theatre had more or less paid its way.

Preoccupied as he was with the practicalities of direction (he had somehow managed to get forty-four plays of varying lengths on to the stage during the season, sixteen of them being new productions), Ibsen had had little time for writing poetry. During January he published three occasional pieces in *Illustreret Nyhedsblad*, an elegy for the author Ole Vig, a *Festsang* and an *Ode to the Memory of Carl Johan*, all echoing his nationalistic work at the theatre and devoid of serious merit. These, as far as we know, were the only new poems he wrote during his first year in Christiania, though he published for the first time (also in *Illustreret Nyhedsblad*) several poems which he had written in Bergen, including *A Bird's Song*, *Earth Flowers and Potted Plants*, and *Building Plans*, the original version of which (though he was to alter it significantly when preparing his collected poems in 1871) runs thus:

I remember as well as if it had happened today
The time I saw in the paper my first poem in print.
I sat there in my room puffing my pipe,
Exuding smoke in blest complacency.

I hummed and I read for surely the twentieth time
That paper, finding it strangely interesting.
And imagination played its restless game—
Well, what is life without a little madness?

I built a dream castle. The work went swiftly and well.
I set myself two aims, one little and one great.
The great aim was to become an immortal man.
The small, to own a lovely water-lily.

I thought it a noble and harmonious plan,
But then confusion entered into it.
As I grew sane, the whole plan went quite crazy.
The great aim shrank to nothing. The other was all that mattered.[1]

In June, a few days before the season at the Norwegian Theatre ended, Ibsen went to Bergen to marry Suzannah Thoresen. The wedding was celebrated quietly on 18 June 1858, under melancholy circumstances, for only seven days previously her father, the Dean, had died at the age of fifty-two. His death cannot have been unexpected, for the obituary notice in *Bergens Adressecontoirs Efterretninger* speaks of 'grievous physical suffering'. No eye-

---

[1] A note accompanying this poem, *A Bird Song* and *Earth Flowers and Potted Plants*, when the three were first printed in *Illustreret Nyhedsblad* on 14 March 1858, states that they 'belong to an earlier period in his life'. It has generally and I think rightly been assumed that *Building Plans*, like the other two, was written either during or shortly after Ibsen's short-lived association with Rikke Holst in 1853. When Ibsen revised the poem in 1871 he re-wrote it as follows:

I remember as well as if it were yesterday
That evening when, in the paper, I saw my first poem in print.
I sat there in my garret puffing my pipe
And dreaming dreams of blest complacency.

'I shall build a cloud-castle. It shall shine over the North.
Two wings shall it have; one little and one great.
The great wing shall shelter an immortal poet.
The small wing shall be a young girl's bower'.

I thought it a noble and harmonious plan,
But then confusion entered into it.
As the master grew sane, the castle went all crazy.
The great wing shrank; the small fell into ruins.

witness account of the wedding ceremony has come down to us; small loss
probably, for who ever reported anything interesting about a wedding?
Ibsen took Suzannah back to share his life in Christiania, taking the opportunity
as the steamer touched at Grimstad to introduce her to his old friend Christopher Due, and Magdalene Thoresen, before very long, returned to her native
Denmark, where the sorrows of widowhood do not seem greatly to have
inhibited her.

On 23 August the new season began at the Norwegian Theatre. Both it and
the Christiania Theatre had decided on a policy of more new plays, to the
pleasure of the newspapers; and the open quarrel between Ibsen and Borgaard
seems to have had a good publicity effect, for both theatres found themselves
playing to increased business. Every week, we learn, the Norwegian Theatre
presented something new, if only a one-acter. On 1 October Ibsen was praised
by a critic in *Morgenbladet*, who pointed out that he was answerable not only for
the staging of the plays but also for the coaching of the younger and less
talented of his players, 'and has therefore much more responsibility than his
Danish counterpart'. Such productivity, declared the writer, can only be the
result of 'a harmonious co-operation between the director and his company,
and a ceaseless striving towards a mutual goal'. So extensive a repertory, the
article concluded, might be supposed deleterious to the actors; but this was
not the case. The plays were well rehearsed 'and the roles well memorised'.
It is evident that Ibsen was, at this stage, pursuing his task with energy; and the
public, too, was well pleased.

Yet the plays themselves were little more exciting than before. The staple
fare continued to consist of light comedy, musicals and vaudevilles, mainly
Danish adaptations from the French. Thus, one of the chief successes of the
new season was *Zoë, ou l'Amant Prêté*, by Scribe and Mélesville, of which a
critic wrote that 'the presentation was uncommonly agreeable and the instruction excellent'. Madame Døvle, he declared, gave a 'handsome and lively'
performance in the title role, and her marked progress was attributed to 'Herr
Ibsen's talent for using her abilities, and those of the rest of the company, in
the best manner'. Another success was *Seven Girls in Uniform*, an adaptation
by J. L. Heiberg of a German adaptation of a French comedy by Francis,
Dartois and Théaulon entitled *Les Jolis Soldats; Aftenbladet* wrote (30 October)
that 'one cannot praise too highly Herr Ibsen's energy in arranging so excellent
a repertory and one must admit that he has been highly successful in choosing
plays that suit the talents of his company'. The premiere of *Seven Girls in
Uniform* on 27 October seems to have been especially well attended, for the
reviewer complains of the 'oppressive heat, and undue crowding'. It achieved
twenty-one performances that season.

Ibsen now decided to risk his company in *The Vikings at Helgeland*, rather than wait a year in the uncertain hope of the more experienced Danish players performing it. *Morgenbladet* (1 October) doubted the wisdom of attempting so difficult a play on so small a stage and with a company virtually devoid of experience outside comedy and vaudeville. However, in one of his letters to the press complaining of Borgaard's rejection of the play, Ibsen had observed that 'only by seeing their plays performed can dramatists discover their faults and learn for the future', and Botten Hansen took the opportunity to remind readers of *Illustreret Nyhedsblad* how warmly the play had, when printed, been received outside Norway. Public interest was excited, and when *The Vikings at Helgeland* received its première at the Norwegian Theatre on 24 November 1858 the house was full and people had to be turned away.

The production, amazingly, proved a success. 'That this uncommonly imaginative work, long known to readers, should succeed on the stage in its own right,' wrote *Morgenbladet*, 'was to be expected. What was not expected was that the Norwegian Theatre would give so worthy a performance ...The whole presentation is virtually free from serious criticism, something that seldom occurs in our theatres when a tragedy with so large a cast is staged.' The management had gone to the expense of new decor and costumes, spending as much as 500 specie-dollars (£125) on the production. At the final curtain there was loud cheering, and 'the author, Herr Ibsen, was called for, and was thunderously applauded'. *Aftenbladet* remarked that the production was the first essay that the Norwegian Theatre had attempted in 'the higher dramatic art', and that the result exceeded all expectations. 'No effort had been spared by the actors to see that the play should succeed, and encouraging outbursts of applause occurred not infrequently. It did one good to hear the powerful language of the play spoken in the homely accents of our mother tongue. The diction was clear and none of the play's content was lost...The winter decor with the open, turbulent sea in the background was beautiful, and the scenic arrangements were generally successful.' Botten Hansen in *Illustreret Nyhedsblad* noted the significance of 'a national play being presented with every technical advantage that stage management can provide', and took the opportunity to quote a laudatory comment upon the play by a German critic.

The evening had, in fact, been a triumph for Ibsen, the last that he was to know for over five years. Both the play and his production of it had been acclaimed almost unanimously. Admittedly, a supporter of the rival theatre wrote an article in *Aftenbladet* on 11 December accusing Ibsen of plagiarising the work of 'a younger and more talented fellow-countryman' (a reference to Bjørnson's *Between the Battles*),[1] and condemning the performance as 'destroying the image one has hitherto cherished of the characters in the Sagas'; but this evoked an eloquent retort in *Morgenbladet* on 16 December, and a party was arranged to celebrate Ibsen's success as both dramatist and director, at which a speech of congratulation was delivered by Professor M. J. Monrad. The first four performances were well attended, with takings totalling 460 specie-dollars(£115), a quarter of which was allotted to Ibsen as honorarium.

But in spite of the excellent reviews and the attractions of the new decor and costumes, the play proved to have a limited appeal. There was not the same public in Christiania for a tragedy as for a comedy or a vaudeville, and only four more performances were given that season, compared with the twenty-one of *Les Jolis Soldats*.

Nevertheless, by the end of 1858 the hopes with which Ibsen had come to Christiania must still have been high. He had written a few poems for special occasions during the autumn—for the fiftieth anniversary of a society, for the inauguration of new school buildings in Lillehammer, for a student ballet performance, receiving as payment now a silver mug, now a punch bowl with matching glasses—and the tone of these is vigorous and optimistic, almost Kiplingesque in its naïve nationalism. In December he wrote a more interesting poem in the same mood, *Gull Cry*. The Danes were objecting that the Norwegians, by their chauvinism, were isolating themselves from the rest of Scandinavia and obstructing a closer union between the four countries. Ibsen, in his poem, retorts that the cry of the Norwegian gull is not beautiful, but that it makes that sound because it must; it is its nature. In passing, he rebuked the Danes for allowing their culture to fall so deeply under German influence. The language of this poem is deliberately very Norwegian, using several words and forms with which a Danish reader would be unfamiliar. One is reminded of the young James Joyce, fifty years later, similarly caught up in the toils of a nationalism which diverted his genius, and who, likewise, was not to fulfil himself until he had escaped from it into a self-imposed exile.

In January of the New Year (1859) Ibsen revived two Holberg comedies, *Jeppe of the Hill* and *The Peasant in Pawn*, and in March he produced, for the first time at the theatre, a Molière, *Les Fourberies de Scapin;* but, characteristically, none of these proved as popular as a slight vaudeville by Erik Bøgh

---

[1] Ibsen had almost certainly read *Between the Battles* before writing *The Vikings at Helgeland*, since Bjørnson had unsuccessfully offered the former to the Bergen Theatre in the winter of 1856–7, not long before Ibsen began his play. But *The Vikings at Helgeland* is no more imitative of *Between the Battles* than Shakespeare's *Richard II* is imitative of first critic to confuse imitation with stimulation.
Marlowe's *Edward II*. Hartvig Lassen, the author of the article in *Aftenbladet*, was not the

called *All Possible Parts*, based on a French original but set locally at 'the Hotel Nord in Christiania', which achieved twelve performances that spring. Then, emboldened by the reception of *The Vikings at Helgeland*, (which had also been staged at Trondhjem on 10 February and at Bergen on 4 March, the latter production being directed by Bjørnson, though with no great success[1]), Ibsen decided to see what his company could do with *Lady Inger of Østraat*.

Unfortunately, *Lady Inger* defeated the talents of the Christiania actors as completely as it had those of the company at Bergen. More than any other of Ibsen's early plays, *Lady Inger* requires, especially in the title role, the kind of acting between and against the lines that he was to demand in the prose plays of his maturity. This was something to which the inexperienced players of the Christiania Norwegian Theatre were not equal without the kind of forceful instruction which Ibsen was too shy to give them. Neither the press nor the public liked *Lady Inger* when it was presented on 11 April 1859, and the second performance, two evenings later, was so poorly attended that it was withdrawn and never revived. From the reviews of the play we learn amongst other things that contemporary Norwegian taste found it difficult to stomach what we would nowadays regard as a typical Ibsen ending; they wanted a play to conclude in calm and reconciliation. To remedy the financial loss incurred by this failure, the theatre engaged two English dancers, a pair of sisters named Agnes and Christine Healey, who filled the theatre night after night.

The success of the Norwegian Theatre hereabouts caused the directors of the Danish Theatre to rethink their policy. On 13 January 1859 *Aftenbladet* had declared that a milestone had been reached in Norwegian theatrical history, in that the directors of the Christiania Theatre had decided 'to convert our country's leading theatre into an entirely Norwegian organisation, emancipating it from Danish influence and...henceforth to make every effort to

---

[1] 'The play hasn't succeeded, though it may seem from a distance to have...Ibsen has a little clique of admirers headed by *Nyhedsbladet*. But every time he has to face the general public everything goes wrong and I've had to go to his aid twice, because Ibsen despite his aberrations *is* a poet. And I hope some day to get him to be himself and turn away from all this damned pastiche. The day Ibsen admits *he is small* he'll become a perfectly enchanting poet. I've told him as much pretty plainly, but the result is, he's jealous. He's done all sorts of little things to annoy me, and does still. He's angry that I haven't put *The Vikings at Helgeland* into my repertory...I haven't read his poem, *Gull Cry*; I've heard it's rather affected stuff, and was written largely because a Danish monthly said he was a lesser writer than me. Now that's exactly the kind of thing that always distracts Ibsen from what he ought to be and do. The point is, he's a rather small and gnomish (*tusset*) little chap, with no chest or rump, so he feels that as he has no other gifts he has to strain most frightfully (*tage saa forfærdelig i*) when he writes. And so he doesn't write what he'd really like to, and could.' (Bjørnson to Clemens Petersen, Bergen, 5 March 1859).

recruit Norwegian actors, and not in the immediate future to engage any more Danish staff'. *Morgenbladet* took this information with a pinch of salt, observing (on 19 January) that it was excellent news 'if this pronouncement is true', but warning the Norwegian Theatre not to place too much trust in these 'magnificent promises'. This scepticism proved to be justified, for the Christiania Theatre, when it came to the crunch, decided against dismissing their most experienced players, and the feud continued.

At the annual general meeting of the Norwegian Theatre on 2 July 1859, Ibsen presented his report, which was fully quoted in *Christiania-Posten* (on 4 July). Surprisingly neglected by his earlier biographers, it gives us a detailed insight into his feelings at this time about his work as a theatre director. At the close of the previous year, he reminded his committee, he had been called upon to present more new plays; during the season just completed, he has staged no less than thirty-one, and now people are saying that he has gone too far in this direction. But it is not merely the number of new productions that matters.

'A theatre can be as active in a year in which it presents ten new plays as in one in which it presents thirty. The question is whether one wishes to see plays that have been adequately or inadequately rehearsed...In the theatre one learns to be practical, to admit the power of circumstance and, when absolutely necessary, to abandon one's higher ideals...This necessity arises, alas, all too often in a theatre such as ours, which has no means of support other than its daily takings, and where every possible economy must be exercised in every possible direction. It is this consideration that has guided my policy during the past year. Under the continual strain of three or four performances a week, the company has been forced practically throughout the season to start rehearsing a new play each Wednesday for performance the following Wednesday; so that it is understandable enough if the first performances of plays presented under such circumstances should prove more satisfactory financially than aesthetically. The physical conditions under which we perform add to our difficulties. In a large auditorium one may aim at a general effect, but in one as cramped as ours an actor must concentrate more upon detail, and this demands a lengthier preparation and more thorough study if the result is to please.

'While therefore all possible credit must be paid to the company for their enthusiasm and endurance, the ceaseless activity of the past year should not, from the theatre's viewpoint, be a matter for unqualified praise. One may accept it as necessary; but everyone who does not regard aesthetic considerations as irrelevant must, not merely for the company's sake, but for the sake of our theatre, hope that this state of affairs will prove to be transitory. To express unqualified approval would be as irrational as was last year's allegation of insufficient activity because, it was said, too few new plays were being presented. I must therefore disassociate myself from the view that those allegations caused me to alter my policy. I was, even before my arrival here, too experienced in practical theatrical matters not to have determined the principles I had to follow.'

Ibsen then recapitulates the conditions under which he took up his post.

'I arrived here just as the season was about to begin. Nothing was prepared, and anyone who knows anything about such matters must realise that no theatre director can prepare a repertory for a company of whose capacities he is ignorant. If the selection of a repertory consisted merely of assembling a casual miscellany of plays and putting them on one after the other, the problem would be easy. But that is not the case. One must, as I say, know the material with which one is to work; one must also, regrettably, to some degree take into account public taste; one must seek a suitable balance between different types of play (so many with music, so many without, so many full-length, so many short, etc.); ideally, moreover, different schools of literature and different periods should be represented; and, finally, the parts must be fairly shared among the various members of the company. All this should of course have been prepared during the course of the summer, at least in outline; but I was not and could not have been prepared. The season began, and there was nothing new to begin with. I must therefore refute the accusations made at the last annual general meeting...'

Ibsen concluded his report by stressing the need for enlarging and improving the theatre.[1] Economically as well as artistically, he explained, this would prove advantageous, 'since it is an accepted rule that a larger theatre attracts a larger public, and through a larger public, and only thus, can we expand our technical resources so as to achieve the artistic result towards which we must hope to strive.'

But if the results of the season had not satisfied Ibsen's 'higher ideals', they had, financially, proved highly successful.[2] The one hundred and thirty-one

---

[1] *Morgenbladet*, on 16 October 1859, commented on a production of Holberg's *Jean de France* that the stage was so small that four people seemed a crowd, while anyone who stood alone in the wings 'looks a Goliath'.

[2] They were, in fact, doing better than the Bergen Theatre under Bjørnson, whom we find complaining in *Bergensposten* on 8 March 1859: 'Talent and enthusiasm have been wasted the whole winter on houses a half, a quarter, an eighth and even less full; the actors and the directors are losing heart'.

performances given had produced takings of just over 11,000 specie-dollars (£2,750), a much larger figure than in any previous year since the theatre had opened. Admittedly, this had resulted in a loss on the year of 1,048 specie-dollars (£262), but this was partly accounted for by the rebuilding of the stage machinery and various expenses inseparable from new productions, such as fees to authors and translators, new decor and costumes (on occasion), and the cost of gas for the many extra rehearsals. The main item of expense, however, was the rent. The committee had been offered the freehold of the theatre for 15,000 specie-dollars (£3,750), and on 12 April they had announced in the press a 'national subscription' to help raise the money. An upper limit of five specie-dollars (25s.) per person had been set, and by 12 June 2,000 specie-dollars had been contributed.

That summer, after the season at the Norwegian Theatre had ended, Ibsen paid a brief visit to Skien, not to see his family but to ask for financial help from his half-uncle, and most prosperous relative, Christopher Blom Paus, a merchant in the town. Hanna Olsen, at that time a maidservant of Paus, re-called to J. Brunsvig[1] nearly seventy years later how Ibsen had arrived in a top hat and frock coat. 'He looked sad and dispirited; his clothes were somewhat worn, but neat and well cared for, so that one did not immediately notice that they were far from new. In his whole demeanour there was a suggestion of suffering which we servants could not but mark. We realised that things were going hardly for him, and pitied him. When he left we stood in the window watching him go.' She added that he did not sleep at his uncle's, but ate his dinners there, and took many walks in and around the town, out to Venstøp and up to Bratsberg. He did not, she said, visit his parents; he had stayed in the neighbourhood about a week, and his uncle had suggested that he should come and work in his shop, but Ibsen had refused. 'As he walked through the streets, he kept to himself, seemingly deep in thought. It was as though he knew no one and no one knew him. But people turned and looked at him; for he stood out from the generality with his neat clothes and shrewd and learned mien.'

Ibsen himself never referred to this visit; in a letter to his sister Hedvig in 1891 he refers to having last been 'at home in Skien' in 1850 (on his way from Grimstad to Christiania). Halvdan Koht[2] rejects Hanna Olsen's evidence on the strength of this statement, and the fact that Ibsen and Hedvig, and his father and another uncle, Christian Paus, several times later write of having last met in 1850. But this proves nothing except that Ibsen did not see them during any visit he may have made, which falls in with Hanna's statement that he did not

---

[1] *Fremskridts* Ibsen-nummer, 17 March 1928.
[2] Koht: *Data om Henrik Ibsen i Skien* (*Ibsen-årbok 1954*, Skien 1955).

call on his parents; and Ibsen's letter of 1891 specifically states that 1850 was the last time he was *at home*. Koht, who had been appointed one of Ibsen's literary executors, was inclined to reject, sometimes rather high-handedly, anything that redounded to his old master's discredit. Hanna's account is very detailed, and Oskar Mosfjeld, who met her and was a critical judge of witnesses, found her testimony convincing.[1] She also told him that Christopher Paus visited Ibsen in Christiania later during the year and, on his return to Skien, reported that Ibsen was living in humble circumstances, with a 'chicken-ladder' leading up to his room.

---

[1] Mosfjeld, *op. cit.*, p. 162.

SEVEN

✄ The Thousand Beaks

(1859–1862)

THAT SUMMER OF 1859 marks a turning-point during Ibsen's second sojourn in Christiania. Up to now he had faced the difficulties of trying to run a national theatre with inexperienced actors, and no worthwhile plays to produce, hopefully. From now on the obstacles became too much for him, and the next three years are a sad story of administrative failure and creative barrenness. He wrote no plays at all between *The Vikings at Helgeland* in 1857 and *Love's Comedy* in 1862, the longest period of inactivity as a dramatist that he was to know until the first of his strokes incapacitated him in 1900, six years before his death.

He staged nothing of interest at the Norwegian Theatre during the autumn after his return from Skien, preferring mainly to revive the light successes of the previous season. For this policy he was attacked in the press. Why, asked *Morgenbladet* on 9 September, did he allow his company to waste their talents on such trivialities as *Le Chevalier des Dames*, a farce by Marc-Michel and Labiche, and *Frontin, Mari, Garçon*, a vaudeville by Scribe and Mélesville? The fact that the public seemed to enjoy them, declared the critic, was no excuse. Thus Ibsen, for the only time in his life, found himself rebuked for truckling to the box-office. The chief new success of the season was *A Caprice*, not Alfred de Musset's comedy of that name (though Ibsen was to direct that two years later), but a 'dramatic divertissement with song and dance' by the prolific Erik Bøgh, which had been a triumph in Copenhagen with the Spanish danseuse Pepita d'Oliva,[1] and for which Ibsen engaged a celebrated German performer called Bianca Bills. This ran for the unprecedented number of twenty-four performances before the end of December, and for a further eleven in the spring. Its reception encouraged Ibsen to present a similar

---

[1] Pepita had already, in 1852, embarked on a liaison that was to last nineteen years with an English diplomat, Lionel Sackville-West (later the 2nd Lord Sackville). They never married, but she bore him seven children before dying at the age of 40 in 1871. One of her granddaughters, Victoria Sackville-West, wrote a delightful book about her (*Pepita*, London, 1937).

entertainment in November, *The Two Comets*, a vaudeville by Hans Peter Holst, in which Fräulein Bills was joined by another dancer with the even more exotic name of Dobsen St Louis. This achieved eleven performances.

It was especially ironical that Bøgh's play should have revived the fortunes of the Norwegian Theatre, for it poked considerable fun at the extravagances of nationalism: one of the characters was a Norwegian ballet-master who spoke broad *pipersvik* dialect and whom the other characters consequently found difficulty in understanding. But it is characteristic of Ibsen that he should have encouraged a parody of what he himself had been preaching, as though in warning against the dangers of extremism; just as a quarter of a century later he was to underline, in *The Wild Duck*, the dangers of that 'claim of the ideal' which was seemingly the cornerstone of his teaching. The implications of *A Caprice* bitterly offended Bjørnson, who had by now left the Bergen Theatre, after two tumultuous years as Ibsen's successor, and had returned to Christiania as co-editor of *Aftenbladet*, living for a while in the same house as the Ibsens on Akersgaden. Never a man to tolerate mockery of his convictions, Bjørnson published a sharp attack on the Norwegian Theatre's policy. 'This theatre', he wrote, 'which but lately was going cap in hand around the country with the appearance of being about to drop dead from starvation…has, in the space of a month, not merely raised itself to its feet but has even found the strength to dance…In the process it has cast overboard the heavy burden of honest nationalistic intent with which, last year, it seemed likely to throttle itself, and has hired a pair of foreign dancers who have achieved a thunderous success…In short, it is dancing away its youth.' *Morgenbladet* joined in the attack, suggesting on 18 September that if Ibsen regarded his company as inadequate for better plays he might consider trying to recruit some actors from Bergen where, especially since Bjørnson's departure, economic conditions were now so bad that they might well be glad to move to Christiania. The article concluded, somewhat unethically one might feel, by advising Ibsen to exploit his friendship with the Bergen players and use 'a little personal persuasion'.

These newspaper attacks continued throughout the autumn. On 9 October *Morgenbladet* declared that 'the so-called Norwegian Theatre no longer exists', and that the public was attending 'in blind devotion to the cause which the Norwegian Theatre is supposed to be advancing, but which it no longer raises a finger to support…It is declining into a kind of amusement ground for the lower classes…We are amazed that the theatre should be allowed to slide lazily and without apparent resistance onto the well-greased chute of Danish mediocrity—under the guidance of a *Norwegian* poet.'

Ibsen retorted to these criticisms by producing, on 12 October, Holberg's five-act comedy *Jean de France;* but this was the only play of any quality that he staged before the end of the year, and the newspaper attacks were soon renewed. Bjørnson defended him, with his usual eloquence, on 26 November in *Aftenbladet;* on 7 December, however, the most vituperative attack yet on the Norwegian Theatre appeared in the form of a poem in *Morgenbladet* by one H. Ø. Blom[1] (ostensibly a farewell tribute to the Danish actor Anton Wilhelm Wiehe, who was leaving the Christiania Theatre). Ibsen replied in *Aftenbladet* three days later, likewise in rhymed verse; whereupon Blom came back at him with another poem, of twenty-two strophes, using his seniority to deliver the magisterial rebuke:

> But here's the difference. I am H. Ø. Blom,
> And you are Henrik Ibsen, nothing more.

Blom had himself been at school at Skien, and may have been hitting at Ibsen's being the son of a virtual bankrupt; the lines quoted suggest a sense of more than literary superiority. Ibsen's reply was so violent that Bjørnson thought it best not to print it.

This undignified controversy had, however, one concrete result. Ibsen told Henrik Jæger in 1887 that when he took his reply to Blom's first attack to the *Aftenbladet* office (presumably on 9 December, since it was printed the following day), he, Bjørnson and Bjørnson's co-editor, Richter, had a conversation in which 'the view was expressed that the time was ripe for the establishment of a group to work for nationalistic aims'.[2] Within a few days, Bjørnson and Ibsen, with the former as prime mover, had established Det Norske Selskab (The Norwegian Society). At first its aims were purely artistic. A special committee was set up, with Ibsen as a member, to try to assemble a national team of the best Norwegian actors from the three theatres in Christiania and Bergen to give a series of special performances in the capital during the summer (when the three theatres would normally be closed). Another of the Society's vaguely stated aims was to tempt all Norwegian actors who worked at the Bankpladsen

---

[1] Blom was a great admirer of Scribe, whom he had declared (in *Morgenbladet* on 1 November 1859) to be 'the prince of playwrights', deprecating the current 'Scribophobia' in Christiania.

[2] Midbøe, *op. cit.*, p. 150. Bjørnson recorded (in *Aftenbladet*, 28 December 1859) that he had been thinking of founding some such society during his last year in Bergen, but that when he came to Christiania he found the atmosphere so different from what he had expected that he had lost interest, and that nothing would have happened 'had not Herr Ibsen been of the opinion that the mere act of founding such a society would start a movement that would achieve several desirable ends...He took all the necessary measures, and to him must all the honour be given.' An older Norwegian Society had been formed in Copenhagen in 1772, with the writer J. H. Wessel as its leading figure, and this had moved to Christiania after the break with Denmark in 1814; but, according to Vinje in *The Dalesman*, it was now only 'an excuse for social get-togethers with food, drink and cards'.

Theatre to leave, though no one seems to have had any clear idea how this was to be done. Opposition was also expressed to the so-called Dusseldorf school of painting. As stated, it had for some time been the custom for Norwegian painters of any talent to emigrate to Dusseldorf, where J. C. Dahl, who had helped Ibsen in Dresden, held sway, and where, so Bjørnson and other purists felt, they came too much under foreign influence! The absurdity of this view deterred several moderate minds from joining, Botten Hansen among them.

Under Bjørnson's energetic leadership, however, the Society soon acquired a hundred members, artists, scientists, journalists and, before long, politicians, including Ole Bull (who was giving a series of concerts in Christiania and who, naturally, played at the first meeting), Vinje, Sars, Johan Sverdrup and, surprisingly, Ibsen's enemy H. Ø. Blom. They met on Tuesday evenings, ate, drank punch, made speeches and, as always seems to happen in Norway at even the most esoteric gatherings, invariably ended up singing. Ludvig Daae, later to become an eminent scholar as well as an active politician, found the meetings ridiculous and thought that Ibsen and one other member, a Dr Bidenkap, were 'the only people who talked any sense'.[1] Gradually, as more and more members of the Storthing joined, the Norwegian Society acquired a more political aspect, and Ibsen began to lose interest in its proceedings.

He was beginning, like so many writers before and after him, to find nationalism cramping to his talent. The occasional poems which he wrote during these first years in Christiania, with their naïve exhortations, ring somewhat hollow. An extreme point was reached the month after the founding of the Norwegian Society, in January 1860, when he wrote a poem called *Life in the Mountains* to be spoken on the stage of the Norwegian Theatre as an accompaniment to a *tableau vivant* 'in which', a contemporary tells us, 'several of the city's most feted ladies appeared'.[2] Ibsen couched this poem in such extremely Norwegian language that, according to Yngvar Nielsen,[3] the eminent Danish actor Anton Wilhelm Wiehe refused to read it, saying that he could not understand many of the words, and Laura Gundersen had to take his place. From about the beginning of 1860 Ibsen seems to have begun to grow sceptical about nationalism; but it was to be some time before he grew finally disillusioned with it, and

---

[1] W. S. Dahl, the biographer of Johan Sverdrup, describes Ibsen at these meetings as 'quietly in attendance, listening to every word spoken but himself scarcely uttering a syllable'; and another member of the Society, O. Hansen, recalled over fifty years later that Ibsen 'never made any speech but listened, and walked to and fro, smiling slightly'. (Christen Collin, *Bjørnstjerne Bjørnson, hans barndom og ungdom*, II, Christiania, 1904, pp. 482 and 487).
[2] Yngvar Nielsen, *En Christianiensers erindringer fra 1850- og 1860-aarene* (Christiania, 1910), p. 315.
[3] *ibid.*, p. 315.

with no other job in sight he was in no position to give up his job at the Norwegian Theatre because of a lack of faith in its ideals.

Of Ibsen's private life at this time, we know virtually nothing; it remained,
as it was always to remain, a closed book to the outside world. Such scanty
evidence as we have suggests that, now as later, Suzannah was a source of
extraordinary strength to him. 'She is just the kind of character I need,' he
wrote to Peter Hansen in 1870, 'illogical, but with a strong poetical intuition,
a bigness of outlook and an almost violent hatred of all things petty. My
fellow-countrymen understood nothing of all this.' And their son was to declare: 'It is probably true, as has been suggested, that he sometimes rebelled
against her will and wished himself far away so that he could lose himself in
his daydreams. I am thinking particularly of their first years together. But if
he had lost her for good he would have been inconsolable; he would have been
miserable had she withdrawn her will. He was the genius, she was the character.
His character. And he knew it, though he would not willingly have admitted
it until towards the end. But she knew it the whole time, and so was uncon-
cerned by what people said, and by the criticisms of friends and acquaintances.
She knew what fate had entrusted to her care, and she regarded it as her life's
task. Let them call her a kill-joy when bad friends, in my father's younger days,
wanted to drag him out with them—or self-willed, when she was old, and kept
the fire still burning in him. She knew that ultimately, her will was his will.'[1]

This son was born to them on 23 December 1859. They called him Sigurd,
after the hero of *The Vikings at Helgeland*, and Bjørnson stood as godfather.
Bjørnson's wife Karoline asserted to numerous acquaintances during the next
three-quarters of a century (she died in 1934, in her ninety-ninth year) that, as
they were returning from the christening, she heard Suzannah loudly declare
that she would never have another child—a statement which, at that time, as
Fru Bjørnson never failed to point out to her listeners, was taken to mean that
a woman had decided to cease sexual relations with her husband. But there is
no record that Fru Bjørnson began to spread this story until much later, when
her dislike of Suzannah and jealousy of Ibsen had become marked; and her
relish in the telling of disparaging stories about them once Ibsen's fame had
began to surpass that of her husband makes her not the most credible of witnesses. 'Anyone who has ever done me any wrong', wrote Bjørnson of her on
5 March 1859 to Clemens Petersen, 'is immediately, and for ever, her most
implacable enemy.' Whatever Suzannah Ibsen's faults may have been, dis-
loyalty to her husband was never one of them, and it seems extraordinarily unlikely that, if she had decided to give up sleeping with her husband, she would

---

[1] Bergliot Ibsen, *op. cit.*, p. 185.

have said so out loud in public, particularly with Karoline Bjørnson around.

Much more to Ibsen's liking than the Norwegian Society was a group which Paul Botten Hansen had gathered round him, and which Ibsen, during this same winter of 1859–1860, began to frequent. Botten Hansen was a passionate bibliophile, who had already amassed a fine library when Ibsen had first met him in 1850; he had had to sell it all the following year to pay his debts, but in the eight years since, by assiduous attendance at book auctions, he had built up another, of no less than fourteen thousand volumes.[1] With his 'pale, angular face and irregular gait', as Ludvig Daae[2] describes him, he had a remarkable flair for discovering rare and often valuable books in the most unlikely places; it used to be said that the most obscure provincial could not die owning one worthwhile book without Botten Hansen hearing of and acquiring it. 'Damn that Dutchman, he has his spies everywhere!' said Ludvig Daae of him, quoting Holberg. The name caught. Botten Hansen came to be known as 'the Dutchman', and his circle, consequently, as 'The Learned Holland'.

The aims of 'The Learned Holland' were almost diametrically opposed to those of the Norwegian Society. Its members were, in the main, critics and scholars rather than creative writers. A kind of cross between the Bloomsbury Set and the Fabian Society, they distrusted naïve plans for the future, and submitted them to sceptical analysis. They strongly opposed some of the Norwegian Society's more cherished and chauvinistic aims, especially in the field of language: such as Bjørnson's passion for injecting Norwegian words and turns of style into the established *riksmaal* (a habit with which, as we have seen, Ibsen also had become infected), and Vinje's attempts to establish a Norwegian *landsmaal*. Mutual admiration was frowned on; criticism was the purpose of the gatherings, which took place on Monday evenings. They would assemble at Botten Hansen's apartment, Raadhusgaden 28 (known as Pipersgaarden, 'probably the oldest three-storey house in Christiania'),[3] where he had two large rooms on the second floor, with books everywhere, including the hall and passages; even the bed was in an alcove of bookshelves. From there they would proceed to one or another café: Nibbe's, the Hotel Angleterre, Engebret Christoffersen's at the corner of Raadhusgaden and Kirkegaten, Peter's Restaurant, which they facetiously nicknamed St Peter's, or, most often, L'Orsa's, a small Swiss café with a convenient back parlour.

Here Ibsen met rising young scholars, such as J. E. Sars and his own wife's cousin, Ludwig Daae, both later to become eminent historians; Asbjørnsen, the

---

[1] His landlord forbade him to bring in any more books lest the floor should give way, and he had to smuggle them in when the landlord was out (Daae, *op. cit.*, p. 339 n.).

[2] *ibid.*, p. 335.

[3] *ibid.*, p. 342.

N

collector of folk lore; his old professor, the poet J. S. Welhaven; and other lively minds, such as Jakob Løkke, Michael Birkeland and Olof Rygh. Vinje, though they stood for everything that he did not, occasionally attended, for old friendship's sake; so, even, did Bjørnson, who found the sceptical mood of the gatherings by no means to his liking. Another promising new author to be seen there was the young Jonas Lie, a Charles Lamb-like figure with whom Ibsen soon struck up a lasting friendship. Lie later recalled Ibsen at these Holland meetings 'in that dark, closed cape and felt hat, his face framed by an outlandishly dark head of hair and beard...Apart from those moments when, in a fit of euphoria, he would hold forth, there was something knotted about him.'[1]

Holberg, the supreme iconoclast, was, not surprisingly, the principal idol of the Holland group. Some of the members knew his comedies almost by heart, and his style and vocabulary influenced their conversation, so that they would often talk a kind of Holberg pastiche. They gave each other nicknames taken from his characters, and Ibsen became known as Gert Westphaler, after the talkative barber in the play of that name. This does not seem to have been applied to him in sarcasm; Christopher Due, Jonas Lie and Lorentz Dietrichson have all testified that, when the mood took him, he could, like many depressives, hold forth with passionate eloquence. He loved, at these gatherings, to quote hypothetical paradoxes; imagine, he would say, an owl afraid of the dark, or a fish intolerant of water; being at the earth's centre, and not knowing the difference between up and down; and whether two and two would make four on, say, Sirius. Six years later, in *Brand*, he was to recall this mood:

> When I was a boy, I remember,
> Two thoughts kept occurring to me, and made me laugh.
> An owl frightened by darkness, and a fish
> Afraid of water. Why did I think of them?
> Because I felt, dimly, the difference
> Between what is and what should be; between
> Having to endure and finding one's burden
> Unendurable.
>
> > Every man
> Is such an owl and such a fish, created
> To work in darkness, to live in the deep;
> And yet he is afraid. He splashes
> In anguish towards the shore, stares at the bright
> Vault of heaven, and screams: 'Give me air
> And the blaze of day!'

---

[1] *Henrik Ibsen: Festskrift i anledning af hans 70de fodseldag*, edited by Gerhard Gran (Bergen, Stockholm and Copenhagen, 1898), pp. 15–16.

One of Ibsen's early biographers, Gerhard Gran, half a generation younger than the Hollanders, knew most of them well and has left an interesting comment upon them. 'They were', he writes, 'almost without exception, distinguished for learning rather than for original ideas, for intelligence rather than energy or vitality, for critical ability rather than creative fertility. The ideals they worshipped were old and dying ideals; they clung tightly to the old Danish traditions, from which others were seeking to emancipate themselves, they abased themselves before the classical education which even then was beginning to show cracks in its seams, they worshipped the concept of Scandinavianism, which was soon to be proved bankrupt. The river of progress passed them by, and, clinging to the past, they watched it glide—each according to his temperament, some in hopeless surrender, others bitterly resentful—certain that their country was moving swiftly towards perdition.' No wonder that Bjørnson hated them; but Ibsen, as Gran says, 'felt at home in this atmosphere which Bjørnson found poisonous. Ibsen had no reason to look on life with a hopeful eye; the iron had, not unnaturally, entered deep into his soul, he had little faith left, and he was, like so many of those others, cynical; he shared readily in their causticity. There was in Ibsen's highly complex make-up a strong measure of conservatism...radical as he was in matters of the spirit and in his championship of individuality, he was indifferent, even antagonistic towards anyone with a bombastic passion for external reforms. He, who was so shy and silent, was by nature suspicious of facile enthusiasm and loud-mouthedness...Eloquence was to him an empty jingle, a politician synonymous with a self-seeker, a patriot with a screeching monkey; he hated nothing so much as silken phrases. One can easily understand why such a man found himself at home among the Hollanders...He shared their antipathies, at any rate to a degree. He found in their circle an echo of his contempt for the poverty of Norwegian political and cultural life.'[1]

Ibsen's preference for the Holland group over the Norwegian Society is confirmation of his growing disillusionment with nationalism. Under the circumstances, it is hardly surprising that his work at the theatre was soon to deteriorate; a man can hardly be a good theatre director if he has doubts about its policy.

Ibsen's associates in 'Holland' and the Norwegian Society were in the main acquaintances rather than friends; he did not make friends easily, and that autumn he lost one of the few he had. Ole Schulerud, who had published *Catiline* at his own expense and shared his small means with Ibsen in their student days, died in October at the age of thirty-one. He was one of the few

---

[1] Gran, *op. cit.*, I, pp. 103–6.

people with whom Ibsen had been, or was ever to be, really intimate, and Ibsen composed a simple and moving little poem to be sung at his graveside. Eleven years later, on 9 June 1870, he wrote Schulerud's widow a long and, for him, unusually personal letter recalling the debt he owed to her husband:

...He was a true friend to me, unstinting, unqualified and loyal. When I look back, there was no one so closely bound up with my youthful development as he. And amidst the successes which I have since achieved it has been a great grief to me that he could not be here among us and share my joy with me. He was the friend I needed in the days when one had to make certain renunciations and prepare oneself for the future; and how few such one has in times like those! There are plenty of people who take note of one when things go well; but the likelihood of failure was every bit as great as that of success when he joined his fortunes to mine with all his loyal and noble heart. Then our lives parted; we seldom wrote to each other; we didn't seem to need to; now that I think back, we never really exchanged a word about friendship or anything like that. What existed between us arose quite spontaneously and developed into something completely unforced, and it never occurred to us to think it could be otherwise. And then, when we met again, our time together was so sadly brief.

But a loss has its exaltation, as it has its grief. The sharpened memory, the inward truth, remain; what parting robs us of is inessential...I should deeply love to have a portrait of Ole, if you can spare one; I have none...

In warmest friendship,

Henrik Ibsen.[1]

The picture we have of Ibsen at this stage in his career, when he was approaching his thirty-second birthday, is of a writer distracted. At the age when an author is commonly at his most fertile, if not at his best, he found his creative energies diverted by the claims of two ideals which he was gradually finding to be false: the ideal of nationalism, and the ideal of creating a worthwhile theatre. Both demanded something that he lacked, and that Bjørnson revelled in; gregariousness, the love of being with and working with other people. To Ibsen, torn between his ideals and his daily work on the one hand, and his instincts and nature on the other, the problem was especially tormenting; and during the last months of 1859 he managed, heaven knows how, to find the leisure to write a long poem of three hundred and eighty-four lines in which he dramatised his dilemma. He called it *On the Heights*, and it is perhaps the finest of his non-dramatic works.

---

[1] This letter is unexplainedly omitted from the Centenary edition (Vol. XVI, Oslo, 1946), though it had been printed in Sigurd Høst's *Ibsens diktning og Ibsen selv* nineteen years previously (Oslo, 1927).

The narrator, a young man, leaves his mother 'with scrip on back and gun in hand' to seek solitude in the mountains. On the way he sees a girl, spends the night with her, and promises to return and marry her. But once in the mountains, he feels different:

> All passions dark, all wild desires
> Are driven from my thoughts.
> I'm born anew. Up here I stand
> Near to myself and God.

Among the peaks he meets a stranger. 'Tears play in his laughter. His lips, when silent, speak'. His eyes are like the mountain lake, born of, and caged by, the glacier. He teaches the young man a 'new wisdom'; the old desires and longings lose their power over him. On Christmas night he looks down and sees his home burn, with his mother in it; but the stranger, by his side, views the scene through his hollowed hand and points out the beauty of the red flames in the moonlight. He loses all desire to return to the life of the valley below. Finally, at midsummer, he sees the girl he loves riding to church to marry another man, and shades his eyes with his hand, like the stranger, better to appreciate the aesthetic effect of the gay clothes against the white birch-trees. He is now freed from all foolish emotional ties, and senses in his heart 'full evidence of petrifaction'. The poem ends:

> I am steeled. I am done with the lowland life.
> Up here on the heights are freedom and God.
> Men do but grope in the valley.

On the Heights is one of Ibsen's most personal poems; and again, as with so many of his best, the English poet whom it most calls to mind is Thomas Hardy, with its changing rhythms, frequent use of dactylic metres, strong dramatisation, economy of narration and extreme simplicity of statement that trembles on, yet never quite oversteps, the cliff-edge of banality. The problem of whether an artist should plunge into life or withdraw from it had been exhaustively and comparatively recently examined by Kierkegaard in (among other works) Either-Or; yet this temptation of total withdrawal is one that has confonted writers in every age, whether as Aestheticism (Kierkegaard), Apollonianism (Nietzsche), the Ivory Tower (Yeats) or, in our own time, non-commitment. At the same time, Kierkegaard was one of those thinkers whose ideas were certainly discussed in the Holland circle, and Ibsen may well, as at other times, have been infected by them at second-hand. The dilemma of commitment or non-commitment remained with him, as it had to while he continued with his grind at the theatre; and he now, in the first month of 1860, began to plan a play on the theme—*Love's Comedy*, which, however, he was not to finish until 1862.[1]

This question of Kierkegaard's influence on Ibsen is one that no student of either writer can sidestep. On the one hand, it has undoubtedly been exaggerated by critics who seem ignorant of the frequency with which authors distrustful of and hostile to each other's work have followed parallel paths to the same goal; and Ibsen, as we have seen, when questioned in later life as to this influence, replied testily that he had 'read little of Kierkegaard and understood less'. This statement was probably true, for Ibsen was never much interrested in philosophical writing. On the other hand, he shares with Kierkegaard such striking similarities not merely of thought but of phrasing that the matter cannot be allowed to rest there.

Ibsen, though a freethinker from a very early age, had, like Kierkegaard, been brought up in an atmosphere of deep pietism and, again like Kierkegaard, regarded the Christian doctrine with a mixture of fear and admiration. Julian the Apostate, in *Emperor and Galilean*, was to voice this duality: 'Whoever has once been in His power can never completely free himself from it.' Ibsen must often have felt, as Kierkegaard did, that he could never fight his way out of the stranglehold which the Galilean system of ethics had put on him; and Kierkegaard's stern conception of Christianity, contempt for the established church and insistence that religion was a matter for the individual soul must have appealed very strongly to him. The two men had, moreover, much in common psychologically. Both were ugly, and shy of close human relationships. Kierkegaard had written (in his journal for 1841): 'The curse which rests on me is never to be allowed to let anyone join themselves to me deeply and inwardly', just as Ibsen had apologised to C. J. Anker in 1858 for being 'walled about with a kind of off-putting coldness which makes any close relationship with me difficult'. Both despised the masses, and were suspicious of so-called liberalism and all party lines; both tended to ask questions rather than give answers; both were oddly addicted to reading newspaper advertisements. Many ideas receive almost identical expression in their writings: Kierkegaard's 'Truth is in the minority' and Dr Stockmann's 'The minority is always right'; Kierkegaard's 'The great thing is not to be this or the other, but to be oneself, and of that every human being is capable if only he wills it', and Brand's:

---

[1] 'Not until I married', wrote Ibsen to Peter Hansen on 28 October 1870, 'did my life achieve a weightier content. The first fruits of this was a longish poem, *On the Heights*. But the demand for freedom which runs throughout this poem did not find full expression until I wrote *Love's Comedy*.'

To be wholly oneself! But how,
With the weight of one's inheritance of sin?...
It is not by spectacular achievements
That man can be transformed, but by will.
It is man's will that acquits or condemns him.

Kierkegaard had stressed, as Ibsen was frequently to do, the necessity of self-liberation as opposed to liberation from without, and the need for an artist to experience sorrow (though Keats had also stressed this, and he had died when Kierkegaard was eight). And Kierkegaard had stated, in *A Seducer's Diary* (in *Either-Or*) that: 'When two people fall in love and decide that they are destined for each other, then they must have the courage to break it off. For to continue is to lose everything and win nothing'; which was to be precisely the theme of *Love's Comedy*.

Such similarities could be coincidental; Strindberg and Freud share as many, yet Strindberg almost certainly never read a word of Freud,[1] and Freud came to his conclusions without Strindberg's help. (As Coleridge remarked when Hazlitt accused him of plagiarising Shakespeare: 'Is there no such thing as two men's having similar thoughts on similar occasions?'). But many of Ibsen's friends were ardent Kierkegaardians. In June 1857, towards the end of Ibsen's stay in Bergen, Magdalene Thoresen wrote to a friend that she read Kierkegaard 'unceasingly', so that Ibsen can hardly have avoided hearing a lot of him through her. Kierkegaard was also much discussed by Ibsen's friends in the 'Holland' circle; and the young priest Christopher Bruun, with whom Ibsen was to have close contact during his first year in Rome, was another enthusiastic disciple. In short Kierkegaard's ideas were everywhere in the air around Ibsen during the latter's formative years and, bored and puzzled as he may have been by Kierkegaard's philosophical processes, he must have found many of his own half-formed thoughts crystallised there.

Meanwhile, now that he had written *On the Heights*, the Norwegian Theatre continued to occupy most of his time and energy. He had, as we have seen, been under fire from the press; but towards the end of 1859 the repertory began to show signs of improvement. On 11 December, the day after he published his long verse counter-attack on H. Ø. Blom (how on earth did he find the time for that during the last days of rehearsing a new production?), he

[1] There is no mention of Freud in Strindberg's twenty thousand surviving letters, which are full of references to what he was reading, nor is there any work of Freud's in Strindberg's library; and he always bought rather than borrowed books, even when he could least afford them. Freud's *The Interpretation of Dreams* was scarcely reviewed at all when it appeared in 1900, and took eight years to sell its first edition of 600 copies, so that Strindberg, though he did not die till 1912, had probably never heard of Freud's name.

staged Holberg's full-length comedy, *Jacob von Thyboe* (about a boastful soldier), and followed it ten days later with a new Danish one-acter, Carit Etlar's *When the Sun Goes Down*. On 3 February 1860 he directed *Ole Shut-Eye*, a comedy by Hans Andersen requiring elaborate staging and scenery, and this proved a popular as well as a critical success, being performed thirteen times that month and nineteen in all before the end of the season. Another new play, Thomas Overskou's *The Devil's Master* (after Mélesville's *Le Fils de la Vierge*) followed in March, and this, too, was a success; the critics went out of their way to praise the production, which included several tableaux of 'witchcraft', with 'Bengal candles'. 'The acting in general', wrote *Aftenbladet* (on 10 March) surveying the theatre's recent productions, 'bears witness to such conscientious instruction that the performances give considerable satisfaction.' Dumas *père's Les Demoiselles de St Cyr*, in April, achieved only two performances, as did Joseph Bouchardy's *Le Sonneur de St Paul* the following month. No one could now complain that the theatre was not presenting new works, even if disappointingly few of the required quality were being written by native dramatists.

On 18 May the Storthing rejected another appeal from the theatre for a state grant. Some time during the summer Ibsen had again to humiliate himself by asking his uncle, Christopher Blom Paus, for money.[1] He visited the latter at his country estate, Buslaaten, in Gjerpen, just outside Skien. We do not know whether he succeeded in his mission, and he does not seem to have visited his family on this occasion either. That summer there were floods in Skien which caused widespread destruction, and the last memory he took away of his native town (for he was never to visit it again) may have been of the great waters pouring through the streets. No wonder he later remembered Skien as 'the town of the storming, soughing, seething waters'. There is also a local tradition that at about this time he applied to the Skien town council for help;[2] but many of the council papers were destroyed in the fire of 1886, so that this cannot be confirmed or denied.

On 1 July he wrote a song for the winners at the summer festival of a rifle club to which he belonged in Christiania; this was published in *Illustreret Nyhedsblad* on 8 July. On 6 August he applied, together with Bjørnson and Vinje, for state travel grants. Ibsen's application reads pathetically:

To the King!

Henrik Johan Ibsen most humbly begs that he may be granted a sum of 400 (four hundred) specie-dollars from the fund set aside for artists and scholars for foreign travel,

---

[1] According to Hanna Olsen, Paus's maid, who, as a very old woman, gave the information to Oskar Mosfjeld (*op. cit.*, p. 162).

[2] *ibid.*, pp. 162–3.

for a six months journey to London, Paris, the larger German cities, Copenhagen and Stockholm, to study dramatic art and literature.

During ten years of literary activity, and an earlier period of preparation for this work, the study of dramatic art and literature, its principles, system and histories, has absorbed the greater part of my time and constituted my main occupation. The criticisms of my dramatic works which have during this period been published by foreign as well as native judges may, I trust, present sufficient testimony that these efforts have not been fruitless; as the sympathy with which the public has received my various plays, several of which have also been performed in Sweden and Denmark, may testify to a talent for the vocation which I have chosen...

Your Majesty's most humble servant,

Henr. Ibsen.

The Akademiske Kollegium, to whom the applications of the three writers were referred, at first rejected them all. The head of the Ministry for Ecclesiastical and Educational Affairs, Christian Birch-Reichenwald, persuaded them to reconsider their decision in the cases of Bjørnson and Vinje, though each received only half the amount applied for (Bjørnson 500 specie-dollars instead of 1,000, and Vinje 250 instead of 500). But they steadfastly refused to make any grant to Ibsen, whose application had been the most modest of the three. It is interesting to speculate on the influence that a visit to London and Paris might have had on Ibsen at this stage of his career. The London theatre was undergoing a particularly lean period; Harley Granville Barker has described its state during the fifties and sixties as one of 'slovenly chaos'.[1] There were no good playwrights; Ibsen would have been just too early for the 'realistic' plays of T. W. Robertson (who was to write *Caste* in 1867) and for W. S. Gilbert, whose first play, *Dulcamara*, would be produced in 1866; he would have seen nothing more interesting in the way of new plays than the comedies of H. J. Byron and J. R. Planché, which were no better than the trivia he had been directing at home. Nor was it a great period for English acting. Macready had recently ended his career and Henry Irving, though he had just started on his, did not play in London in either 1860 or 1861.[2] The best that Ibsen could have seen would have been Charles Kean, J. L. Toole, Samuel Phelps, Helen Faucit and Dion Boucicault, none of them major talents. Nor would Paris have had much more to offer. Rachel had died in 1858, and Sarah Bernhardt was not to make her début until August 1862. Frédéric Lemaître, now aged sixty, had gone into decline. Of the French dramatists, Ibsen already knew about Dumas *père* and Victorien Sardou; he had produced several plays by the former, and was to

---

[1] See his essay in *The Eighteen Sixties*, edited by John Drinkwater (London, 1932).
[2] See Laurence Irving: *Henry Irving* (London, 1951), pp. 98–110.

stage the latter's *Pattes de Mouche* later that year. He might have seen in Paris a revival of the younger Dumas's *La Dame aux Camélias*, which had been first produced in 1852 (but was not to reach Christiania until 1899). What would most have interested him, however, would have been the plays of Emile Augier. Augier's plays, with their contemporary themes and settings, such as *Gabrielle*, *Le Gendre de M. Poirier*, *Le Fils de Giboyer* and *Lions et Renards*, today seem scarcely more 'realistic' than *La Dame aux Camélias*, or *Caste*, or *The Second Mrs Tanqueray*. The characters seem shallow, the plots melodramatic. But they dealt, however superficially, with current problems; they castigated contemporary morals, and even introduced contemporary politics. No doubt Ibsen, even without any French, would have been delighted to see such things on the stage. But since he himself was to do exactly these things in his next play, *Love's Comedy*, and since his dramatic technique was already much superior to Augier's, it is difficult to imagine that seeing the latter's plays acted would have had much, if any, influence on him.

As things turned out, Ibsen was never to visit England; nor, although he was to live for twenty-seven years in Italy and Germany, was he to enter France, except to pass briefly through in 1869 on his way to and from the opening of the Suez Canal.

So he stayed in Norway, and on 17 August that year, 1860, we find him again in the role of hack poet, writing a song to greet visiting members of the Swedish Parliament. A week later, on 25 August, J. L. Heiberg died, and Ibsen wrote a moving elegy[1] to the memory of the man who had received him courteously in Copenhagen eight years before, and whose plays had been among the few that it can have given him any pleasure to direct. Ibsen retained his admiration for Heiberg, and for his actress wife, all his life.[2] He also, in the role of unofficial local laureate which he so curiously filled, wrote a poem to be spoken on the day of the new King Carl XV's coronation, and yet another greeting to the Swedish M.P's, this time to a deputation from them which was visiting Trondhjem. All of these pieces, except the Heiberg elegy, are naïvely, even (to an outsider) embarrassingly patriotic, with frequent exhortations to 'Men of Norway' and 'Norway's Heroes'. Sir Henry Newbolt is not a poet whom one would immediately associate with Ibsen; but these poems, *mutatis mutandis*, might almost have come from his pen. Needless to say, they delighted most of his contemporaries. 'Thank Ibsen for his poems!' wrote Vinje to Botten Hansen (who had published three of the worst of them in *Illustreret Nyhedsblad*) on 8 September. 'They are the most Norwegian of all!'

On 29 September Ibsen presented his annual report to the board of the

---

[1] See p. 116.

[2] *cf.* e.g. John Paulsen, *Samliv med Ibsen* (Christiania and Copenhagen, 1906), p. 46.

Norwegian Theatre. It is very defensive in tone, and consists largely of an attempt to answer criticisms of the repertory during the early part of the season. 'Fräulein Bills's engagement', he stated, 'was entered into in September with an especial eye to the presentation of the one-act plays, A Caprice and The Two Comets. These two plays, which were performed (as they had to be) continuously over the next two months, since her contract did not extend beyond that period, had naturally to be accompanied by pieces which would not occupy a whole evening. The repertory during this period had therefore to consist mainly of short works, a state of affairs which could not be remedied except by the already remarked concentration of full-length plays towards the end of the season.' Ibsen concluded by admitting that some of the new plays could have been better performed, but pleaded as an excuse various sicknesses within the company.

Despite the criticisms, the season had proved financially the most successful that the theatre had known. The takings had amounted to some 12,000 specie-dollars (£3,000), about 860 specie-dollars more than in the preceding year. Expenses, however, had exceeded income by 2,000 specie-dollars, which meant dipping into the 3,500 specie-dollars raised by the national appeal.

Ibsen seems, however, around this time to have become apathetic about his work at the theatre. That summer the theatre was being rebuilt, at considerable expense, and Knud Knudsen, the language instructor who was also on the board, records that Ibsen showed little interest in the theatre's affairs, was lazy during August and September in rehearsing new plays for the coming season (which did not open until the rebuilding was completed in October), and frequently absented himself from board meetings 'for no other reason than that he knew he would be asked what he had done since the last meeting. I remember we once found ourselves holding a board meeting in a rear room at L'Orsa's café in Prindsensgade, because we had heard that he happened to be there.' He recalled that at one board meeting this year he 'gave Ibsen a real dressing-down, the like of which he can never have experienced before or since'; and that Joachim Garborg, another board member, had told him (Knudsen) that he had treated Ibsen 'like a truant schoolboy'. But, says Knudsen, 'Ibsen took what I gave him without saying a word'; and he adds that Ole Bull, now back from Oleana, who himself had spoken severely to Ibsen at the same meeting, told him: 'You've got to be tough with Ibsen if you're to get anywhere'.[1]

Evidence of Ibsen's apathy can be found in the fact that he chose as his

---

[1] Knudsen did not publish his memoirs, but D. A. Seip noted extracts from them in the inaugural issue of Edda (Christiania, 1914).

second production of the new season that tedious nationalistic drama, *The Goblin's Home*, by P. A. Jensen, which he had condemned in such violent terms as a student back in 1851. 'Such nationalism as it contains', he had written then, 'is merely a tacked-on embellishment and has no organic connection with the play...Amongst such nationalistic tinsel we may enumerate a quarterstaff duel, a peasant dance, a few rustic swear-words and some fragments of *patois* which may dazzle the ignorant but which, critically investigated, reveal themselves in all their hollowness and triviality.' This was the play which he now, nine years later, chose to direct, and he may have thought his cynicism justified when the production received enthusiastic reviews and ran for ten performances. The enlarged stage[1] and more elaborate scenic effects that could consequently be achieved were doubtless partly responsible; on 30 October, *Morgenbladet* noted with pleasure that it was no longer necessary for 'one step to signify four, or for lovers to crowd and buffet each other incongruously for lack of space'.

On 25 October Ibsen addressed yet another appeal for assistance to the Storthing on behalf of the theatre. Comparing its circumstances to that of theatres in other countries, he expresses the hope that those who have done so much to encourage the other arts will not neglect that of the stage. No art, he suggests, has 'so active and meaningful an influence on the development of a people' as the dramatic; and he begs for support, that they may not be 'driven by oppressive circumstances to strike a false path...Under such conditions a theatre is all too often compelled to *follow* public opinion instead of *guiding* it, to be dragged down by current and often depraved taste instead of controlling it. If our theatre possessed greater resources' he continues, 'it would also be in a position to increase and improve its acting strength, and to give it a more thorough preparation and training. It would be able to discriminate more in its choice of plays and in the performing of them, to reward original writing and thus assist our dramatic literature, and, in general, to work in a more artistic and national spirit than has hitherto been possible.'

Needless to say, the appeal was rejected.

---

[1] A description of the improved arrangements appears in *Christiania-Posten* (nr. 286). Conditions, we are told, are now 'much more comfortable and agreeable for the audience. In the stalls, as in the amphitheatre and the first tier of boxes, every spectator has an individual seat with arms; where, previously, the seating was cramped and displeasing, there is now plenty of room, and although the auditorium has now been sunk into the basement, by which arrangement it has been possible to incorporate a second tier of boxes, the total capacity has not signifiicantly been increased...The theatre is handsomely decorated, the white colours harmonising agreeably with the gilded embellishments; and the new curtain, representing a mountain landscape traversed by a stream, makes a gratifying impression'.

In November Ibsen revived another play which he had seen as an under-graduate in 1851, a five-act German historical drama by Karl Gutzkow entitled *Zopf und Schwert* (*Pigtail and Sword*), set in the court of Frederick William I. It had been badly received then, but he had admired and defended it: 'When one has, like our public, inured oneself year in and year out to the dramatic candy-floss of Scribe & Co., cautiously seasoned with a ration of bogus poetry, it is not to be wondered at that this more solid German fare should prove indigestible even to the ostrich stomachs of Christiania audiences.' The play was newly translated, by Suzannah Ibsen, and was sympathetically reviewed; but the public liked it no better than they had in 1851, and it was withdrawn after only four performances.

No wonder Ibsen was feeling apathetic towards his work. The public had made it clear that it had little appetite for serious drama, and that what it wanted, and what the theatre needed if it was to remain solvent, was a virtually unbroken diet of comedy, preferably with music and dancing. Even Sardou's *Pattes de Mouche*, being without music, proved too much and ran for only three performances that November; and *The Foster Brothers*, an adaptation by J. L. Heiberg of a comedy by Karl Töpfer based on an adaptation by J. R. Planché of William Rowley's 1632 comedy. *A New Wonder, A Woman Never Vext* (the list of credits underlines the kind of material with which Ibsen had to work, even when the original was of some quality) managed only four in January. A reviewer of the Sardou complained that the actors seemed to 'lack instruction', to which Ibsen replied in *Aftenbladet* (5 December) that 'under me, no debutant has appeared on the stage without sufficient preparation. It is another thing for beginners to show lack of experience, which your reviewer has confused with lack of instruction.' On 22 November, meanwhile, he had learned that his application for a travel grant had been rejected.

During the autumn of 1860 the theatre had, greatly daring, started a ballet school, and on New Year's Day 1861 a 'dance divertissement' was presented. *Morgenbladet* (3 January) complained that the performers 'have not yet acquired the first rudiments of dancing...Granted that the performance found its public; a storm of applause was heard from the gallery when the curtain fell, and the dancers appeared with happy faces...But we would ask the artistic director to consider whether the Norwegian Theatre and the superior public that it has lately acquired are not somewhat beyond "dance divertissements" of this quality.'

Bowing to the public taste, Ibsen presented in February a 'folk comedy' entitled *The Builders*, an adaptation of a French piece by Théodore Cogniard and L. F. N. Clairville, *Les Compagnons de la Truelle*. The play, as adapted, was set locally in Christiania, and this caused the greatest excitement. The public, we learn, were amazed and delighted to see 'their own windows' on the stage, and the presentation of Frederiksberg and the Klingenberg gardens with their famous Apollo *salon* evoked 'a storm of spontaneous enthusiasm'. There was a scene in Storgaden 'at eventide', another against the background of the fortress of Akershus, and, the grand climax, a bird's-eye view of the whole city. *Morgenbladet*, which seems to have acquired a new and caustic reviewer at the beginning of this year, complained that this was merely 'the photographic language of reality...as if one were to present masons with chalk dust on their faces or a blacksmith with dirty fingers'; a reminder that every age has its critics who object to what they regard as excessive realism. The same gentleman also felt that the humble diction of the actors was unsuited to the representation of upper-class Christiania society, though he appears to have accepted it in the portrayal of foreign royalty and aristocrats, But the public liked the show, and it ran for twelve performances that season.

This was, however, almost the only success of the New Year. *Erasmus Montanus*, another of Holberg's best comedies, achieved only three perform-ances, and H. P. Holst's adaptation of Charlotte Birch-Pfeiffer's *Das Glücksind* four. Ibsen fell back on farces and vaudevilles, but attendances at the theatre declined badly throughout that winter and spring. This was partly because the Christiania Theatre had engaged the toast of Copenhagen, Pepita d'Oliva, and was presenting her in Bøgh's *A Caprice*, in the role in which she had taken the Danish capital by storm. Even the re-engagement by Ibsen of the two English dancers, the Healey Sisters, could not compete with this.

Throughout this winter and spring of 1861 Ibsen was violently and repeatedly attacked in the press for his conduct of the Norwegian Theatre. His new enemy in *Morgenbladet* was particularly to the fore. 'Amidst all the joy and enthusiasm which the Spanish Sennora [*sic*] is spreading over Christiania', he wrote, 'the lesser theatre stands forgotten, thanks to the very bad plays which the artistic director thinks fit to present week after week. A visit to the Norwegian Theatre is like a kind of aesthetic visit to a hospital; to wander down the long empty corridors to the empty rows of stalls and boxes is "a journey through the abodes of misery and the vales of sorrow". Things could scarcely be worse if the artistic director strove his utmost to make the repertory as unattractive as possible.'

At the beginning of March Ibsen wrote a series of four articles for *Aften-bladet* under the general title *The Two Theatres of Christiania*. Asking whether the Danish-controlled Christiania Theatre was equipped 'to fulfil the Nor-wegian people's justifiable demand for a national dramatic art form' (it is as wordy as that in the original), he critically examined its repertory, its artistic achievements and its attitude towards nationalistic sentiment.

Concluding his final article, Ibsen indicated that he might, at some future date, continue with these criticisms; to which the rival newspaper *Morgenbladet* reacted by printing a triple headline in heavy type repeating thrice the request: HERR IBSEN! MORE THEATRE ARTICLES, PLEASE! followed by a short piece demanding that he justify the criticisms he had made. Ibsen did not reply, and his silence was the signal for further attacks on him. On 28 May, *Christiania-Posten* joined in the fray. 'Lucky the man', declared this newspaper, 'who has a beautiful idea to fight for, and when that idea is a whole people's, and the people have chosen this man to carry their idea towards fulfilment, then that man must be adjudged doubly lucky. Herr Theaterdirektør Ibsen has such an idea to fight for, the Norwegian people have made him controller of their national theatre; *he* is to have charge of this youthful cultural centre, he is, as best he can, to create a national art and elevate our dramatic literature. Such, surely, was the original plan, such surely the principles on which a Norwegian Theatre was to be organised?' But when the rebuilt theatre opened, 'one lacked any sense of overall direction, the theatre stood tottering, the acting was bad, the repertory bad'. After castigating the unnecessary expenditure on redecorating and redesigning the interior of the theatre, the writer contrasts 'the Herr Ibsen who wiites in *Aftenbladet* with the Herr Ibsen who presides in the Norwegian Theatre, the Norwegian Theatre Herr Ibsen describes in the newspaper with the Norwegian Theatre which Herr Ibsen directs', and ends by concluding that 'Herr Ibsen is not the man to direct our theatre'.

The author of these words continued his attack in two further articles, Ibsen defended himself in *Aftenbladet* on 1 June, listing the Norwegian plays, the classics (such as Holberg) and the new foreign plays that he had presented. His anonymous opponent, however, wrote three more lengthy articles in *Christiania-Posten* that month, the first of which began: 'There is a kind of person who supposes that merely by showing himself, merely by stepping forward with an avowal of good conscience and saying "*Hier bin ich*", he will fell his adversary to the ground. Such a person is Herr Ibsen. He thinks that simply by writing a string of articles in *Aftenbladet* he can get people to believe, not merely that he understands about such things, but that he cherishes a living interest in our theatre.'

Ibsen replied in *Aftenbladet* on 12 June, but the feeling that he had neglected his duties was evidently fairly widespread. Knudsen records in his memoirs that on 14 May Ibsen had been rebuked by the board for holding no rehearsals at all between 29 April and 10 May; and a correspondent in *Morgenbladet* asked what Herr Ibsen had done with two new Norwegian plays, J. L. Sundt's *Niels Lykke* (a new treatment of one of the chief characters in *Lady*

Inger of Østraat) and a drama entitled *From the Fjord*, both of which had been submitted to him as long ago as 1859 and which he had promised would be performed that season. 'Herr Ibsen has thus repeatedly discouraged his authors, flaunted his committee and vexed his public. One cannot but ask whether such behaviour is becoming in Herr Ibsen, who recently took such offence because the directors of the Christiania Theatre found themselves compelled to postpone for a few months the production of his own play, *The Vikings at Helgeland.*' An even more damaging attack, however, came in the form, not of an article, but of a lecture by a member of his own company named Døvle.[1] While the five unpaid members of the board, asserted Døvle, had done all that could reasonably be expected of them, this could not be said of the sixth, paid, member, who was receiving a salary of approaching 1,000 [*sic*] specie-dollars a year, and whose direction of the theatre during the season had been 'somewhat negligent'. Another correspondent in *Morgenbladet*, in an article carrying the headline BRING BJØRNSON HOME! demanded that Ibsen be ejected from a post which he seemed to regard as a sinecure and that Bjørnson be put in his place. The news of this campaign, when it reached Bjørnson in Ariccia, did not please him. 'Colonel Bassøe', he wrote to Ditmar Meidell, one of the co-editors of *Aftenbladet*, that summer (the letter is again, maddeningly, undated), 'says that Ibsen is running the theatre badly. That's ill news indeed.'

To these last attacks Ibsen remained silent, and it fell to his old friend Paul Botten Hansen, in *Illustreret Nyhedsblad*, to speak out in his defence. He made the interesting assertion that, apart from Døvle's lecture, all the attacks on Ibsen, while purporting to come from the same source, were in fact being written by the same pen, and declared that 'people are destroying the good name of the press by pretending to speak with a multitude of voices from selfish political motives'. The public, he went on, should not forget the difficulties under which Ibsen has had to work: 'box office considerations, ideals, artistic considerations and unsuitable material all make their own special and powerful demands.' He admits that Ibsen might perhaps show a little more energy; but, whatever Ibsen may or may not have achieved for the Norwegian Theatre, he is not 'a man whom any schoolboy may treat as an equal, even if the wind of opinion should be blowing against him'. By writing such works as *The Vikings at Helgeland*, and others, Ibsen has laid claim to 'a position in our literature which demands a modicum of reason from his opponents, whether they be members of his own company or whether they be undergraduates'. Botten Hansen concluded: 'These vulgarians of art and letters who have spoken so

---

[1] Reported in *Morgenbladet*, 30 May 1861.

scornfully of Ibsen should have sufficient insight into the future and sufficient sense of their own poverty of talent to realise that this man, so viciously attacked by them, will live in Norwegian literature long after moss and grass have grown over their own graves and nettles over their literary reputations.'

Nevertheless, even if all the newspaper attacks were, as Botten Hansen claimed, written by the same pen, it seems likely that they were at least in part justified. It must have been more than a mere difference of opinion that caused Døvle to speak out; Ibsen told Henrik Jæger that Døvle was angry because 'his wife was not getting enough to do',[1] but one notes that no other member of the company raised his or her voice in public to contradict him. And Ibsen had, as we have seen, been rebuked by his board. Moreover, he was now drinking heavily. At least once students returning to their rooms at night saw his bearded figure lying senseless in the gutter.[2]

If it was any comfort, the Christiania Theatre had been doing little better. It was clear that so small a town as Christiania then was could not profitably support two theatres. Indeed, the previous autumn (1860), when things at the Christiania Theatre were especially bad, a feeler had been put out to the Norwegian Theatre concerning the possibility of a merger. This had happened, however, when the Norwegian Theatre was in the middle of its rebuilding operations, which the board hoped would solve their problems; besides which, they feared that a merger would simply result in their being swallowed by the larger organisation. So the Danish offer was rejected. But as the season had progressed, and neither theatre had prospered, there had been a good deal of unofficial testing of opinion from both camps. The possibility remained in everyone's mind as they broke for the summer vacation.

During the summer, Ibsen started trying to rewrite *Olaf Liljekrans* as an opera libretto, and on 18 July he sent the first scenes to the composer M. A. Udbye in Trondhjem. The pages that have survived show that he had worked on the text to make the language as 'Norwegian' as possible; he was still evidently under the influence of the nationalistic movement. But Ibsen, with his poor ear for music, had little idea, despite his earlier youthful article on the subject, of the problems of libretto writing, and despite Udbye's en-

---

[1] Midbøe, *op. cit.*, p. 161.

[2] Told by H. Koht (whose father saw Ibsen thus) to A. E. Zucker, and recorded by the latter in *Ibsen, The Master Builder* (London, 1929), pp. 94 and 310-11 *n*. Professor Francis Bull writes: 'I realised how Ibsen was regarded by the bourgeoisie of Christiania in the eighteen-sixties when generalkonsul Andresen Butenschøn told me that as a young man, in 1864, he had been encouraged by his uncle to subscribe to a fund so that "the drunken poet Henrik Ibsen" might go abroad and be rescued from his misery.' (*Tradisjoner og minner*, 3rd edition, Oslo, 1963, p. 100).

O

couragement he left the project unfinished. He wrote only one poem that summer, a completely worthless exhortatory piece to be sung on 17 May (Independence Day), which opens 'We are a people, our land is free', and gets no better.

The new season at the Norwegian Theatre opened on 14 August, and Ibsen seems to have taken some at least of the criticisms to heart, for the repertory for the first few weeks contained several new plays; but their reception was hardly propitious. The first, a French comedy by P. Dinaux and G. Lemoine, *La Dotte de Suzette*, was described by *Morgenbladet* as 'one of those mediocre products which unfortunately seem to constitute the principal diet of our capital's theatres, and which, even more regrettably, appear to attract the public'.

It didn't, for it ran for only three performances. On 13 September the long awaited *Niels Lykke* was at last performed, and proved a disaster. The critics annihilated it (*Morgenbladet* called it 'an example of how not to write a play'), and it, too, was withdrawn after three performances. On 25 September Ibsen presented a third play new to Christiania, Gustav Freytag's five-act drama *Count Waldemar*, which had been successfully performed at practically every theatre in Germany. Suzannah Ibsen translated it, the critics welcomed it and praised Ibsen for having had the enterprise to produce it; but the public again showed its distaste for anything remotely serious by staying away, and it, too, lasted for only three performances. The experiences of this month alone underline, if any underlining were needed, the impossibility of Ibsen's position. He was abused for not presenting new plays, or plays of sufficient quality; when he tried to do so, they emptied the theatre. It was a situation with which other directors of experimental theatres over the next hundred years were to become increasingly familiar.

At the annual general meeting of the Norwegian Theatre on 19 September 1861, Ibsen presented his report in what must have been an uncomfortable atmosphere. Owing to the fact, he says, that his new actors were not engaged until the end of September, he was unable to plan his repertory ahead, since this was dependent upon what players he might have at his disposal. The departure of several members of the old company had meant that, whereas previously he had a repertory of about a hundred plays which he could revive at short notice, he was now left with only one which would not require recasting and, consequently, protracted rehearsals. Then, the old decor did not fit the new stage, and had to be 'enlarged and repainted', and was not ready until after it was needed. The company, with so many new members, was unused to playing together, and there had been a number of illnesses, as a result of which five performances had had to be cancelled and seven replanned.[1] Despite all this, the theatre had presented more new plays during this seven-and-a-half-months season than in the previous season of nine months. As regards complaints about the economic situation, he presented figures to remind the board that takings had considerably increased since he had taken over the artistic directorship.

Ibsen's defence does not read altogether convincingly at this distance of time. One cannot help feeling, and no doubt the board felt, that, while the difficulties had been considerable, they were of the kind with which a theatre director must more or less expect to be faced, and that a more energetic and resourceful man might have overcome them more successfully. Bjørnson's achievements during his two years as Ibsen's successor at Bergen had become a legend, fostered, we may be sure, by those actors who had recently joined Ibsen's company from there, and that newspaper headline BRING BJØRN-SON HOME! must have been in the mind's eye of many a person present. The chairman of the board, Judge Hansteen, expressed his opinion that 'the artistic director has not shown the zeal that might have been wished for'.

Undeterred by the failure of the three new plays with which he had opened the season, Ibsen presented on 9 October Bjørnson's latest work, *King Sverre*, a three act historical drama written the previous spring. The Christiania Theatre had thought of staging it, but had renounced their rights, and were probably congratulating themselves; to confront the Christiania public with another historical play after the failure of *Niels Lykke* and *Count Waldemar* must have seemed like asking for trouble.

However, the evening after the premiere of *King Sverre*, a gala performance was given to celebrate the laying of the foundation stone of the new Storthing building. The cabinet and members of the Storthing were invited, the house was full and the evening was a triumph. When the final curtain fell, Johan Sverdrup, the Liberal leader, led three cheers for Bjørnson from the stalls. 'It is refreshing to see this kind of dramatic writing as a change from the welter of comedies', commented *Aftenbladet*. The acting, as well as the play, was praised, though no one bothered to mention the direction. *King Sverre* was played six times during the season which, if nothing compared to the runs of comedies and musicals, was reckoned good for a serious play. Bjørnson, now in Rome, must have felt grateful to Ibsen. Advising Clemens Petersen on the

---

[1] To make matters worse, though Ibsen did not mention this, the cost of rebuilding and redecorating the theatre had so exceeded the original calculations that in February the board had found themselves compelled to summon a meeting of all the actors and staff and announce a reduction of salaries by one-sixth for the next four months; if necessary, they were prepared to postpone this reduction until 1 April, to avoid hardship, but the actors and staff agreed to accept it forthwith.

arrangements for the unveiling of a statue to Oehlenschläger, he wrote: 'Ibsen can't make a speech, but if he comes, you get hold of him. Believe me, that man can *think*'.

On 30 October Ibsen, continuing his policy of new plays, staged Alfred de Musset's *Un Caprice* (translated into Norwegian as *En Fantasie*, so as not to confuse with Erik Bøgh's *En Kaprice*, which had been such a success during the two previous seasons). This delicate conversation piece, requiring high comedy acting of the most skilled order, was a bold choice, and the newspapers, to give them credit, praised Ibsen for attempting it. But the public, not surprisingly, found it lacking in action, and four performances were all that it could muster. Financially, the new season was proving a disaster. The mediocre Bøgh, however, came to the rescue with a musical adaptation of Victor-Hugo's *The Hunchback of Notre Dame* entitled *Esmeralda*. Ibsen provided an elaborate production, with processions and choirs, and the play ran for thirteen performances. A new Norwegian play, *The Brothers*, by H. O. Hansen, achieved only three, but *Don César de Bazan*, a five act drama by Philippe Dumanoir and Eugène Dennery, paid its way with six, and both productions were praised for their careful acting. Indeed, the newspapers were being as favourable to the productions at the Norwegian Theatre as they had been critical the previous year; perhaps Ibsen's enemy on *Morgenbladet* (and on *Christiania-Posten* too, if we are to believe Botten Hansen) had got the sack. *Aftenbladet* called on the Christiania Theatre to note 'how neatly and attractively costumed their colleagues at the impecunious Norwegian Theatre always appear', and *Christiania-Posten* remarked: 'If one has censured the Norwegian Theatre in previous years for lack of enterprise, it has certainly shown during the current season energy which fully deserves the appreciation and encouragement which the public, by its regular attendance [!] has given it. During the few months since the opening, it has, apart from revivals, presented a number of plays that are either new or at least new to Christiania—and no one can say that the Theatre has shrunk from the demands that this policy has involved, or from the obstacles that have had to be overcome'.

But the strain was beginning to tell on Ibsen. On 5 December a notice appeared in the press that the artistic director was ill and therefore unable to perform his duties. 'Ibsen is sick, I see?' wrote Vinje to Botten Hansen on 13 December. Magdalene Thoresen, as an old woman in the next century, recalled his illness in her novelettish style:

'He had a violent attack of nervous fever. He, who had hitherto possessed a body of granite, resistant to all the buffets of fate, found himself for once in a situation in which he required care and nursing. He was now a married man with a home, so that all the help he needed was to hand. But he absolutely refused to accept any. He left his home each morning and wandered around in the winter air, planless, alone, dazed with fever. And he came through. The sickness gradually left him. But when, after this test of strength with the enemy of life [Magdalene had grown Ouida-like in her old age] he had become himself again, it was as though he had covered a part of his journey as a writer underground, and had come up into the daylight again in another place. Henceforth Henrik Ibsen was to steer a new course. It is no longer in the open pages of history that he seeks his themes; from now on he follows a personal path, and strides forth as a cleanser, with a scourge in his hand'.[1]

Magdalene always, even as a young woman, preferred the melodramatic to the prosaic explanation. Ever since his teens, Ibsen had been intensely interested in contemporary problems, whether political, social or personal. It was the tide of nationalism, plus the convention that high tragedy usually concerned the dead, that had caused him to seek his themes in the pages of history; and in any event, it was to be another twelve years before he finally turned his back on historical drama. He had always been by nature a cleanser; it was simply that from now on, he was to use the drama instead of journalism as his medium for this.

The first work that he wrote after his illness,[2] though, was as uncontemporary as it could be: a long, patriotic historical poem entitled *Terje Vigen*. Set during the Napoleonic Wars, when Norway was blockaded by the Allies, it tells how a wild youth of that name was changed by the birth of a daughter into a responsible citizen. To save his wife and child from starvation, he tries to break the blockade in a rowing-boat, but is intercepted by an English 'man-of-war' (the poem is studded with English words, such as 'Stop!', 'Mylord' [sic], etc.) and spends five years in prison. When he is freed, he returns to Norway and finds that his wife and child have starved to death. He becomes a pilot; and one night an English yacht is shipwrecked. Terje, by now grizzled, rows out to save the occupants, and who should they be but the English 'Mylord' who had arrested him, with his 'Mylady' and child. Conscience and the desire for revenge struggle within him; conscience wins, and he brings them

---

[1] *Om Henrik Ibsen og hans hustru*, published in *Juleroser* (Copenhagen, 1901). According to Julius Elias, who had it from Suzannah and Lorentz Dietrichson, Ibsen meditated suicide during this illness (Elias, *Christiania-Fahrt*, in *Die Neue Rundschau*, XVII, 1906, p. 1464); how seriously is not known.

[2] Though he may have written it just before. It was published on 23 February 1862, as a rather belated New Year's supplement for *Illustreret Nyhedsblad*'s subscribers, but the exact date of its composition is unknown. Ibsen told Halvorsen that he wrote it at the end of 1860, but this must be an error; cf. Koht, *Eit diktarliv*, II, p. 303.

safely to land, for, as he explains, 'the little one's sake'. If, without knowing, one were asked to guess the author of this curiously sentimental and conventional ballad, the last name that would come to mind would be Ibsen's; yet the poem, perhaps because it is one of the few tolerable patriotic works that he wrote, is held in Norway in extraordinary affection. Victor Sjöström, one of the pioneers of the silent cinema, made a film of it in 1916, only ten years after Ibsen's death.[1]

In the New Year of 1862, Ibsen presented several more new productions at the Norwegian Theatre: Melesville's comedy *Sullivan*, Emile de Najac's *Une Croix à la Cheminée*, *More than Pearls and Gold* (a romantic comedy freely adapted by Hans Andersen from both F. Raimund's *Der Diamant des Geisterkönigs* and *The Thousand and One Nights*), and two new Danish plays, J. C. Hostrup's *A Night in the Mountains* and Meïr Aron Goldschmidt's *Rabbi Eliezer*. *More than Pearls and Gold* ran for seven performances, *Sullivan* for six; the others for only two, four and two performances respectively. Bjørnson's historical verse drama, *Lame Hulda*, in April, managed only three.

On 14 March, Ibsen applied to the Akademiske Collegium for a stipend of 120 specie-dollars (£30) 'to make a journey during two of the summer months through outer Hardanger and the districts around the Sognefjord, northwards to Molde and back through Romsdal, to collect and annotate such folk songs and tales, old and new, as may still be extant. On 24 May this application was granted, though the College cheeseparingly knocked 10 specie-dollars off the amount asked.

The economic position of the Norwegian Theatre was by now critical. On 18 March the board had to ask the actors to renounce their holiday pay during the summer, in return for being allowed to lease the theatre free during these months and share the proceeds. In April the orchestra announced that they would not perform until their wages had been paid. That catastrophe was averted; but Ibsen himself was being dunned by creditors, and on 14 May he wrote to J. B. Klingenberg, the treasurer:

If, as promised, you have met any members of the board or would be willing to act on your own account, you would do me the greatest possible service if you could possibly send me by messenger some of the money that is due to me. A warrant of distraint has been served on me for last year's tax (11–12 specie-dollars), and I am threatened with the removal of my possessions. This is more than hard, since I am owed a considerable part of my salary, and I therefore place my trust in you as the only person to whom I can turn.

Your obedient servant,
Henr. Ibsen

---

[1] Sjöström lived long enough to act the leading role in Ingmar Bergman's film, *Wild Strawberries*, in 1957.

A sad note by Klingenberg that same day in the record books of the theatre shows that they had no more than fifty-three specie-dollars (£13) in the till. 'Last week', concludes Klingenberg's note, 'I had to pay 126 specie-dollars from my own pocket to settle salaries and other essential debts concerned with the running of the theatre'.[1]

But by now the Norwegian Theatre had reached the point of no return. The rebuilding operations, on which they had embarked with such hopes, had crippled them, and they now found themselves with debts amounting to 28,000 specie-dollars (£7,000). The board approached the Christiania Theatre to reopen the question of a merger. Among the conditions they proposed were (1) that the artistic director of the combined venture 'shall never be a Dane or other foreigner' (2) that 'the standing rule that only Norwegian actors and actresses may be engaged shall not be broken'. The Christiania Theatre replied recalling that they had themselves suggested a merger in 1860, but that 'although this proposal appeared to have been favourably received, the directors of the Norwegian Theatre withdrew from further negotiations, so that the opportunity of uniting without either side incurring an impossible financial debt was lost'. The Christiania Theatre (the letter continued) felt unable to take over the very considerable debt now owed by the Norwegian Theatre; if, however, the latter should succeed in selling its building for some non-theatrical purpose, and could arrange for its debt to be paid off in annual instalments of 1,500 specie-dollars, agreement might possibly be reached.

These terms, especially in view of the high-handed manner in which they were worded, the Norwegian Theatre found unacceptable. It was decided to file a petition of bankruptcy, and Ibsen and his company were given notice as from 1 June. The actors, however, decided to remain together and lease the theatre as an independent concern for the coming season for a payment of 18 specie-dollars (£4-10-0) per performance.

So Ibsen's career as a theatre director ended. If his six years at Bergen had been hard, these five years at Christiania had been harder. For him, of all people, so fastidious in his tastes and so shy of human contact, to produce this succession of featherweight farces and musicals with an inexperienced company, contemptible rehearsal time, and hopelessly inadequate financial and technical resources, abused in the press, attacked from within his own company and condemned by his board, it must indeed have been a protracted nightmare. His own dramatic talent, instead of flowering as he had hoped, had gone barren; and now, with a wife and son to support and no private means, he was without a job.

Moreover, he was now being blamed in some quarters for the theatre's

---

[1] Ø. Anker: *Ibseniana og Bjørnsoniana fra Kristiania-teatrene* (*Edda*, 1956).

failure. Knud Knudsen, in his unpublished memoirs, makes no bones about the matter. They should, he said, have got rid of Ibsen much earlier, and had only not done so 'because (1) we had no one else to turn to (2) we always hoped that the pressure exerted by the board must some time take effect (3) he undeniably *understood* the work better than anyone else we could possibly hope to get (4) we were unwilling to make a man, in other respects so deserving, jobless...People would hardly credit that an author who could create so strong-willed a character as Brand could have been so slack and lethargical in practical matters'.

Knudsen's condemnation probably goes too far. We know that he and Ibsen had disagreed violently from the beginning about how far the theatre could go in being 'Norwegian'; Knudsen was a fanatic on this subject, and there is evidence that, in common with a curiously high proportion of linguists, he tended to become paranoiacally hostile to anyone who opposed him on his pet subject. If one peruses the newspaper reactions to the hundreds of productions which Ibsen presented at the Norwegian Theatre, one finds him praised more often than blamed; frequently we read that the scenic arrangements are 'especially handsome and tasteful', the ensemble playing excellent, the costumes attractive (he was always especially meticulous about other people's clothes as well as his own). Not only the standard of acting and production, but also the box-office takings improved markedly during his tenure of office, except during his last season, and the falling-off then was almost certainly directly due to his pursuing a policy of new plays on the orders of his committee. Under his direction, the Norwegian Theatre soon found itself able to compete on equal terms with, and sometimes even surpass, the Christiania Theatre, which had a better building and stage, a smarter position, much more experien-ced actors and an established audience. When Ibsen arrived, the annual takings at the Norwegian Theatre had averaged 7,000 specie-dollars; during his first year this rose to 9,000 and over the next few years it rose to 12,000—an increase of more than 70 per cent. If the board had not overreached themselves by their decision to rebuild, and so saddled themselves with a debt they could never hope to pay off, they would probably still, eventually, have had to merge with the Christiania Theatre, because the city could not support two theatres run-ning roughly similar repertories; but Ibsen would at least have been recognised as having done the job he had been appointed to do, namely, to raise the Norwegian Theatre to the same level as the Christiania Theatre. He was not the first nor the last theatre director to become a scapegoat for the failings of his committee and the preferences of his audience for light entertainment rather than serious drama.

Nowhere, probably, in Europe could he have found a less inspiring town to work in. 'Christiania during the late eighteen-fifties and early eighteen-sixties', wrote Gerhard Gran, 'must have been a sadly jejune place...All observers from this time agree in their condemnation of its spiritual indifference.'[1] J. E. Sars called it 'a temple of puritanism and narrow-mindedness, a community of the old, granting youth no rights whatever'.[2] Henrik Jæger, writing in 1887–1888, noted: 'It is significant that none of our living Norwegian authors choose to live in the capital. They have arranged to live in the country...or have buried themselves in a small town. And usually they have chosen to exile themselves for a shorter or longer period'.[3] The most eloquent condemnation of nine-teenth-century Christiania, however, comes from one of Norway's most distinguished novelists, Henrik Wergeland's sister, Camilla Collett:

> 'O great and little city! What a cold and surly sky broods over you! You are great enough, with your thousand beaks! great enough slowly to peck to death the man who no longer diverts you, or against whom you bear a grudge. But not so great that one of these unhappy creatures can find a corner in which to hide...You have all the consuming passions, yearnings and pretensions of a great city; and yet you are so small, and so petty, that you cannot gratify one of them...We, your children, must live off one another, feed on one another...' [*The Judge's Daughters*, 1854–1855].

In the long run, however, we must be grateful that things happened as they did. If Ibsen had been successful and happy in his work in Christiania he might, with his lifelong dislike of travel, never have uprooted himself from Norway and spent the greater part of his working life abroad; and, as with so many creative writers, it was only when he transplanted himelf to foreign soil that his genius really began to flower.

---

[1] Gran, *op. cit.*, I pp. 86–7.

[2] Quoted by Gran, *op. cit.*, I p. 87. He does not specify where in Sars's writings this reference occurs, nor have I succeeded in tracing it.

[3] Jæger, *op. cit.*, p. 163.

EIGHT

❧ Out of the Tunnel

(1862-1864)

On 20 June 1862 Ibsen signed a contract with Jonas Lie, who by now had taken over the ownership of *Illustreret Nyhedsblad* (though Botten Hansen was still its editor) for the publication of a new play, his first for five years; and on 29 June the magazine announced that 'a modern verse comedy in three acts by Henrik Ibsen' would constitute its New Year supplement. The idea for this play had first come to Ibsen as early as 1858, and in 1860 he had begun to write it under the title of *Svanhild* (the name of the heroine). About sixteen pages of this draft have survived; apart from a song which opens it, a solo with choruses, it is in prose, a modern satirical comedy set just outside Christiania. But during 1860 he had been overwhelmed by a general feeling of apathy towards his work, and had abandoned the project. Now, during either the spring or, more probably, the early summer of 1862, he had taken it up again, this time writing it in verse, which, one can scarcely repeat too often, came to him as a young man more easily than prose, not least in the composing of dialogue. It has usually been assumed, on no evidence that I can find, that he had completed the first draft by the time he signed his contract. But that spring had been a particularly hectic time at the Norwegian Theatre, and it seems likelier that he merely showed Lie and Botten Hansen the draft of *Svanhild*, or a few pages of verse rewrite, and that they, knowing his past achievements and perhaps wishing to give him an additional incentive, commissioned the play, which he eventually re-titled *Love's Comedy*.[1]

---

[1] Ibsen only just got the final version ready in time for it to be published on 31 December; after he had handed in the first two acts, he was so long over the third that Lie only managed to extract it from him by threatening: 'If I don't get it now, I'll write it myself'. Now this final version differs very little from the first verse draft, and the only substantial changes occur in Act One. Ibsen had nothing else to occupy him after his return to Christiania in early August except a little casual journalism, and it seems more probable that he spent those next five months completing his first draft and then revising it than that he devoted them purely to the revisionary work, which we know to be slight. Moreover, the announcement in *Illustreret Nyhedsblad* on 29 June gives no title, which suggests that at that stage it was merely begun or proiected.

On 24 June, he left Christiania on his trip northwards to gather folk-lore, for which the Akademiske Kollegium had granted him a stipend. He travelled partly by coach, partly on foot, partly by fjord steamer and partly by rowing-boat. A brief diary which he kept during the first three weeks, barely a thousand words all told, was discovered as late as 1932, and enables us to follow him, in the company of a newly-engaged young law student and a stern Catholic priest, to Lillehammer, along the valley of Gudsbrandsdalen and across the Sogne mountains; thence he voyaged along the Sognefjord, northwards through the spectacular landscape of Sunnfjord and Nordfjord, over the mountains from Breim to Sunnylven, by steamer to Søholt, on to Vestnes in Romsdal, and back through Gudbrandsdalen to Christiania. The harshness of life in the remoter areas astonished him. He came to one valley where the parsonage had been destroyed by an avalanche. The wife, who had just given birth to a child, occupied a screened-off corner, while the husband transacted the business of the parish in the rest of the room. Another house lay at the foot of a precipice so sheer that the inhabitants had no fear of avalanches; the stones, they told him, always fell at a slight angle so that, hugging the rock, the house was safe. From the Jotunfjeld he looked straight down on a steeple hundreds of feet below, and could see no possible way of descent; but there turned out to be a path cut in the face of the precipice, and he descended this with his Catholic priest and a sick woman tied to a horse. He mistook two Swedish fellow-travellers in succession for the young Swedish poet Carl Snoilsky, who that year had published his first book of poems (and who was to become his close friend a quarter of a century later); was depressed by the heavy rain which followed him everywhere; commented on the varying quality of his lodgings; took showers when he could, bathed, fished and collected stories.

Some of these he dismissed as fabrication, such as the sea-serpent caught in Lysterfjord and sold for 300 specie-dollars to an Englishman, who got his money back; 'for' (records Ibsen), 'he knew where the sea-serpent hides in its belly all costly objects of gold and silver which it swallows, and slit it open and took them'. But others seemed more authentic; and he found two especially rewarding informants. One was a free-thinking peasant known as Steins-Knut, whom Ibsen described as 'the wisest countryman he had ever met'; the other, at Solnær, was a local historian named Peder Fylling, to whom Ibsen was introduced by his wife's cousin, Ludvig Daae. From Fylling he scribbled down over a hundred pages of legendary anecdotes, most of them dealing with supernatural visitations. Many of these centred on an eighteenth century priest named Peder Strøm; he had studied the 'Black Book' at Wittenberg, as was common among churchmen of those days, for the ability to perform seemingly impossible tricks enabled them to impress and convert otherwise sceptical

peasants. Thus, Ibsen learned, Peder once sank an unbeliever in the earth up to
his shoulders and freed him only when he had promised to follow the true faith.
He terrified the local witches by telling them that, if they were in league with
the Devil, blood would run from their butter when he cut it with his knife;
'and those present saw a new sight, for the blood not only ran from the butter
but drenched the whole table'. Then there was the story of St Olaf's pig; the
Saint left it with a peasant, and at first the animal thrived, 'but as the rumour
spread that the Saint was dead, the pig began to pine, and finally so sickened
that it turned into stone, and so it may still be seen standing there today'. There
was the witch who, as they took her to the stake, swore that no living thing
would grow for as far as she could see as she burned, 'wherefore they deemed
it expedient to bandage her eyes'; and the ignorant charcoal-burner, whose
one desire was to become a priest, though he could neither read nor write. By
a trick played on the King, he managed to obtain a living, but his ignorance was
so patent that the parishioners petitioned the Bishop to remove him. Knowing
the Bishop to be a lecher, he feigned death, having bidden his wife to sit alone
with the Bishop watching over his coffin. Then, as the Bishop began to fondle
her, the charcoal-burner rose from his coffin and denounced him, as a result
of which 'the Bishop had to let him remain as priest, although he could not
read the Book'.

In addition to these notes, Ibsen made drawings of the landscape, and when
he returned to Christiania in early August, four of these (two of Gudbrandsdalen, one of Vestnes and one of Nordfjord) were published in *Illustreret
Nyhedsblad*—the only time, so far as we know, that he ever received payment
for any artistic work. They are excellent realistic studies; Ibsen had continued
with his painting all the time he had been in Christiania, even, when he could
ill afford it, taking lessons from a feckless painter named Magnus Bagge who
was to be one of the models (there were several, for it is a common enough
Norwegian type) for Hjalmar Ekdal in *The Wild Duck*. He accompanied
these drawings with stiff little descriptive sketches, of the kind expected from
nineteenth-century travellers. He also wrote up for *Illustreret Nyhedsblad* four of
the stories that Peder Fylling had told him, and on 17 November signed a
contract with the bookseller and publisher Johan Dahl to make a book of them,
of two hundred and fifty pages, for an honorarium of 160 specie-dollars (£40)
—a project which (surprisingly, in view of his need for cash) he never completed. Now that the Norwegian Theatre had closed he was without a job,
and had to support his wife and son by casual journalism, plus whatever he may
have saved from his travel stipend. There cannot have been much left from the
110 specie-dollars; but Ibsen (and Suzannah, too) were, all their lives, the
thriftiest of people, and they seem to have managed somehow.

Ibsen wrote eight long articles for *Illustreret Nyhedsblad, Aftenbladet* and even *Morgenbladet* (which had been so hostile towards him) before the end of the year. The first two, on *The Crisis in the Theatre* (that perennial subject) include, in addition to an indictment of the public for indifference, a bitter attack on the complacency of actors. 'Our players', he wrote, 'have not as yet experienced the blessing of privation, which no man escapes with impunity. The man of ideas who lacks the opportunity to starve or suffer is thereby deprived of *one* way of becoming great.' He went on to express his personal faith in a vivid image. 'When Vesuvius erupted and destroyed Pompeii with earthquake and ash, a Roman soldier stood guard at the temple. Slaves and anyone, anything that could flee, fled past him; but the soldier remained at his post, bound by his duty, guarding his trust. The rain of ash rose and rose around him, inch by inch, and rose so high that it buried him; he could not flee, for *he had not been dismissed*! Such action is spiritual, it is a revelation of the spirit that should rule in art as in the army or the Church...to remain at one's post and guard one's trust.'[1] He was, though he did not know it, about to be given a further opportunity to test the strength of his belief in his calling.

On 31 December 1862 *Love's Comedy* was published, as *Illustreret Nyhedsblad*'s special New Year supplement for their subscribers. Ibsen received 100 specie-dollars, 'at that time a goodish fee', noted Henrik Jæger.[2] Apart from *St John's Night*, it was the first play he had written with a modern setting.

The action takes place in the garden of a villa just outside Christiania, owned by Mrs Halm, the widow of a civil servant. She has married off seven nieces from this house, and is anxious to do the same for her two daughters, Anna and Svanhild; which ambition seems about to be fulfilled, for they are being courted by her lively young student lodgers, Lind and Falk. Falk, however, believes that marriage and love are incompatible; marriage, he declares, is 'a galley of chains and thralldom', and as though to prove his point the local Pastor Strawman enters with his wife and eight of their twelve children. Once he had been a burning young idealist like Falk; now he has faded into dullness and conventionality, and the girl he loved has become a plump housewife. 'Everything's burned out, dead!' cries Falk. 'Where's the green joy of life?' He calls on Svanhild to join her life to his, but without the bond of marriage. 'If you must die, live first! Be mine, in God's green spring!' With her to inspire him, he knows he could become a great poet. Like the falcon whose name he bears:

---

[1] *Aftenbladet*, 31 August 1862.
[2] Midbøe, *op. cit.*, p. 164.

> I must fly against the wind to reach the heights,
> And you're the gust to carry me...
> Be mine, be mine, until the world shall claim you!
> And when our tree grows bare, why, then we'll part.

SVANHILD: You think of me as a reed that a child cuts
Into a flute to play on for an hour,
Then casts away.

FALK: Better that than to stagnate in the marsh
Till autumn comes and chokes you with grey fog.

But she, the first of those imaginative yet realistic girls whom Ibsen was to create, the predecessor of Agnes in *Brand*, Solveig in *Peer Gynt*, Dina Dorf in *The Pillars of Society*, Nora when the scales have fallen from her eyes, replies:

> You called yourself a falcon...
> Another image came into my mind.
> I saw you as no falcon, but a kite,
> A poet's kite of paper, that is nothing
> Without its string...impotently beseeching:
> 'Send me aloft, that the strong winds may bear me!'

She leaves him; and impulsively he decides that he must, after all, marry her.

But in the second act his disillusionment returns. His friend Lind, whom Anna has by now accepted, begins to show the marks of domesticity; and Pastor Strawman does not help by descanting on the joys of marriage. Falk, inexasperation, denounces marriage to the assembled company. Love, he says, anticipating T. S. Eliot, has to cross the desert; to marry is to turn one's back on that desert. Marriage is to love 'as is a potted plant to fresh field flowers'. The company is scandalised and departs into the house; only Svanhild remains, awed by his fury as Agnes was to be by Brand's, and says that, if he still wants her, she will go with him. He tells her that they will show the world that there is a love which marriage need not destroy, takes off his ring and puts it on her finger.

This is where most dramatists of the age would have ended the play; but Ibsen, even this early in his career, had something up his sleeve for the final act. Pastor Strawman, hitherto merely a figure of fun, tells Falk that the latter's denunciation of marriage has reminded him of his own lost ideals, and begs him, somehow, to give him (Strawman) back his faith. Falk says he cannot. But now Guldstad, a rich but kindly business man, and himself an admirer of Svanhild, steps in. He reminds Falk of what the latter had said yesterday, about the incompatibility of marriage and love; has he really changed his views? The only possible foundation for a happy marriage, says Guldstad, is the kind of love that is based on other things than passion; it is not inferior to passionate love, and it grows where the other fades. He leaves Falk and Svanhild alone to make their decision. Svanhild asks Falk if he would not still cherish her if and when his love died; to which he replies: 'No. When my love died, all else would die too'. She asks whether he can promise her that he will love her for ever; he answers: 'For a long time'. She says that the kind of love she and Falk bear for each other can only survive if the lovers part when it is at its full, and keep it as a memory. This memory will do more for Falk as a poet than if they should stay together and their love fade. She kisses his ring, throws it into the fjord and tells Guldstad that she will marry him; and is left sadly seated as the others congratulate her, while Falk, free as he has always longed to be, goes off into the mountains with his illusions.

Love's Comedy was, both structurally and in the depth of its characterisation, by far the best play that Ibsen had yet written. Why is it never acted today, in Scandinavia any more than elsewhere? The reason lies in the form which Ibsen employed. It is written throughout in rhymed verse, of remarkable concentration and ingenuity, but of an extreme formalism, as though by a modern Alexander Pope. Admittedly, Ibsen was to use rhyme throughout both Brand and Peer Gynt, but in both those plays he employed it far more flexibly than in Love's Comedy. In them the characters speak dialogue, in Love's Comedy they deliver set pieces packed with epigrams. To work on a modern stage, the play would have to be translated into free verse; and even then, the effect of set pieces would remain. Attempts to revive it in this century have never proved successful, and are never likely to; it remains a brilliant dramatic poem rather than a poetic play. It is crippled by the untheatricality of its form, just as Olaf Liljekrans is crippled by the untheatricality of the ballad form and The Vikings at Helgeland by that of the saga style.

The day after Love's Comedy was published, on 1 January 1863, Ibsen took up a part-time employment as aesthetisk konsulent to the Christiania Theatre, which had decided to bow to public opinion and go Norwegian. The Danish manager, Carl Borgaard, had been dismissed, and negotiations were in progress for the services of the actors of the Norwegian Theatre who, since that body had declared itself bankrupt, had been giving performances at the Møllergaden Theatre as an independent company. Most of them were to move to Bankpladsen in the summer. Ibsen's duties in his new post included, as well as literary advice, supervision of the historical accuracy of the decor and costumes and, when required, stage direction. His salary was pathetically small, 25 specie-dollars (£6) per month, and since even this small sum was dependent on the box office takings exceeding a certain figure, he in fact received only a fraction of it.

On 8 January he offered *Love's Comedy* to the theatre at Trondhjem for the modest honorarium of 60 specie-dollars (£15), and while he was awaiting their reply a notice appeared in *Illustreret Nyhedsblad*, on 25 January, to the effect that the play was shortly to be staged at the Christiania Theatre. But during February and March reviews of the most unfavourable nature began to appear in the press. Professor M. J. Monrad, who had welcomed the appearance of *Catiline* thirteen years earlier, warned Ibsen in *Morgenbladet* that he would destroy himself if he became 'a mouthpiece for the loose thinking and debilitating nihilism that is now fashionable'. The play, he asserted, was 'an offence against human decency…The underlying theme, that marriage and love are irreconcilable opposites, is not merely basically untrue and, in the loftier sense of the word, immoral, in that it denigrates both love and marriage; it is also unpoetical, as any viewpoint must be which claims that idealism and reality are incompatible'.

In *Aftenbladet*, Ditmar Meidell called *Love's Comedy* 'a wretched specimen of literary dilettantism', and said that Ibsen had 'abandoned himself to a wild pursuit of effects, not shunning the most fanciful and tasteless paradoxes to achieve his goal'. Ibsen, he continued, 'does not possess genius, but merely talent…He could develop into a pleasing poet, since he has a facility for modelling himself on good masters and an ear for verbal music', but 'he sets out deliberately to portray marriage and family life as the darker side of human existence, nay, as the very cause of all the misery that this world contains, since the state of marriage, in his view, extinguishes true love and closes men's eyes permanently to all ideals'. Botten Hansen, as always, attempted to defend his friend in *Illustreret Nyhedsblad*,[1] but the public was left in no doubt that *Love's Comedy* was an immoral work (just as, eighteen years later, they were to receive a like warning about *Ghosts*). The Christiania Theatre, never (then or later) renowned for flying in the face of public sentiment, decided that they dare not perform it.

Ibsen never forgot the abuse with which his compatriots had received *Love's Comedy*, and the effect it had had on him. When, three years later, following the success of *Brand*, *Love's Comedy* came to be reprinted, he decided to hit back at his attackers in a preface. 'I made the mistake', he wrote, 'of publishing it in Norway. Both the time and the place were ill chosen. The play aroused a storm of hostility, more violent and widespread than most books could boast of having

---

[1] A caricature in the weekly magazine *Vikingen* (7 March 1863) shows Botten Hansen, pierced with arrows and quill pens, using *Illustreret Nyhedsblad* as a shield to defend Ibsen against the attacks of *Aftenbladet*.

evoked in a community the vast majority of whose members commonly regard matters of literature as being of small concern. This reception did not really surprise me...When, in my comedy, as best I could, I cracked the whip over the problem of love and marriage, it was only natural that the majority should rush shrieking to the defence of those institutions. Not many of our critics and readers have acquired the intellectual discipline and training which enable a man to recognise delusions'. In a letter to Peter Hansen on 28 October 1870, he recalled: 'People brought my personal affairs into the discussion, and my reputation suffered considerably. The only person who approved of the play was my wife...I was excommunicated. Everyone was against me'. Perhaps partly because of the hostility of its reception, he retained a particular fondness for the play. 'Structurally', he wrote to Hartvig Lassen on 24 October 1872,[1] I am more than ever convinced that it cannot be faulted, and has not in this respect been bettered in any of my other plays. All in all, I reckon *Love's Comedy* to be among the best things that I have done'—and this was after he had written *Brand* and *Peer Gynt*.

Ibsen admitted that his wife had been the model for Svanhild. 'Illogical, but with a strong poetic intuition, a bigness of outlook and an almost vehement hatred of all petty scruples' was how he was to describe Suzannah (in the letter to Peter Hansen quoted above); and the description would apply equally to Svanhild. (Similarly, he declared Suzannah to have been the model for Hjørdis in *The Vikings at Helgeland*, because Suzannah, like Hjørdis, thought that the highest thing that a woman could do was to accompany her loved one into battle and 'set his vision aflame'). He may have taken the name Svanhild from the Volsungasaga, one of his main sources for *The Vikings at Helgeland;* in that, there is an innocent young girl named Svanhild who has to suffer a tragic fate because of the crimes of her family, just as Ibsen's Svanhild was to suffer because everyone around her had sinned against the true concept of love.

Ibsen's finances were now at rock bottom. They had, as we know, been bad enough when he was receiving 50 specie-dollars a month from the Norwegian Theatre; now he was forced to resort to money-lenders, and to making further applications for grants and stipends. On 6 March he applied to the Akademiske Kollegium for a renewal of the stipend allowed him the previous year for the collection of folk lore. He asked 120 specie-dollars and was granted 100. Four days later he addressed a petition to the King: 'Henrik Ibsen', it begins, 'most humbly begs...that he be granted an annual pension of 400 (four hundred) specie-dollars, to enable him to continue his literary activity'.

---

[1] This letter is not in the Centenary edition, but was printed by Øyvind Anker in his article *Kjærlighedens Komedie på Christiania Theater* in *Edda*, lxi, 1961, pp. 59–81.

P

The document makes sad reading. Ibsen describes his career up to this point; how he had started work at fifteen, 'my parents being in needy circumstances'; how he had prepared himself for his matriculation; and then lists his publications and the plays which he has had staged, naming the various salaries he has enjoyed.

My salary at the Bergen Theatre amounted to 300 specie-dollars annually, and I was compelled to leave the city in debt. My appointment at the Norwegian Theatre of Christiania carried with it an annual salary of about 600 specie-dollars, but the theatre's bankruptcy involved me in a loss of over 150 specie-dollars, together with all permanency of occupation. At the Christiania Theatre I have been allotted a nominal salary of 25 specie-dollars per month, but the payment of this is dependent upon higher takings than the theatre has achieved during the current winter, My financially most successful work, The Vikings at Helgeland, *which occupied me for nearly a year, brought me in all 277 specie-dollars. Under the circumstances I have incurred debts of some 500 specie-dollars, and since I have been unable to envisage any prospect of improving my financial situation in this country, I have felt compelled to make the necessary preliminary arrangements to emigrate this spring to Denmark. To leave my native land and abandon a career which I have hitherto regarded, and still regard, as my true vocation, is, however, a step which I find inexpressibly distressing, and it is in the hope of avoiding this step that I now, as a last resort, most humbly beseech that a proposal signed by Your Majesty be laid before the present Parliament granting me an annual pension of 400 specie-dollars, whereby I may be enabled to continue a career in the service of letters which I have reason to believe that the public would not wish to see brought to an end.*

Your Majesty's most humble servant,
Henrik Ibsen.

This appeal was rejected; not, as some biographers have suggested, because of *Love's Comedy* (though one member of the grants board, a cleric named Riddervold, declared that the man who could have written such a play deserved not a grant but a thrashing). The records of the Department of Education (who had, after all, granted his folk lore application the previous year) show that in their report they admitted that 'the applicant's literary achievements must be agreed to be of no small importance to our literature, and would have wished that Ibsen could be granted support to enable him to continue his work under more favourable circumstances; but, since we must hesitate before recommending new grants that are not of immediate urgency, Parliament having been assembled for so long, we cannot feel that there is the same urgency to make such a recommendation as in that of the grant for Bjørnstjerne Bjørnson', who had applied simultaneously. The memorandum added a reminder that Ibsen's request in 1860 for a travel grant had not been acceded to, and concluded: 'We feel it is probable that he will be favourably considered at the next allocation of stipendia, though this statement naturally cannot be regarded as binding'.[1]

On 27 May he made a further application, this time for a grant of 600 specie-dollars 'to spend a year, principally in Paris and Rome, studying art, art history and literature'. The petition continues: 'The many and great difficulties with which an author has to contend in this country are increased still further by the almost total absence of opportunity to obtain the necessary grounding in general culture which everywhere else is regarded as an essential condition for the successful and profitable continuation of the work which I believe to be my vocation. I venture to observe that travel grants of this nature have been granted to every Norwegian writer who has devoted himself exclusively to authorship except myself, and I therefore most humbly beseech that I may be allotted six hundred specie-dollars from the Fund for Foreign Travel in the Pursuit of Art and Science'.

'Ibsen can rely on a bigger grant than Bjørnson, surely!' wrote Vinje to Botten Hansen on 11 June; but he was wrong. Although, on 12 September, the Akademiske Kollegium at last acceded to his request, they did so as grudgingly as possible, giving him the last place on their list and recommending that the award be reduced to 250 specie-dollars. This sum struck even the Department of Education as miserly, and they recommended that it be increased to 400 specie-dollars 'which, though considerably less than the amount applied for, may be regarded as sufficient to ensure some satisfactory return, which can scarcely be said of so small a sum as that suggested by the Kollegium'.[2]

The result of this latest application was not made known to Ibsen until mid-September, and he existed that summer, we must suppose, largely on the 100 specie-dollars which he had been granted to continue his study of folk lore, and which he in fact never used for that purpose. O. Arvesen describes how Ibsen could be seen in his shabby clothes entering L'Orsa's café punctually at two o'clock each afternoon to drink coffee and read the foreign newspapers, and adds: 'That this man with the threadbare coat, old, soft mormon hat and profoundly unassuming mien would become one of Norway's and Scandinavia's greatest men was an unimaginable thought'.[3]

The tide was, however, about to turn.

In June Ibsen received an invitation from students to attend a choral festival at Bergen, at which over a thousand singers were to gather from various parts of Norway. He accepted, and wrote a song which the three choral groups

---

[1] Statssektetariatets Arkiv, quoted by J. B. Halvorsen (*op. cit.*, p. 13).

[2] *ibid.*, p. 13.

[3] O. Arvesen, *Oplevelser og erindringer* (Christiania, 1912), pp. 128–9.

from Christiania learned for the occasion. The news of Ibsen's imminent return aroused no enthusiasm in Bergen. A list of those requiring accommodation was posted in the town; those willing to offer hospitality were asked to sign against visitors whom they would like to have, and, we are told, Ibsen's was the last name to be taken up. Ignorant of this, he left Christiania with the three choirs by ship on 12 June, and reached Bergen two days later.

The voyage in the company of these people, and the festival itself (which lasted four days) had a remarkable effect on him. For the first time in his life, he was lionised. The critics, especially of late, had been hostile to his works, the cultural authorities had repeatedly negatived his applications, and, living, as he did now, a comparatively solitary life, he can seldom have heard a word of praise except from those he knew well, and that one never quite believes. But now, forced into the company of this largely youthful gathering, he, who had previously felt isolated and rejected, found himself surrounded by sympathy, friendship and spontaneous admiration. One incident especially moved him. At a banquet in Bergen on 16 June, Bjørnson paid him a most generous public tribute, speaking out handsomely in praise of his writing and denouncing those people who had tried, as critics will in every age that contains writers of comparable stature, to turn them into adversaries. 'Have I not experienced', cried Bjørnson, 'that my friend Ibsen has been held up against me for the purpose of disparaging me, and I against him, to disparage him?' His speech was followed by the song which Ibsen had written for the occasion, dealing, it so happened, with the importance of naturally dissimilar people living together in harmony— a coincidence which Ibsen, no more than anyone else, can have missed. Four days after his return to Christiania, on 25 June, he wrote to his host at Bergen, a shipping agent named Randolph Nilsen:

> It is eight days to the hour since we said goodbye, and, God be praised, I still carry within me the spirit of the festival, and I hope I shall long keep it. My hearty thanks to you and your good wife for all the indescribable warmth and friendliness you showed me. The festival up there, and the many dear and unforgettable people whom I met, are working on me like a good visit to church, and I sincerely hope that this mood will not pass. Everyone was so kind to me in Bergen. It is not so here, where there are many people who seek to hurt and wound me at every opportunity. This powerful feeling of elevation, of being ennobled and purified in all one's thoughts, must I think have been common to all who attended the choral festival, and he would indeed have something hard and evil in his soul who could remain insensitive to such an atmosphere.

Further encouraging things were to happen that summer. On 18 July, the young Danish critic Clemens Petersen published a long review of *Love's*

Comedy in the Copenhagen magazine *Fædrelandet*. It occupied half the issue, and was by no means altogether favourable; indeed, it summed the play itself up as 'a failure'. Petersen praised the skill of the verse, but thought, rightly, that there was too much virtuoso rhyming, and that the reasoning was sometimes glib. He also asserted, one would think less correctly, that Ibsen only wrote well when he wrote 'in the shadow of some accepted prototype', saying that he was 'unsure and hit-or-miss' when left to his own resources; he thought that Ibsen had striven to compete with Bjørnson, at the same time imitating him and trying to do the opposite to him. What Ibsen ought to do, concluded Petersen, 'with his fine eye for a prototype and his rich talent for carrying on where others have left off' was to unite the old traditions with the new. Although, therefore, Petersen ultimately came down against *Love's Comedy*, his review made it clear that he regarded Ibsen as a writer of both accomplishment and promise, to be taken seriously; and this, from the most influential critic in Scandinavia, must have seemed praise indeed compared with the kind of criticisms which Ibsen had been getting in Norway.

The following day, 19 July, a long 'profile' of Ibsen was published in *Illustreret Nyhedsblad*. These weekly profiles were a feature of the magazine; notabilities thus honoured that summer included Lamartine, Liszt and Stonewall Jackson, so that to appear in the series was something of a distinction. Paul Botten Hansen was the author, and the piece, some 2,500 words in length, was accompanied by the first likeness of Ibsen to be printed, a clumsy linocut 'after a photograph by Petersen', not easily distinguishable from one of Vinje, similarly bearded and melancholy, which was published in the next issue, and much inferior to a large illustration of Princess Alexandra of Denmark's arrival in London for her wedding with the Prince of Wales which appeared in the same issue as Ibsen's profile. Pointing out that Ibsen now has no fixed income other than his uncertain salary as *aesthetisk konsulent* to the Christiania Theatre, Botten Hansen continued: 'He is consequently mainly dependent on such honoraria as his writing may bring him. But this, Ibsen being the kind of author he is, can never prove a rich source, for he is one of those individuals whom external circumstances, and even privation, cannot readily incite, except as the expression of a temporary inspiration. The reason for this is a self-criticism which often rejects not merely long-matured plans, drafts and works already commenced, but even completed *œuvres* which, when he considers them coldly and at a distance, no longer satisfy him'. Botten Hansen went on to compare Ibsen's lyrics with those of Heine, but said that his dramatic works were his most important, and concluded with the information that Ibsen 'is at present busied with a new saga-play set in Norway in the Middle Ages'.

A further reference to this latest project occurs in a letter which Ibsen wrote on 10 August to Clemens Petersen, thanking him for his notice of *Love's Comedy:*

Mr Clemens Petersen.

I don't like writing letters, largely because I suspect that the criticisms which you make, rather harshly I feel, of my prose in general may justly be levelled against my efforts in this field. However, I must write briefly to thank you warmly and sincerely for your review of my book. I thank you both for what I agree with (which isn't only the flattering bits) and for what, if I ever have the good fortune to meet you, I shall at any rate try to dispute. I am especially grateful to see that you are not in general as opposed to my work as I had instinctively imagined; this has for me an importance which is perhaps difficult for you to understand who do not know how frighteningly alone, in a spiritual sense, I feel up here. My 'friends'' opinion of me doesn't hurt; in matters where I myself am concerned, I see far more clearly than all my friends—and the result is far from flattering. I am now engaged on a historical drama in five acts—but in prose, I cannot write it in verse. You do me a little injustice when you suggest that I have tried to imitate Bjørnson; Lady Inger of Østraat *and* The Vikings at Helgeland *were written before Bjørnson had composed a line. (N.B. It is possible that* Between the Battles *was in existence by the time I wrote* The Vikings, *but I did not and could not have read it). As regards* Love's Comedy, *I can assure you that if ever an author had to get a mood and a subject off his chest, it was the case when I sat down to write that. I shall follow your kind advice to offer* Lady Inger *to the Royal Theatre* [at Copenhagen]; *please heaven I handle the matter in the right way, and it comes off. I feel compelled to send you these lines of thanks because I feel most warmly and sincerely that you have done me a great kindness in not putting my book aside in silence.*

Yours gratefully,
Henr. Ibsen.

This 'historical drama', or, as Botten-Hansen had described it, 'saga-play' on which Ibsen was now engaged was his first really major dramatic work: *The Pretenders.*

He had begun to plan this work as early as five years previously, in the summer of 1858. The idea seems to have come to him then through reading Volume Three of P. A. Munch's *History of the Norwegian People*, which had been published the previous year, and which dealt with the civil wars between 1177 (the date of the accession of King Sverre, the hero of Bjørnson's play of that name) and 1240, when the chief character of *The Pretenders*, Duke Skule, died. According to a letter which Ibsen wrote to J. B. Halvorsen (18 June 1889), he had also worked on it during 1860. But he had put the project aside, and it needed the tonic effect of the Bergen Festival, and his meetings there with

Bjørnson, to get him into the mood to write it. He seems to have begun it almost immediately on his return to Christiania from Bergen towards the end of June (1863), and he completed it in six to eight weeks. It was published by the Christiania bookseller Johan Dahl towards the end of October (though, by an error, the date 1864 appears on the title page of the first edition). In a letter (12 February 1870) to his later publisher, Frederik Hegel of Gyldendal, Ibsen described how this publication came about:

> One day early in September 1863, with the fair copy of The Pretenders under my arm, I met Johan Dahl on the street in Christiania, told him I had written a new historical play, and offered it to him for publication. Dahl immediately expressed his willingness, and agreed without demur to my request for an honorarium of 150 specie-dollars for the first edition. Dahl took the manuscript, the printing began forthwith, and on 15 September I signed the contract in Dahl's bookshop...I later heard...that 1,750 copies of the book were printed.[1]

The Pretenders is set in Norway during the first half of the thirteenth century. The King, Inge, has just died leaving no legal heir, and there are several claimants to the throne. Of these, the two strongest are Earl Skule, brother to the dead King, a famous warrior and a skilled statesman, and Haakon Haakonsson, a boy still in his teens who claims to be the dead King's illegitimate son. The Grand Council votes Haakon king; he, to win Skule's friendship, takes Skule's daughter to be his Queen, and gives Skule a third of his kingdom. But the villainous Bishop Nicholas, whom sexual impotence has twisted into evil, and who is anxious that 'there must be no giants in Norway, for I was never one', sows discord between them. He incites Skule to rebel against Haakon, hoping that they will destroy each other. Skule proclaims himself King, and civil war breaks out. At first, things go Skule's way. He is the more experienced soldier and statesman. But he has one fatal defect, and Haakon one supreme advantage. Skule has, when it comes to the crunch, no real belief in himself; he lacks single-mindedness. Haakon, on the other hand, never has a moment's doubt that 'he is the one whom God has chosen.' It has been Skule's fate, throughout his life, to vacillate when success was within his grasp; and so it is now. He is defeated and killed. Haakon is left King of, for the first time in its history, a united Norway.

Such is a brief outline of the plot, but it gives little idea of the richness and complexity of the play, of its intense poetic imagination (though it is written in prose) and epic sweep, working remorselessly towards the superb climax in

---

[1] In fact 1,250 copies were printed. It sold poorly, and six years later Dahl still had 200 copies on his hands.

the abbey, where Skule has taken sanctuary with Haakon's baby son as hostage and the peasants are waiting outside to lynch him. It contains, in Skule, Haakon and Bishop Nicholas three characters comparable in stature with any that he was to create later, and a dozen splendidly drawn minor parts: Peter, Skule's illegitimate son, a former priest whom blind belief in his father has turned into a ruthless killer; the lonely bard, Jatgeir; the young Queen, Margaret, torn between love of her husband and of her father; Ingeborg, Skule's former mistress and Peter's mother; and the Cassandra-like figure of Skule's sister, Sigrid. Ibsen's previous plays, from *Catiline* to *Love's Comedy*, had been range-finders; *The Pretenders* is the first of the great epic quartet that was to embrace *Brand*, *Peer Gynt* and *Emperor and Galilean*.

Stylistically, too, it marks an important stage in Ibsen's development as a dramatist. Of his previous nine plays, four (*Catiline*, *The Warrior's Barrow*, *Norma* and *Love's Comedy*) had been written in verse, and three (*St John's Night*, *Lady Inger of Østraat* and *The Vikings at Helgeland*) in prose (apart from songs, etc.), while *The Feast at Solhaug* and *Olaf Liljekrans* had been composed in a mixture of the two. Although he had managed here and there to achieve a colloquial prose, he had limited it to his peasants and lower class characters; his princes and chieftains had spoken a formal dialogue, and in *The Vikings at Helgeland* he had, as stated, deliberately imitated the antique language of the sagas. Bjørnson had disapproved of this experiment, and Ibsen himself, in a review of Bjørnson's historical drama *Sigurd Slembe* published in *Illustreret Nyhedsblad* on 21 December 1862, had expressed his conviction that the language of a historical play should be living and colloquial, whoever might be speaking. In *The Pretenders* he attempted to create such a dialogue, retaining formal language only when the characters use a deliberately formal mode of address—as in the opening exchange between Haakon and Skule—and occasionally for special effect. He succeeded, not indeed completely, but to a considerable degree.[1] The play is full of terse, colloquial statements that we do not find in *Lady Inger* or *The Vikings*, and that shock by their unexpectedness; as in the exchange between Skule, when his fortunes are at their height, and the bard Jatgeir:

SKULE. There seem to dwell two men in you, Icelander. When you sit among the warriors at a feast, you draw cap and cloak over every thought. But when a man is alone with you, you seem the kind of man one would choose to have as a friend. Why is this?

---

[1] Not least in the delightfully easy rhymed verse given to the Bishop's ghost in Act Five, and dismissed by some critics as 'doggerel'. If this is doggerel, so is much of *Peer Gynt*.

JATGEIR. When you go to swim in the river, my lord, you do not undress where the people walk to church. You seek out a lonely place.

SKULE. Of course.

JATGEIR. My soul is shy. So I do not bare it when the hall is full.

SKULE. Hm. (*Short pause*). Tell me, Jatgeir, how did you come to be a singer? From whom did you learn your art?

JATGEIR. The art of song cannot be learned, my lord.

SKULE. Then how did you acquire it?

JATGEIR. I received the gift of sorrow, and found myself a singer.

SKULE. Is that what a singer needs?

JATGEIR. I needed sorrow. Others may need faith—or joy—or doubt—

SKULE. Doubt too?

JATGEIR. Yes. But then he who doubts must be strong.

SKULE. And whom would you call a weak doubter?

JATGEIR. He who doubts his own doubt.

SKULE (*slowly*). That sounds to me like death.

JATGEIR. It is worse. It is twilight.

...SKULE (*grips him by the arm*). What gift do *I* need to become King?

JATGEIR. Not the gift of doubt, or you would not have asked.

SKULE. What gift do I need?

JATGEIR. My lord, you *are* King.

SKULE. Are you always sure that you are a poet?

JATGEIR (*looks at him silently for a moment, then asks*). Have you never loved?

SKULE. Yes, once. Passionately, beautifully; sinfully.

JATGEIR. You have a wife.

SKULE. I took her because I wanted a son.

JATGEIR. But you have a daughter, my lord. A gentle and noble daughter.

SKULE. If my daughter had been a son, I would not have asked you what gift I needed. (*Passionately*). I must have someone by me who will obey me instinctively, believe in me unflinchingly, stand close by me through good days and evil, live only to give light and warmth to my life—someone who, when I fall, must die! What shall I do, Jatgeir?

JATGEIR. Buy a dog, my lord.

In a sense, that last line of Jatgeir's is the beginning of modern prose drama.

The Pretenders is one of Ibsen's most personal plays; there can be little doubt that the conflict between Skule and Haakon reflects Ibsen's sense of bitterness at the contrast between his failure (at the time he wrote it) and the younger, less gifted but utterly self-confident Bjørnson's success. This contrast must have seemed especially painful in that summer of 1862, when his fortunes were at their lowest, and he portrayed it very recognisably in *The Pretenders*, in which a man of great gifts invalidated by self-distrust is worsted by a potentially lesser man who possesses the supreme virtue of believing in himself. Bjørnson was very much the model for Haakon (whom, incidentally, he had praised in a speech at Bergen as 'Norway's best king'), and Ibsen put much of himself into Skule and also, by his own admission, into the bard Jatgeir. 'I know I have the fault', he was to write to Bjørnson from Rome on 16 September 1864, echoing the words he had used earlier to Carl Johan Anker, 'that I can't make close contact with those people who demand that one should give oneself freely and competently. I am rather like the bard Jatgeir in *The Pretenders*, I can never bring myself to strip completely. I have the feeling that, where personal relation-ships are concerned, I can only give false expression to what I feel deep down inside, and that is why I prefer to shut it up within me, and why we have sometimes stood as it were observing each other from a distance.' And to Peter Hansen, on 28 October 1870, he wrote: 'The fact that everyone was against me, that there was no uncommitted person who could be said to believe in me, could not but give rise to the strain of feeling which found utterance in *The Pretenders*'.

The Pretenders received mixed reviews when it was published in October 1863, including a disappointing one from Clemens Petersen; but the Christiania Theatre accepted it for production the following January. It was presumably this last turn of events which caused Ibsen to delay his departure for the south; on 8 October he had asked for an advance of 100 specie-dollars from his pension to send his wife and son to Copenhagen, to stay with Magdalene Thore-sen, and on 27 October he applied for a further 300 specie-dollars, 'since it is my intention to leave during the next few weeks by steamer for Hamburg'. But a production of his new play was something which he could not afford to miss.

Ibsen directed the production himself—the last time that he was ever to direct a play of his own or anyone else's—and it received its first performance at the Christiania Theatre on 17 January 1864. Halvdan Koht has described the premiere. 'It was not a really integrated performance. The young Sigvard Gundersen had not yet the strength or assurance to give King Haakon the assurance of victory that is begotten of genius. The Danish actor Wolf played Duke Skule better than any role he had previously attempted…but in general it was the strong hero that he presented rather than the soul-sick doubter… Nevertheless the play gripped the public. Although it lasted for nearly five hours—later they managed to reduce the playing time to four—we are told that "from start to finish it was followed with excited attention" and that "after the fall of the curtain there was a general cry for the author who, when he appeared, was rewarded with thunderous applause". In less than two months [adds Koht] *The Pretenders* was performed eight times, a success unique for a play as long and serious as this in a town as small as the Christiania of those days...Now for the first time he rested in a full and free confidence in his own ability to write, and in his calling as a poet.'[1]

Between the writing of *The Pretenders* and its production, however, larger and more far-reaching issues had arisen to occupy Ibsen's mind.

On 15 November 1863 King Frederik VII of Denmark had died without male issue, and been succeeded by a collateral member of the family, Christian IX. The old and grisly problem of the Duchies of Schleswig and Holstein now reared its head. They disputed Christian's claim to be their ruler, since they had always accepted the Salic Law and denied claims through females. The German states, who had long resented the Danish suzerainty over the Duchies, maintained that the rightful ruler of them was now the Duke of Augustenburg, and Bismarck, supported by Austria, championed the German cause. In December the armies of the German League attacked Holstein; in mid-January the Prussians issued an ultimatum to Denmark; and on 1 February the Prussian forces invaded Schleswig. It was the first testing of Bismarck's new army, which Lord Palmerston had recently scorned ('all military men who have seen it at its annual reviews of late years have unequivocally declared that the French could walk over it and get without difficulty to Berlin'),[2] and which Franz Josef and Napoleon III were similarly, and more disastrously, to underrate.

The young King of Sweden and Norway, Carl XV, and his foreign minister, Count Manderström, had continuously and openly professed support for Denmark in this matter of the Duchies, and Manderström had made several pronouncements, notably one in July, which left no doubt in most Scandinavian minds, including Ibsen's, that, if Danish independence were threatened, Sweden and Norway would come to her aid. A few days after Manderström's July statement, Carl XV offered Denmark a military alliance. But, not for the last time in Swedish history, strong forces within the government advocated a policy of isolationism, and the King found his hands bound. The Norwegian students held a big meeting on 12 December, at which they sent a

---

[1] Koht, *op. cit.*, I, pp. 214–16.

[2] Sir Spencer Walpole, *History of England from the Conclusion of the Great War in 1815* (rev. edn. London 1890, Vol. II, p. 388, note 1). The campaign was planned and finished off by the great Moltke who might, had he chosen differently forty years earlier, have been fighting on the other side. His father, a Mecklenburger, had become a Danish subject and he himself was educated in Holstein and Denmark, became a page at the Danish court and entered the Danish army in 1818. But three years later, unfortunately for millions of unborn Europeans, he transferred to the Prussian army.

declaration to the Swedish students asserting that all Scandinavians must now
regard the Danish cause as their own, and a week later a gathering of three
thousand citizens in Christiania sent the King a message of support for any
military action he might take in support of the Danish cause. But the Storthing
would go no further than to make a promise of financial aid to Denmark, and
that conditional on one of the great western powers joining the alliance.
Palmerston had declared in the House of Commons that autumn that any
nation which challenged the rights of Denmark 'would find in the result
that it would not be Denmark alone with which they would have to contend',
but for any effective intervention the co-operation of France was essential,
and Palmerston could not face the prospect of a French conquest of Prussia.
When the crisis came, Denmark found herself alone.

Ibsen's feelings towards his countrymen, already strained, became considerably aggravated by this, as he thought, chicanery. He had had hard things
to say about Denmark in the cultural field in recent years, but this example of
aggression against a small neighbour by a bullying power angered him as
much as that similar situation had done in 1848, when, as now, the Swedes
and Norwegians had uttered professions of sympathy but had sent no help.
On 13 December, the day after the student meeting in Christiania, Ibsen published in *Illustreret Nyhedsblad* a furious indictment of his fellow-countrymen.
He called the poem simply *To Norway*.

> Those generous words that seemed to gush
> From bold hearts swelling high
> Were but a flood of empty gush,
> And now their stream is dry!
> The tree, that buds of promise bore
> Beneath the banquet's light
> Stands stripped and smitten to its core,
> A graveyard cross upon the shore
> That's ravaged in a night.
>
> 'Twas but a lie in festal song,
> A kiss that Judas gave,
> When Norway's sons sang loud and long
> Beside the Danish wave.[1]

The poem continued in such vehement terms that Botten Hansen, who
wished to print it in *Illustreret Nyhedsblad*, asked Ibsen to tone it down; and a
comparison of the Norwegian people to Cain was modified, as was a sug-

---

[1] Edmund Gosse's translation.

gestion that they would do well in the future to deny their nationality since the stigma attached to the word 'Norwegian' would be such that even the country's flag would be shunned like a plague pennant. Ibsen has sometimes been condemned for compromising in this fashion especially since his next play after *The Pretenders*, *Brand*, was largely an indictment of compromise; but in that tiny community it was fairly certain that no one but Botten Hansen would have published the poem in any form, and it was presumably a question of getting it printed in a modified version or not at all. And Botten Hansen, himself no coward, may have been right in thinking that the poem would be more effective if it made Norwegians ashamed rather than angry. It appeared in *Illustreret Nyhedsblad* on 13 December 1863, and shortly afterwards Ibsen wrote an elegy to King Frederik VII which developed into a moving expression of sympathy with the beleagured Danes. This was sung at a meeting in the Christiania Students' Union on 13 January 1864, and printed in *Illustreret Nyhedsblad* four days later on the day of the premiere of *The Pretenders*.

Christiania was icebound that winter until early April, so that Ibsen had to kick his heels for ten weeks, separated from his wife and son, before starting on his journey. He occupied part of his time in planning a new historical drama to succeed *The Pretenders*; some notes have survived which he copied from history books about Magnus Heineson, a sixteenth century freebooter from the Faroe Islands who ended his life on the executioner's block. But he never completed or, as far as we know, even began this work, though he was still talking about it as late as 1870.[1] Meanwhile, Bjørnson, who had returned to Christiania the previous autumn, had, with characteristically impulsive generosity, set about raising a fund to augment Ibsen's small grant and, we may suppose, to help pay off his outstanding debts in Norway. He used his powers of eloquence to such effect that he managed to gather 700 specie-dollars, and thus more than double Ibsen's finances. Johan Sverdrup, the future Prime Minister, was among the subscribers.

On 2 April the Learned Holland group gave a banquet at the Hotel Nord, partly to celebrate Paul Botten Hansen's recent appointment (on 7 March) as University Librarian, and partly to say farewell to Ibsen. Of this surely interesting occasion there is, infuriatingly, no record whatever. Three days later, in the early morning of Tuesday 5 April, 1864, Ibsen left Christiania with Botten Hansen in the first southbound steamer of the year. The next day he joined his

---

[1] P. A. Rosenberg remembered Ibsen speaking of the Magnus Heineson project at his (Rosenberg's) father's house in Copenhagen during the summer of 1870. Rosenberg, then a boy of twelve, asked who Heineson was. 'Ibsen looked at me, and I noticed that one of his eyes was larger than the other. Slowly and weightily he replied: "He was a great scoundrel" '. (*Nationaltidende*, Copenhagen, 28 July 1926).

wife and son in Copenhagen; it was to be ten years before he set foot in Norway again, and a further seventeen before he returned to live there.

On 17 April Ibsen wrote from Copenhagen to Bernhard Dunker, a lawyer who had helped Bjørnson to organise the fund for him,[1] thanking him for the money and adding: 'On Wednesday I leave for Lübeck, and shall proceed thence to Trieste. I have gained much pleasure and profit from my stay here; as soon as I reach Rome I shall work on a new five act play, which I hope to have ready by the end of the summer'. This, presumably, was the abortive project about Magnus Heineson.

The next day the Prussians stormed Dybbøl, and the brave Danish resistance was ended. Two days later, on 20 April, Ibsen sailed to Lübeck, leaving Suzannah and Sigurd to follow him later, and continued on to Berlin. There, on 4 May, he saw the Danish cannon captured at Dybbøl led in triumph through the streets while Germans lining the route spat at them. 'It was for me', he wrote a year later, 'a sign that, some day, history would spit in the eyes of Sweden and Norway for their part in this affair':[2] and the idea for a new play, unlike anything that he had hitherto written, grew in him, 'like a foetus'.

From Berlin he took the railway to Vienna, and thence southwards across the Alps. Thirty-four years later, in a speech in Copenhagen on 1 April 1898, he was to recall his first sight of Italy. 'I... crossed the Alps on 9 May. Over the high mountains the clouds hung like great, dark curtains, and beneath these we drove though the tunnel and, suddenly, found ourselves at Mira Mara, where that marvellously bright light which is the beauty of the south suddenly revealed itself to me, gleaming like white marble. It was to affect all my later work, even if the content thereof was not always beautiful.' He described his emotion at that moment as 'a feeling of being released from the darkness into light, emerging from mists through a tunnel into the sunshine'. He travelled on through Trieste, Venice and Milan, Piacenza, Parma, Bologna and Florence; what impression these cities made on him we do not know, apart from the fact that he admired Milan Cathedral. Otherwise, of these six weeks in May and early June of 1864, when Europe was opening itself before him, no record exists; the letters which he must have written to Suzannah were, like all his early letters to her, destroyed. 'Our relationship concerns no one but ourselves'. At last, in the middle of June, he reached Rome.

---

[1] He had been Marcus Thrane's defending counsel.
Letter to Magdalene Thoresen, 3 December 1865.

APPENDIX A

Ludvig Holberg

Baron Ludvig Holberg, the father of Danish and Norwegian literature, was born in Bergen in 1684. After studying there and (after Bergen was
destroyed by fire in 1702) in Copenhagen, he spent two years (1706–1708) in
Oxford, keeping himself by giving lessons on the violin and flute. It was in
the Bodleian Library that it first occurred to him 'how splendid and glorious
a thing it would be to take a place among the authors'. He then tutored and
lectured all over Europe, touring much of it on foot; in 1715 he walked from
Rome to Paris, across the Alps. In 1717 he was appointed Professor of Meta-
physics at Copenhagen University. Hitherto his writings had been confined to
history and law, but he now published several brilliant poetical satires on contemporary manners, rather in the manner of Alexander Pope; the fourth of
these, *Peder Paars* (1719–1720), is regarded as the first Danish classic. In 1722
the first public theatre in Copenhagen was opened, and in the next eighteen
months Holberg wrote fifteen comedies for it, the first plays of any note in
Danish. In all, he wrote over thirty plays. Modelled principally on Molière and
the Latin dramatists Plautus and Terence, they are, by modern standards, a
little short on plot; they usually have no sub-plot, creating a single situation
and then working it out with wit and style, but without much in the way of
dramatic surprises. But Holberg's lively, simple prose, short, rapid scenes and
robust characterisation have survived the test of time, and a dozen or so of
his plays still work today if acted with Brechtian panache: *Jeppe of the Hill,
The Woman of Whims, The Scatterbrain, The Masquerade, Erasmus Montanus,
Henrik and Pernilla, Gert Westphaler, The Political Tinker, Jean de France, The
Lying-in Room, Pernilla's Brief Mistress-ship, The Peasant in Pawn.* It has been
said of Holberg that he found Denmark bookless and left it a library. He died
unmarried in 1754. Statues of him stand outside both the National Theatre
in Oslo and the Royal Theatre in Copenhagen; both countries claim him as
their own. He was one of the very few authors whom Ibsen admitted to
admiring.

Norwegian *v.* Danish: The Linguistic Problem

IN AN APPENDIX to *Britain and the British*, a lively survey of contemporary life and manners in England and Scotland which Vinje wrote in English[1] and which was published in Edinburgh in 1863, he well summarised the peculiar linguistic problem which faced Norwegian authors. From the end of the fourteenth century, he explains, when the Norse crown descended to the Dane, 'functionaries entrusted with the administration were trained in Danish universities, a Danish literature rose into fashion, and the old Norse, forced to yield to a more powerful rival, retreated to the dells and mountains...Thus it was that the Norse language was displaced by the Danish, as the Anglo-Saxon was by the French, with this important difference, however, that the relationship between Norse and Danish was closer than that between French and Anglo-Saxon. Norse and old Danish differed very slightly at first, but in the lapse of time their features became more and more unlike...[The] Germanic tendencies of Denmark produced a marked change upon her language. German words and idioms were received into it, until it became totally corrupted. These corruptions were partly imported into the Bible translation which Norway had received from Denmark, and which continued in use there down to 1814. At this period Norway became separated from Denmark and became united, under one King, with Sweden. The political separation from Denmark did not, however, prevent Danish literature from still maintaining its former sway.

'Among the Thelemorkish folk there were, until recently, still preserved in their original beauty and purity many fine old Norse songs. The collection of these words and melodies was the task of different individuals at different times. Far and wide, throughout that romantic land of lakes and mountains, men wandered on their linguistic tours; writing down from the faltering lips

---

[1] In his introduction Vinje thanks an unnamed British friend for correcting his style, and the helper did a good job, for Vinje's own letters in English to Welhaven, on which the book is based, are far less fluent.

of its aged inhabitants many a musical and literary treasure—snatched thus, like brands from the burning...Among these songs are some of the old ballads known at an early stage in most literatures of Europe—but the greater part of them are indigenous lyric, and some half-dramatic. They have been handed down orally from generation to generation, improved in their descent by touches from master-minds, and arriving at us in a state of perfection and preservation beyond all praise. These will, I maintain, form the nucleus of our regenerated literature, and the more so, as the dialect is pure, rich and living. This is the language which I am in the habit of writing...For the space of three years I have, with some slight interruptions, put forth weekly a newspaper written in this Norse. My readers were at first sorely puzzled. The spelling of many known words is completely altered, and I am often forced to use words never before seen in print by those not conversant with old Norse. Even, however, to those tolerably well read in that literature, new words are constantly turning up, for it possesses great facilities for the formation of such new words, the old roots being clear and comparatively pure; whereas in Danish they are corrupted and settled, and, therefore, organic growth is no longer possible...We always see that vice, weakness and cowardice are the causes of corruption of languages. Had not our exhausted Norway, in the fifteenth century, yielded to Denmark, there would have been no room for our present linguistic strife and struggle'.

APPENDIX C

Vaudeville

IN HIS BOOK *Concerning Vaudeville*, J. L. Heiberg explains the difference between vaudeville and (a) opera comique (b) ordinary musical comedy. In the latter two, he says, the dialogue merely links and introduces the music, whereas in vaudeville the dialogue is the main feature. In the one, the dialogue temporarily replaces the music, in the other the music temporarily replaces the dialogue; for which reason, he suggests, one should employ simple and familiar tunes, 'since the attention of the audience should not be distracted by the musical element but should remain concentrated on the words, which these familiar tunes buttress and clarify, since the memory of them puts the audience into the required mood...Vaudeville is drama of situation, with characters loosely outlined...It cannot be tragic, since tragedy depends on character development... It exists mainly in the realm of comedy...The music and the text... should seem inseparable. A vaudeville should not have too broad a scope, nor demand elaborate theatrical effects. I have therefore written all my vaudevilles in one act, with no changes of scene'—though, he adds, they are long enough to have been divided into two or three acts if he had so wished.

Heiberg adds that comedy had become divorced from reality to the extent that it was only found acceptable if it took place in a foreign setting with foreign characters. He wanted to make it topical, as it had been in Holberg's time, and also to write a type of comedy that would please 'not merely the knowledgeable, but also the ignorant'; and he recalled with pride that his first vaudeville 'not merely pleased the Court and higher circles, but was sung at street corners and in cellars, and drew to the theatre persons from the class that never, or seldom, pays to see a comedy... I say, not in boast, but as a fact, that when my first vaudeville was still a novelty I was addressed in the streets and other public places by people I had never met...and was thanked by members of the humbler trading class because my vaudeville had, to their profit, enticed strangers from the provinces to the capital...The public has found a new interest in local comedy, and the way has therefore been opened for a new national comedy'.

Against the charge that his vaudevilles are farces, Heiberg replies that indeed they are, and so were many of Holberg's best plays, and that he regards
farce as a legitimate and respectable form of drama. He praised the Swedish
poet Bellman's songs as 'extra-theatrical vaudevilles', admiring their mixture
of 'the burlesque and the melancholic', and the inseparability of the words
from the music.[1]

---

[1] *Om Vaudeville og dens Betydning paa den danske Skueplads* (Copenhagen, 1826), pp. 38 *ff.*

Select Bibliography

ANKER, Øyvind. *Christiania theaters repertoire 1827-1899* (Oslo, 1956).

ANKER, Øyvind. *Kristiania norske theaters repertoire 1852-1863* (Oslo, 1956).

ANKER, Øyvind. Ibseniana og Bjørnsoniana fra Kristiania-teatrene in *Edda*, V. (Oslo, 1956).

ARVESEN, O. *Oplevelser og erindringer* (Christiania, 1921).

BEYER, Harald. *Søren Kierkegaard og Norge* (Christiania, 1924).

BJÖRKLUND-BEXELL, I. *Ibsens Vildanden, en studie* (1962, unpublished).

BJØRNSON, Bjørnstjerne. *Grotid (brev fra aarene 1857-1870)*, I, II (Christiania, 1912).

BLANC, T. H. *Norges første nationale scene* (Christiania, 1884).

BLANC, T. H. *Christiania theaters historie 1827-1899* (Christiania, 1899).

BLYTT, Peter. *Minder fra den første norske scene i Bergen* (Bergen, 1894).

BOTTEN HANSEN, Paul. Henrik Ibsen in *Illustreret Nyhedsblad*, 19 July 1863.

BULL, Francis. Henrik Ibsen in *Norsk Litteratur-Historie*, IV (Oslo, 1960).

BULL, Francis. *Studier og streiftog* (Oslo, 1931).

BULL, Francis. *Tradisjoner og minner* (Oslo, 1945).

BULL, Francis. *Essays i utvalg* (Oslo, 1964).

BULL, Francis. Foreningen af den 22 December in *Edda* X (Oslo, 1919).

BULL, Francis. Introductions to *Catiline, The Warrior's Barrow, Norma, St John's Night, The Feast at Solhaug, Olaf Liljekrans, The Vikings at Helgeland* and *Love's Comedy* in *Henrik Ibsen, Samlede verker, hundreårsutgave*, I–IV (Oslo, 1928-30).

BULL, Marie. *Minder fra Bergens første nationale scene* (Bergen, 1905).

COLLIN, Christen. *Bjørnstjerne Bjørnson, hans barndom og ungdom*, I, II (Christiania, 1902, 1907).

DAAE, Ludvig. Paul Botten Hansen in *Vidar* (Copenhagen, 1888).

DERRY, T. K. *A Short History of Norway* (London, 1957).

DIETRICHSON, Lorentz. *Svundne tider*, I–IV (Christiania, 1894-1917).

DOWNS, B. W. *Ibsen: the Intellectual Background* (Cambridge, 1946).

DUE, Christopher. *Erindringer fra Henrik Ibsens ungdomsaar* (Copenhagen, 1909).

DUVE, Arne. *Symbolikken i Henrik Ibsens skuespill* (Oslo, 1945).

EITREM, Hans. *Ibsen og Grimstad* (Oslo, 1940).

FORESTER, Thomas. *Norway in 1848 and 1849* (London, 1850).

GOSSE, Edmund. *Ibsen* (London, 1907).

GRAN, Gerhard. *Henrik Ibsen: Liv og verker* I, II (Christiania, 1918).

GRAN, Gerhard (ed.). *Henrik Ibsen: Festskrift i anledning af hans 70de fødselsdag* (Bergen, 1898).

GRØNVOLD, Marcus. *Fra Ulrikken til Alperne* (Oslo, 1925).

HALVORSEN, J. B. Henrik Ibsen in *Norsk Forfatter-Lexicon 1814-1880*, III (Christiania, 1892).

HAMMER, S. C. *Kristianias historie*, IV (Christiania, 1923).

HEIBERG, J. L. *Om Vaudeville og dens Betydning paa den danske Skueplads* (Copenhagen, 1826).

HØST, Sigurd. *Ibsens diktning og Ibsen selv* (Oslo, 1927).

IBSEN, Bergliot. *De tre* (Oslo, 1948).

IBSEN, Henrik. *Samlede verker, hundreårsutgave*, I-XXI, ed. Francis Bull, Halvdan Koht and Didrik Arup Seip (Oslo, 1928-1958).

IBSEN, Henrik. *Efterladte skrifter*, I-III, ed. Halvdan Koht and Julius Elias (Christiania and Copenhagen, 1909).

JÆGER, Henrik. *Henrik Ibsen, et livsbillede* (Copenhagen, 1888).

JANSON, Kristofer. *Hvad jeg har oplevet* (Christiania, 1913).

KNUDSEN, Knud. Unpublished memoirs.

KOHT, Halvdan. *Henrik Ibsen, eit diktarliv*, I-II (revised edition, Oslo, 1954).

KOHT, Halvdan. Introduction to *The Pretenders* in *Henrik Ibsen, Samlede verker, hundreårsutgave*, V (Oslo, 1928).

LAMM, Martin. *Det moderna dramat* (Stockholm, 1948).

LUND, Audhild. *Henrik Ibsen og det norske theater 1857-1863* (Oslo, 1925).

MCFARLANE, J. W. *Ibsen and the Temper of Norwegian Literature* (London, 1960).

MCFARLANE, J. W. *The Oxford Ibsen*, II (London, 1962).

MIDBØE, Hans. *Streiflys over Ibsen* (Oslo, 1960).

MOHR, Otto Lous. *Henrik Ibsen som maler* (Oslo, 1953).

MOSFJELD, Oskar. *Henrik Ibsen og Skien* (Oslo, 1949).

MØLLER, P. L. *Det Nyere Lystspil i Frankrig og Danmark* (Copenhagen, 1858).

NEIIENDAM, Robert. *Mennesker bag masker* (Copenhagen, 1931).

NEIIENDAM, Robert. *Gjennem mange aar* (Copenhagen, 1933).

NIELSEN, Yngvar. *En Kristianiensers erindringer fra 1850- og 1860- aarene* (Christiania and Copenhagen, 1910).

ORDING, Fr. *Henrik Ibsens vennekreds, Det lærde Holland* (Oslo, 1927).

PAULSEN, John. *Mine erindringer* (Copenhagen, 1900).

PAULSEN, John. *Nye erindringer* (Copenhagen, 1901).

PAULSEN, John. *Erindringer. Siste samling* (Copenhagen, 1903).

PAULSEN, John. *Samliv med Ibsen, 2den samling* (Copenhagen and Christiania, 1913).

PETTERSEN, HJ. *Henrik Ibsen 1828-1928, bedømt af Samtid og Eftertid* (Oslo, 1928)

RUDLER, Roderick. Scenebilledkunsten i Norge for 100 år siden in *Kunstkultur*, 44 årgang (Oslo, 1961).

SCHNEIDER, J. A. *Fra det gamle Skien*, III (Skien, 1924).

SEIP, Didrik Arup. Henrik Ibsen og K. Knudsen: Det sproglige gjennembrud hos Ibsen in *Edda* I (Christiania, 1914).

SKARD, Sigmund. *A. O. Vinje og antikken* (Oslo, 1938).

STEINER, George. *The Death of Tragedy* (London, 1961).

TEDFORD, Ingrid. *Ibsen Bibliography, 1928-1957* (Oslo, 1961).

THORESEN, Magdalene. *Brev fra Magdalene Thoresen* (Copenhagen, 1919).

THORESEN, Magdalene. Om Henrik Ibsen og hans hustru in *Juleroser* (Copenhagen, 1901).

WIESENER, A. M. *Henrik Ibsen og det norske theater i Bergen, 1851-1857* (Bergen, 1928).

WITTICH, W. *A Visit to the Western Coast of Norway* (London, 1848).

WOLF, Lucie. *Mine livserindringer* (Christiania, 1898).

ZUCKER, A. E. *Ibsen, the Master Builder* (London, 1929).

Index

Works by Ibsen are printed in small capitals. For the convenience of readers unacquainted with the Scandinavian alphabet, æ, ä and å have been listed under a, and œ, ö and ø under o.

Botten Hansen, Paul—*cont.*
  him, 167; he defends Ibsen, 177, 181,
  208–9, 212, 224; dislike of Norwegian
  Society, 191; founds 'The Learned
  Holland', 193; letter from Vinje, 202;
  still editor, 218; asks Ibsen to tone down
  poem, 236–7; leaves Norway with
  Ibsen, 238
Bouchardy, Joseph, 200
Boucicault, Dion, 201
Bournonville, A., 111
Boyssen, Jacob, 19
BRAND, 24, 31, 52, 59, 61, 70, 79, 95, 119,
  138, 147, 155–6, 194, 198–9, 216, 222,
  232, 237
'Brandeis', criminal, 25
Brandes, Georg, 140, 148
Bratsberg, 26, 38–9, 69, 70, 186
Bredsdorff, Elias, 14
Bremer, Frederika, 45
Brevik, 69–70
Brun, Johannes, 108–9, 111, 113, 116, 144, 162
Brun, Louise, 106–9, 111, 113, 116, 153
Brunsvig, J., 32, 36, 186
Bruun, Christopher, 199
Büchner, Georg, 122, 124
BUILDING PLANS, 63, 178–9
Bull, Francis, 14, 31, 143, 209, 244–5
Bull, Maria, 100, 244
Bull, Ole; early life, 99–100; founds
  Norwegian Theatre in Bergen, 99–102;
  leaves for America, 106–7; also 122, 165,
  174, 191, 203
Bulwer-Lytton, Edward, 45
Buntzen, Andreas, 112
Butenschøn, Andreas, 209
Byron, Henry J., 201

Calderon de la Barca, Pedro, 108, 167, 174
California, 69
Caprice, A (Bøgh), 188–9, 203, 206, 212
Caprice, Un (Musset), 123, 139, 212
Caricaturist, Ibsen as a, 45, 53–4, 92, 95
Carl, Crown Prince, see Carl XV
Carl XIII, King, 21
Carl XIV Johan, King, 21, 178
Carl XV, King, 150–1, 202, 235
Carron, 51
Casino Theatre, Copenhagen, 114
Caste, 201
CATILINE, 51, 58–65, 67, 70, 72–5, 77–8, 80,
  82, 86, 148, 171, 195, 224, 232

Chanteuse Voilée, La, 167, 178
Charles II of England, 169
Charlotte Corday, 107
Chartist manfesto, 76
Château des Cartes, Un, 149
Chaumière et sa Coeur, Une, 91
Chekhov, Anton, 13
Christian IX of Denmark, 57, 235
Christiania, described, 71–2; Ibsen in,
  71–102, 160–238; *et passim*
Christiania-Posten, 63, 68, 73, 166, 173, 177,
  183, 204, 207, 212
Christiania Theatre ('Danish' Theatre at
  Bankpladsen), 62–5, 78–9, 86–7, 157–8,
  164–5, 167, 173, 176, 183–4, 190–1, 206,
  208, 212, 215–16, 223–4, 226, 229, 234
Christiansborg, 114
Cicero, 58–9
Clairville, Louis François Nicolai, 205
Clara Raphael's Letters, 55
Clifford le Voleur, 178
Cobbett, William, 52
Cod, excellence of Norwegian, 128
Cogniard, Théodor, 205
Coleridge, Samuel Taylor, 75, 199
Collett, Camilla, 217
Collin, Christen, 140, 191, 244
Colman, George, the elder, 108, 173
Columbus, Christopher, 88
Comédie Française, 139
Comedy, Satire, Irony and Deeper Meaning,
  123
Contes de la Reine de Navarre, Les, 136–7
Cooper, Fenimore, 45
Copenhagen, 23, 39, 51, 72, 77, 82, 87, 89,
  108–116, 122–3, 126, 136, 140, 162, 165,
  176, 188, 190, 200–202, 206, 230, 234,
  237–9
Corneille, Pierre, 51
Corsair, The, 77, 87
Costume, 105, 108, 112, 114, 117, 125, 144,
  156, 173, 216, 223; see also Dress
Crawfurd, Elizabeth, 50–2, 60, 81
Crawfurd, Jens, 51–2
Crawfurd, Thomas, 51
Creation, Man and Messiah, 52
Cronborg, Jens, 160, 164, 166
Cudrio, Ulrich, 19

Daae, Ludvig, 191, 193, 219, 244
Dahl, Emma, 102
Dahl, J. C., 36, 116–17, 190